The Twelve Steps

A Spiritual Journey

The
Twelve
Steps

A Spiritual

Journey

REVISED EDITION

A Working Guide for Healing Damaged Emotions

....

Based on Biblical Teachings

R P I   P U B L I S H I N G ,   I N C .
San Diego

Published by
RPI Publishing, Inc.
P.O. Box 1026
Julian, CA 92036
(619) 765-2703

Scripture taken from the Holy Bible, New International Version. Copyright © 1973, 1978, 1984 by International Bible Society. Used by permission of Zondervan Bible Publishers.

The Twelve Steps are reprinted with permission of Alcoholics Anonymous World Services, Inc. Permission to reprint and adapt the Twelve Steps does not mean that AA has reviewed or approved the contents of this publications, nor that AA agrees with the views expressed herein. AA is a program of recovery from alcoholism only—use of the Twelve Steps in connection with programs and activities which are patterned after AA, but which address other problems, does not imply otherwise.

For the purposes of this book, the word "alcohol" in Step One has been changed to read "the effects of our separation from God," and the word "alcoholics" in Step Twelve has been changed to read "others."

NOTICE: This book is designed to provide information regarding the subject matter covered. It is provided with the understanding that the publisher and author are not engaged in rendering individualized professional services. These processes and questions are intended for group or individual study, and not designed to be a substitute for one-to-one professional therapy when such help is necessary.

ISBN 0-941405-44-3 pbk

Printed in the United States of America

Revised Edition

10 9 8 7 6 5 4

In memory of Richard, Edward, and others
whose lives were a struggle with addiction,
and who never discovered a spiritual path to recovery.

For nearly fifty years God has used the healing power
of the Twelve Steps to restore the lives of countless individuals.
He has conveyed this healing message through people
who know what it is to be broken by life
and mended by God.
We dedicate this book to all those
who have found healing through this program
and who continue to choose to share
their experience, strength, and hope
with those yet searching.

A part of the proceeds from the sale of this book
goes to support the work of recovery ministry.

TABLE OF CONTENTS

CHRISTIAN ROOTS OF THE TWELVE STEPS

Alcoholics Anonymous began on June 10, 1935, cofounded by William Griffith Wilson (Bill W.) and Dr. Robert Holbrook Smith (Dr. Bob). Wilson conceived the idea of Alcoholics Anonymous while he was hospitalized for excessive drinking in December of 1934. During his hospital stay, Wilson had a spiritual experience that removed his desire to drink. In the following months, he tried to persuade other alcoholics to stop drinking just as he had. Wilson found his first "convert" in Smith, who was willing to follow Wilson's method to find freedom from alcoholism. Four years later, Wilson and Smith published the book *Alcoholics Anonymous*, that contains the Twelve Steps and a spiritually based program of recovery for alcoholism.

THE OXFORD GROUP

Various sources influenced the formulation of AA's program, as developed and recorded by Wilson. Of these, the British-born Oxford Group movement and its American leader, Episcopal clergyman Samuel Moor Shoemaker, Jr., contributed most significantly to the Christian basis of Alcoholics Anonymous. Both Wilson and Smith attended the Oxford Group meetings and based much of the AA program on this framework.

In the 1920s and 1930s, the Oxford Group movement became a revolutionary answer to antireligious reaction following World War I. Aiming to rekindle living faith in a church gone stale with institutionalism, the Oxford Group declared itself an "organism" rather than an "organization." Group members met in homes and hotels, mingling religion with meals. Despite its freedom from institutional ties, the movement was distinctly ecclesiastical and looked to the church as its authority.

Dr. Frank N. D. Buchman, a Lutheran pastor, is most often cited as leader of the Oxford movement. Yet, if one were to ask an Oxford Group follower, "Who is your leader?" the reply might be, "The Holy Spirit." So confidently did the group believe in the guidance of the Spirit that it had no organized board of officers, but relied instead on "God control" through men and women who had fully "surrendered" to God's will. Buchman emphasized the need to surrender to God for forgiveness and guidance and to confess one's sins to God and others. Oxford Group followers learned also to make restitution for wrongs done and to witness about their changed lives in order to help change others.

The Oxford Group's teachings rested3 on the following six basic assumptions:
1. Human beings are sinners.
2. Human beings can be changed.

3. Confession is a prerequisite to change.

4. The changed soul has direct access to God.

5. The age of miracles has returned.

6. Those who have been changed are to change others.[1]

In addition, Wilson incorporated into AA's philosophy the Oxford Group's five procedures, which were:

1. Giving to God.

2. Listening to God's direction.

3. Checking guidance.

4. Restitution.

5. Sharing, both confession and witness.[2]

EVOLUTION OF THE TWELVE STEPS

While trying to attract more followers to sobriety from 1935-1937, Smith and Wilson attended Oxford Group meetings in New York led by Samuel Moor Shoemaker, Jr. "It was from Sam Shoemaker that we absorbed most of the Twelve Steps of Alcoholics Anonymous, steps that express the heart of A.A.'s way of life," Wilson later recalled. "The early A.A. got its ideas of self-examination, acknowledgement of character defects, restitution for harm done, and working with others straight from the Oxford Group and directly from Sam Shoemaker, their former leader in America, and from nowhere else."[3]

THE TWELVE STEPS OF ALCOHOLICS ANONYMOUS

1. We admitted we were powerless over alcohol—that our lives had become unmanageable.

2. Came to believe that a Power greater than ourselves could restore us to sanity.

3. Made a decision to turn our will and our lives over to the care of God *as we understood Him.*

4. Made a searching and fearless moral inventory of ourselves.

5. Admitted to God, to ourselves, and to another human being the exact nature of our wrongs.

---

[1] Cantril, Hadley, *The Psychology of Social Movements* (Huntington, NY: Robert E. Kruger, 1941), pp. 147–148.

[2] Kurtz, Ernest, *Not God: A History of Alcoholics Anonymous* (Center City, MN: Hazelden Educational Materials, 1979) pp. 48–49.

[3] *Alcoholics Anonymous Comes of Age* (New York: Alcoholics Anonymous World Services, Inc., 1957), p. 199.

6. Were entirely ready to have God remove all these defects of character.

7. Humbly asked Him to remove our shortcomings.

8. Made a list of all persons we had harmed, and became willing to make amends to them all.

9. Made direct amends to such people wherever possible, except when to do so would injure them or others.

10. Continued to take personal inventory and when we were wrong promptly admitted it.

11. Sought through prayer and meditation to improve our conscious contact with God, *as we understood Him,* praying only for knowledge of His will for us and the power to carry that out.

12. Having had a spiritual awakening as the result of these steps, we tried to carry this message to alcoholics, and to practice these principles in all our affairs.

THE TWELVE STEPS

GOAL		STEP
Peace with God	**Step One** is about recognizing our brokenness.	We admitted we were powerless over the effects of our separation from God—that our lives had become unmanageable.
	Step Two is about the birth of faith in us.	Came to believe that a power greater than ourselves could restore us to sanity.
	Step Three involves a decision to let God be in charge of our lives.	Made a decision to turn our will and our lives over to the care of God *as we understood Him.*
Peace with Ourselves	**Step Four** involves self-examination.	Made a searching and fearless moral inventory of ourselves.
	Step Five is the discipline of confession.	Admitted to God, to ourselves, and to another human being the exact nature of our wrongs.
	Step Six is an inner transformation sometimes called repentance.	Were entirely ready to have God remove all these defects of character.
	Step Seven involves the transformation or purification of our character.	Humbly asked Him to remove our shortcomings.
Peace with Others	**Step Eight** involves examining our relationships and preparing ourselves to make amends.	Made a list of all persons we had harmed and became willing to make amends to them all.
	Step Nine is the discipline of making amends.	Made direct amends to such people wherever possible, except when to do so would injure them or others.
	Step Ten is about maintaining progress in recovery.	Continued to take personal inventory and, when we were wrong, promptly admitted it.
Keeping the Peace	**Step Eleven** involves the spiritual disciplines of prayer and meditation.	Sought through prayer and meditation to improve our conscious contact with God *as we understood Him,* praying only for knowledge of His will for us and the power to carry that out.
	Step Twelve is about ministry.	Having had a spiritual awakening as the result of these steps, we tried to carry this message to others, and to practice these principles in all our affairs.

AND SPIRITUAL DISCIPLINES

RELATED BIBLICAL TEXT	DISCIPLINE
I know nothing good lives in me, that is, in my sinful nature. For I have the desire to do what is good, but I cannot carry it out. (Rom. 7:17)	Submission
For it is God who works in you to will and to act according to his good purpose. (Phil. 2:13) Therefore, I urge you, brothers, in view of God's mercy, to offer your bodies as living sacrifices, holy and pleasing to God—which is your spiritual worship. (Rom. 12:1)	Conversion
Let us examine our ways and test them, and let us return to the Lord. (Lam. 3:40) Therefore confess your sins to each other and pray for each other so that you may be healed. (James 5:16a)	Confession
Humble yourselves before the Lord, and he will lift you up. (James 4:10) If we confess our sins, he is faithful and just and will forgive us our sins and purify us from all unrighteousness. (1 John 1:9)	Repentance
Do to others as you would have them do to you. (Luke 6:31) Therefore, if you are offering your gift at the altar and there remember that your brother has something against you, leave your gift there in front of the altar. First go and be reconciled to your brother; then come and offer your gift. (Matt. 5:23–24)	Amends
So, if you think you are standing firm, be careful that you don't fall. (1 Cor. 10:12)	Maintenance
Let the word of Christ dwell in you richly. (Col. 3:16a)	Prayer
Brothers, if someone is caught in a sin, you who are spiritual should restore him gently. But watch yourself, or you also may be tempted. (Gal. 6:1)	Ministry

Those of us who participated in the writing and review of this material are recovering Christian lay people and clergy. Our belief is that Scripture and the Twelve Steps are important healing tools. We believe that if we regularly apply these tools to our lives, we open ourselves to God's healing love and grace. Our intention is to carry the message of the Twelve Steps and Christ's love to all hurting people.

This revised edition reflects the spiritual and emotional growth of its contributors. It is also an expression of their commitment to work their individual programs and apply the principles of the Twelve Steps to their daily lives. The foundation of each contributor's recovery process is his or her relationship with a loving Higher Power, God, as personalized in Jesus Christ.

A central theme and assumption of this work is that healing is possible. To some degree or another, everyone can experience freedom from the damaging effects of a less-than-nurturing environment. As our wounds heal, we become functional members of the community.

Working the Twelve Steps helps us reclaim our birthright as children of a compassionate God. We were created in his image and have the gift of free will. The journey we are about to begin is intended to awaken us to God's grace and give us an opportunity to experience peaceful and productive living. Feelings of unworthiness, anxiety, and inferiority diminish and are replaced by spiritual strength and virtues. Focusing on our new relationship with God transforms our obsessive need for other people's approval. Our attention is, instead, captivated by the promise of new life in Christ.

The Twelve Traditions of Alcoholics Anonymous stress personal anonymity as a vital element of one's recovery. "Friends in Recovery" have chosen to remain anonymous to pursue our own personal growth. We understand the importance of facing ourselves honestly and placing our confidence in the person of Jesus Christ. We offer these materials, not as an end in themselves, but as a means to developing a healthy relationship with God, with others, and with oneself.

Your Story: What personal need brings you to this meeting or step study? The Search for a solution to personal unhappiness / Despite all I do God continues to take care of me

NOTE: The meeting format for Week One is in Appendix One on page 234.

INTRODUCTION TO THE JOURNEY

The revisions in this book are the result of the authors' continued growth and recommendations received from individuals using the book. It is through their willingness to share their experience of working the material that these changes are possible. Improvements in the writing exercises and group techniques are a result of feedback from groups using this book.

The Twelve Steps—A Spiritual Journey is a personal guide to understanding the spiritual power of the Twelve Steps from a Christian perspective. This material is primarily for adults whose childhoods were negatively affected by a less-than-nurturing environment. This environment often resulted when the adults responsible for care were influenced by substance abuse, emotional problems, or compulsive behaviors. The Twelve Steps offer a way to grow beyond the harmful effects of a troubled home environment. Since the founding of Alcoholics Anonymous in 1935, the Twelve Steps have become a way for millions of people to change the course of their lives.

Twelve-Step recovery is not a program sponsored by any religious group or entity. However, people using this program find it in harmony with their own spiritual beliefs. It has no official religious affiliation. It is, however, a program that helps us to rediscover and deepen the spiritual part of ourselves. We also realize through working the Twelve Steps that our spirituality is important. We learn to live our lives according to the guidance of God, our Higher Power. We realize that the void or despair we feel is the result of our ignoring or rejecting our relationship with our Lord, Jesus Christ.

The foundation for this book is the Twelve-Step process. This process has helped countless individuals recover from many forms of addictive, compulsive, or obsessive behavior. This book is also a tool for writing one's personal story of recovery. It brings together the tested wisdom of Bible truths and the proven effectiveness of Twelve-Step principles. The material encourages self-understanding and emphasizes the unchanging love of God for all humanity.

The Twelve Steps—A Spiritual Journey contains scriptural passages that illustrate the harmony between the practice of Christianity and the working of the Twelve Steps. The use of Scripture provides an understanding of the Twelve Steps within a biblical context. When used as intended, the steps are a profoundly powerful process for allowing God to heal damaged emotions. This book is a spiritual tool that helps us regain balance and order, and leads us to improved health and increased happiness through a renewed relationship with God.

As Christians we believe that God reveals much of his plan for each of us in the Holy Scriptures. Both mature Christians and those who are just being awakened to a personal relationship with God can find tremendous value in the Twelve Steps. By regularly applying them to the events of one's life, the steps become a means for enriching one's relationship with God. The steps are especially powerful when used together with the regular Christian practices of prayer, meditation, and Bible study. We will discover the unique ways in which the Holy Scriptures support and expand our understanding of the steps.

Your Story: Describe your practice of prayer, Bible reading, or quiet time. _Mostly_ _in och. on way to/from wk - find mind wonders/excited about idea of_ _reading Bible but rarely follow thru / no planned time - almost non-existent._

The Twelve-Step process of recovery is a spiritual journey. It takes us from a life where we experience confusion and grief to a place of peace and serenity—one day at a time. Many changes can and will come over us, but they won't happen all at once. The process takes time and patience. God, in his time, instills in us the strength of character that only comes from a healthy relationship with him.

Your Story: Describe your present spiritual condition. _Bleak — I know God_ _is caring for me + that I have been saved by Christ_ _but do not feel the joy + peace + love that should_ _accompany this knowledge._

We may have many self-defeating habits or behaviors that need correcting. When looking at our inappropriate methods of relating to others, it is important to remember the ways in which these patterns began. Because of the chaotic conditions of our childhood, we developed behaviors that now sabotage and assault the successful management of our lives as adults. Having grown up in emotionally repressive families, we became accustomed to denying our pain and discomfort. Most of us found it necessary to shut down our feelings and keep everything locked inside. We learned that expressing our own wants and needs caused rejection. This rejection stimulated intense feelings of inadequacy.

Your Story: Recall one painful incident from childhood. _Physical - spanking_ _w/coat hanger. Emotional - the "What will people_ _think" Syndrome._

In our present environments, we may have trouble freely expressing pain, fear, anger, or need. We repress our true feelings because we continue to view our environment the same as we did in childhood. When we openly express our needs, we risk rejection. In order to avoid rejection, many of us compensate for our repressed feelings by doing things to extremes. Our behavior may include preoccupation with relationships, our church, and our job. Or we may cover our true feelings through overwork, overeating, or abuse of mood-altering substances such as drugs and alcohol.

Your Story: What behaviors do you use to compensate for or cover your uncomfortable feelings? _The "mask" - don't give anyone else the_ _power to hurt you / if hurt, do not give anyone the_ _satisfaction of knowing they have hurt you._

How do these behaviors affect the rest of your life? _Fraidy Cat. —_
inability to love freely — judgemental — failed if
anything wrong w/whatever doing.

The healing process begins when we look honestly at ourselves. We see the chaotic conditions of our lives as a result of not being prepared for adult relationships and responsibilities. God has given us free will. We can choose several ways of relating to the people and events in our lives. It is important to set aside some of our negative childhood messages and begin the work of learning new behaviors that will better serve us.

Some of us were taught to believe that, if we are Christians, our lives will "automatically" be in order, and we will experience peace and serenity. Yet many Christians know their lives are in turmoil despite their intense devotion to religion. Time, patience, and commitment to God's principles and ways are required to change. And our Christian experience doesn't magically erase the pain or consequences of the past. Instead, our faith empowers us to live life according to God's will.

For Christians who suffer from an addictive disease, or who are the product of a family with addictive traits, the Church's message can sometimes be perceived as shaming. This can keep a person from seeking recovery. There is rarely confusion, however, when the Church's message is honesty. The Bible modeled this honesty by documenting the strengths and weaknesses of God's people. Unfortunately, for some, to admit to imperfection might mean that we are not good Christians. In reality, to admit to imperfection means _we need God_, and that's OK. True recovery begins as we work the spiritual principles embodied in the Twelve Steps. It is most easily accomplished when we acknowledge our need for help, comfort, and courage to face our problems.

Your Story: Explain how your religious experience reinforced your tendency to deny your need for healing. _Judgemental God who doles out_
punishment - Denial of the sacrement for divorce
(Catholicism)

Working the steps with God's help enables us to acknowledge much of our negative or repressed nature. This process is similar to sunlight and shadow. When we stand in the sunlight, we see that we cast a shadow. In the same way, as we begin to work the steps and measure ourselves by God's standards and principles, we see our need. But standing before the Lord and seeking his healing grace does not automatically relieve us of the consequences of our past behavior. We do find, however, that by asking God for help in facing our old behaviors, we are able to begin the work of change and healing.

Diligently seeking God's will for us and working the material in this book enables us to reexamine our relationship with God. This process helps us discover new ways in which the Holy Spirit empowers our daily lives. We learn to look fearlessly at our "shadow"—that part of us that has been ignored for so long. With the help of God's grace we experience changes in our unwanted behaviors such as people pleasing, repressed anger, obsessive thinking, or inappropriate sexual behavior. Through our relationship with Christ we are able to redefine the limits we set for ourselves, and we discover that "all things are possible" for those who love God.

Thought: God's judgment: we get what we deserve.
God's mercy: we don't get what we deserve.
God's grace: we get more than we deserve.
God doesn't have any problems, only plans.

Your Story: What unwanted behaviors do you see in your shadow? _Failure to_
trust or love — judgemental — some compulsions —
fear

With God's power, the Twelve-Step program can be a tool to relieve our suffering, fill our emptiness, and help us extend God's presence in our lives. This releases energy, love, and joy that are new to us. It is a program we follow at our own pace, in our own way. We walk this journey one step at a time, with God's help and with the support of others in the program. All we need is an open mind. Much of the work is done by God's Spirit working through us. If we work the steps faithfully, we notice improvements in ourselves: our awareness, our sensitivity, our ability to love and be free. Our spiritual and emotional growth may surprise us.

GOD BLESS YOU.

This workbook provides a practical way to use the Twelve Steps as a recovery tool and to fully integrate the steps as an ongoing part of our spiritual pilgrimage. The book uses biblical insight to help us identify and deal with issues that are interfering with our lives. Working through these issues requires that we rely on the dynamics of God's word and the Twelve Steps. If we approach this work seriously, we will experience recovery that nurtures physical, emotional, and spiritual well-being.

Trust in God's guidance is necessary. In this program, it is important to realize that God wants us to be returned to wholeness. He gives us the courage to work, to struggle, and to succeed. God also gives us the comfort we need to give him control of our lives and to surrender to the Twelve-Step process.

If you are new to Twelve-Step support groups, it is important to use other resources to help identify more specific issues that pertain to you. Many anonymous Twelve-Step programs have meetings that are focused on issues of relationships, food, sex, alcohol, drugs, etc. Taking part in groups such as Adult Children of Alcoholics, Co-Dependents Anonymous, or Al-Anon broadens your understanding of recovery issues and exposes you to others who share similar problems. You learn more about your own issues and have a sounding board for matters that may arise in the Step Study. We encourage you to read additional material relating to the issues that are problems for you. This increases your awareness and enhances your ability to participate in the process. The Self-Help Resources in Appendix Two will help you identify an appropriate program for you. Other resources are also available through your library or in the telephone directory under "social service organizations" or "crisis intervention."

Your Story: Describe your past or current involvement in other Twelve-Step support or recovery groups. *Book similar to this — Love is a Choice*

Although the material in this book focuses on the individual, the most often-used format for the book includes forming small "family groups," with a limit of six people per family group. Members of this group are not members of your biological family; however, they become like family for the purpose of mutual support in recovery. These family groups work together for a portion of the meeting, and then gather with other groups during the final segment for general sharing.

NOTE: The meeting format for Week Two is in Appendix One on page 237.

Workshop participation is an important step in breaking out of the isolation often experienced by adults reared in chaotic homes. An important part of this process is feeling safe in the "family group." By using the steps as the central tool, along with the support of the family group, it becomes possible to express long-suppressed shame, anger, and grief. The process involves the release and letting go of the past. It makes room for the "one day at a time" serenity and calmness that are a result of working the steps.

As the title implies, the Twelve Steps are a spiritual journey. They can be used as a way out of self-destructive behavior, and also as a laboratory in which to learn new behavior. The Twelve Steps provide an opportunity to experience feelings, talk openly with others, enjoy life one day at a time, and develop healthy relationships. Working together in a group can be a powerful and transforming process. Loneliness diminishes as friendships among group members develop. Individuals can learn to be close to others by giving as well as receiving comfort and support. Communication outside the meeting is a vital element in the workshop process. Use the telephone and other ways to socialize and support one another outside the regular meeting time.

Relationships formed in the family group are a source of many benefits and rewards. The experience of being in a small family group creates an atmosphere in which healthy, family-type communications can develop. It is a safe environment where trust can be learned. The small family groups provide an arena for quality sharing in which family secrets no longer need to be hidden, and the process of loving self-parenting can begin.

Your Story: What do you need from a support group to feel safe?_____

Anonyminity. Complete trust.

Wherever possible, share your insights with someone you trust. Communicating your discoveries to a trusted person can work miracles in your recovery journey. The leaders of this group are familiar with the steps, and their insights and experiences can be invaluable. You will be working with others in your family group who can provide support and encouragement. As you share with others and build new relationships during this journey, be aware that they are not there to give advice or to fix you. The healing results from developing a relationship with your Higher Power.

During the workshop, various issues will surface. Perhaps problems within the small family group will cause conflicts. These issues can usually be resolved without making changes within the group. The struggles within each family group often reflect the roles and reactions from the family of origin. Leaving the groups intact for the duration of the workshop allows participants to resolve their conflicts, foster growth, and strengthen the bonds within the family group.

As participants surrender to guidance from God, problems are handled more constructively. As adults from dysfunctional backgrounds, we rely on the familiar behaviors of being caretakers, (enablers) or people pleasers. This is usually because of our inability to confront inappropriate, hurtful, or self-defeating behavior. Instead, we tend to be overly nice to each other. In keeping with the need for a safe environment, excessive confrontation is usually not required for the family group members to alter old patterns of behavior. However, straightforward feedback is critically important. Our communication is most useful when we share our personal experience in a situation similar to the issue at hand.

Due to our early exposure to negative behavior, many inappropriate behaviors may appear normal to us (e.g., resentment, greed, sexual abuse, dishonesty, gluttony, envy, laziness). Negative feelings may also seem normal (e.g., self-pity, sadness, insecurity, worry, fear of rejection, fear of abandonment). As we progress through the steps, this habit of seeing negative feelings or behavior as normal will change. We will experience growth in all areas by an increased sense of self-worth and self-esteem. Therefore, honest feelings and thoughts need to be appreciated and encouraged. This makes it possible to air elements of discouragement or distress before they hinder the group's progress.

Your Story: What behaviors do you fear most when you participate in this group? This may be yours or someone else's (e.g. anger, isolation, competitiveness, control, etc.). ___Exposure + vunerability._____

_____

_____

USING THIS BOOK

At the beginning of each step there is a step overview with the following elements: Understanding the Step, Working the Step, Preparing for the Step, and Prayer for the Step. Next, there is a step narrative followed by Personal Reflection, which begins the step's writing exercise. Carefully read the narrative and the Personal Reflection section before answering the questions. Note any areas that are unclear to you and seek assistance if needed. Then turn to the Personal Reflection section and answer the questions. If you feel a question does not apply to you, it is not necessary to answer it. Remember, it is your book and it is your right to use the book to your benefit.

Throughout each step there are "Helpful Hints." These are intended as aids in understanding the scripture or question. The "Helpful Hints" refer to *The Life Recovery Bible* by Tyndale House Publishers, *Meditations for the Twelve Steps—A Spiritual Journey,* and *Prayers for the Twelve Steps—A Spiritual Journey* by RPI Publishing.

At the conclusion of each step there is a section entitled "Key Ideas." This section will help you recall the important concepts from each step. Many of the key ideas center around important words from the step.

In this edition, the weekly writing exercises that were previously in the Appendix have been incorporated into the step. The focus and sharing is on the work done in the step. The weekly meeting formats are in Appendix One. The Serenity Prayer, Milestones in Recovery, Twelve Steps and Related Scriptures, and Common Behavior Characteristics are in Appendix Three. To support this process, we have added a section called "Preparing for Community." This section provides specific questions to aid group interaction.

The suggested "Group Activities" are included to provide ideas for group exercises, to illustrate or reinforce important aspects of each step, and to provide an opportunity for fun. Some activities are spiritual in nature, some are relational, others are emotional, and still others have a physical element. The "Group Activities" are also intended to enliven and support the group experience.

As you proceed through the steps, pace yourself and complete as much of each step as possible. Don't be discouraged if Steps One, Two, and Three seem overwhelming to you—this is a common reaction for persons who are new to the steps. Completion of these three steps forms the foundation for working the program. Allow sufficient time to go through the process of thinking about the questions and exercises. Do a little each day. This may take several days, a week, or longer. Be patient with yourself. Allow ample time to digest the content of each question and reflect on its meaning. Impatience can seriously impair your effectiveness.

You may decide to participage in a Step Study writing workshop more than once. The program is a lifelong process to be used regularly, in part or in whole. This workbook should not be your only involvement. It is just one part of working the Twelve Steps.

The Twelve-Step material used in this book is a framework upon which our own life experiences can be reviewed with love and courage. We realize we have reached this point knowing very little about ourselves. As we develop a deeper relationship with God, more will be revealed to us. Slowly we will be given the strength to put the past behind us and build a new life. The depth of our relationship with God will be increased as our knowledge of him increases (Psalm 119). Our lives can be less complicated if we work the steps regularly and continue to improve our relationship with our Higher Power. When we do this, our lives are blessed with the ongoing gift of God's peace and serenity (John 14:27).

Give freely of yourself and join us. We shall be with you in the fellowship of God's Holy Spirit.

The Participation Agreement establishes our personal commitment during this workshop. Accepting them is your choice. The level of individual success, however, will depend on each person's commitment to the process and cooperation with the group.

The Participation Agreement will be signed in each family group member's book during Week Four. Following is a preview of the agreement with brief explanations to clarify each statement and its value.

I agree to fully participate with my family group in working the Twelve Steps. As part of the agreement I will:

Make this workshop a priority in my life for the designated number of weeks.

- Making the workshop a priority means planning our calendars in advance to avoid conflicts with other events or activities. It also means working hard to provide time and energy for all of the requirements of the step study process.

Participate fully in the group's work, discussions, activities, assignments, and projects.

- Participating fully with our family group requires a serious attitude and sincere commitment. Half-heartedness will undermine our own recovery as well as the group's overall success.

Share my experience, strength, and hope during the meeting.

- One of the fundamental strengths of any Twelve-Step program is the shared experience, strength, and hope of its members. When we share our story with others, we allow others to hear of our experience, to learn from our mistakes, to identify with our struggles, to share our hope, and to feel a sense of community and belonging.

Study the steps as thoroughly as possible by scheduling extra time for step work, reading additional materials, attending other Twelve-Step meetings, and discussing the steps with more experienced members.

- We cannot get a full understanding of the Twelve-Step process just from our involvement in one meeting or workshop experience. We need to expose ourselves to a variety of resources.

Maintain contact with my family group members between meetings in order to foster the fellowship, communication, and support that is developed in the meetings.

- Because of the problems that many of us experienced with our biological family, it is important to establish healthy and nurturing relationships with our family group members. We cannot experience recovery by ourselves, and relationships cannot grow without consistent contact. We need others to help us break through the denial and isolation that have affected our lives.

Support my family group members individually by giving them my respectful attention, emotional support, and spiritual fellowship.

- The golden rule, which admonishes us to treat others as we want to be treated, is a good rule for our interaction with family group members. When others speak in a meeting, we should give them undivided attention; when they are hurting, we should lend support and comfort; and at all times, we should give them our spiritual fellowship.

Be as honest as possible in all things, especially with regard to what I am learning about myself—past and present.

- Because denial is a common problem that all of us in recovery face, we need to commit ourselves to honesty. We all want the respect and approval of others, but in the family group context, we must strive to be honest about ourselves and less concerned about our image.

Express my feelings about myself, my family group and its members, my recovery, and my relationship with God.

- Feelings need to be expressed, and the family group can be a safe place for that expression. It is an opportunity to talk about personal feelings, as well as feelings that relate to other family group members. For example, if we feel discomfort when someone uses excessive volume or profanity in the meeting, we should express our feelings to the group.

Accept any discomfort or unsettling behavior changes that I may experience as a result of working the Twelve Steps.

- Working the Twelve Steps is not easy. Surrender to God, self-examination, confession, amends, and other Twelve-Step work all represent major life changes, and these changes can cause us discomfort along the way. Our commitment to recovery includes a willingness to accept discomfort in the process.

Humbly submit to the recovery process.

- Our wrongful pride and character defects can cause us to exert undue control over every aspect of our recovery process. If we allow that to happen, we will hinder our recovery and damage our family group's harmony. Instead, humility is needed. We should humbly submit to the principles and process of the Twelve Steps and to the ground rules which have been established for the group.

Remember that God loves me and wants me to succeed and that my ultimate goal is to experience God's will in my life.

· The Twelve Steps will not work apart from God. Real healing begins when we surrender our will and lives to God. But that surrender is impossible without the conviction that God loves us and wants what is best for us. We need to remind ourselves and others that God is good and his will is best.

Pray, meditate, and work the first three steps daily.

· Because the Twelve Steps are spiritual, we must be commited to maintaining contact with God through prayer and meditation. We must also be commited to the daily surrendering process of the first three steps, through which we admit our need, believe in God's ability, and surrender to his control.

PARTICIPATION AGREEMENT

I, _____, agree to fully participate with my family group in working the Twelve Steps. As a part of my agreement, I will:

❑ Make this workshop a priority in my life for the designated number of weeks.

❑ Participate fully in the group's work, discussions, activities, assignments, and projects.

❑ Share my experience, strength, and hope during the meeting.

❑ Study the steps as thoroughly as possible by scheduling extra time for step work, reading additional materials, attending other Twelve-Step meetings, and discussing the steps with more experienced members.

❑ Maintain contact with my family group members between meetings in order to foster the fellowship, communication, and support that is developed in the meetings.

❑ Support my family group members individually by giving them my respectful attention, emotional support, and spiritual fellowship.

❑ Be as honest as possible in all things, especially with regard to what I am learning about myself—past and present.

❑ Express my feelings about myself, my family group and its members, my recovery, and my relationship with God.

❑ Accept any discomfort or unsettling behavior changes that I may experience as a result of working the Twelve Steps.

❑ Humbly submit to the recovery process.

❑ Remember that God loves me and wants me to succeed and that my ultimate goal is to experience God's will in my life.

❑ Pray, meditate, and work the first three steps daily.

_____   _____

Signed (Participant)   _____

_____   _____

Date   _____

                                            _____

                                            Witnessed (Family Group Members)

Quality communication and support among family group members is essential for effective completion of the materials. Ecclesiastes 4:9–12 conveys the principle of Christ-centered partnership: *"Two are better than one, because they have a good return for their work. If one falls down, his friend can help him up. But pity the man who falls and has no one to help him up!...Though one may be overpowered, two can defend themselves. A cord of three strands is not quickly broken."*

Writing about and sharing our progress with the steps involves a process of redefining our knowledge and understanding of ourselves. Sharing our recovery story with our family group will reveal how our attitudes about ourselves and others can be founded on faulty information. We learned this information from a number of people: parents, siblings, and other relatives who did not know, or perhaps did not care to know, the truth about their own worth and value, or the beauty of other people.

We are encouraged to be open and vulnerable with our family group. Creating a safe place for one another is a very important part of this process as we come together to be supported and to share our journey. We will identify the fears and resentments of our past. This helps us break the vicious cycle of passing hurtful and addictive behavior on to our own children. If we delay taking responsibility for our need for recovery and change, our own children may be faced with self-defeating behaviors in their lives.

It is a challenge to keep in contact with family group members between weekly meetings. We may be unaccustomed to having people actively interested in improving the quality of their lives. Sharing with members of our family group offers us an opportunity to experience supportive-type relationships. We get to know new "friends in recovery" in the weekly meetings and through contact with family group members.

Your Story: Recall a supportive relationship you've had in the past. Describe one important aspect of that relationship experience. _____

_____

_____

Our sharing requires telling our family group members what we are thinking. They cannot read our minds, and we can become resentful or angry if they do not respond to our problems. Although we may be reluctant to share, it is an opportunity to rebuild our trust. By sharing openly we discover what is in our

NOTE: The meeting format for Week Three is in Appendix One on page 239.

own hearts and minds. The dynamics of discovering what we feel and think often occurs through communication with others. Through the process of sharing, many unexpected changes occur. We experience the courage to let go of our fear of discovery. By asking for and receiving support from others, we feel empowered to allow the past to slip away in order to develop a new life.

As we write and share the working of this material, our stories may be ones we have told in the past. It is important to view our sharing as redefining our past behavior, not telling and retelling the unhappy details of shattered dreams and painful childhood experiences. If we repeat our stories often and dramatically, we may find they are exaggerated. We must examine our motives for retelling the drama of our past. Is it because we feel like victims? Are we blaming others or making excuses? Are we justifying our present problems? Are we wallowing in our past miseries and recharging old resentments? Part of our recovery is letting go of our old behavior. This means taking time to listen carefully to what we are sharing and asking the family group members to give honest feedback. If what we are talking about does not support our recovery, there is no reason for sharing it.

Some of us have never overcome the fear of revealing our true feelings. We justify this fear by stating that we have nothing to offer. This is not true, because the quality of our relationships will be determined by the honesty of our sharing. We must each learn how to feel comfortable with others in our family group. By sharing openly and allowing ourselves to be vulnerable, we show our family group that we trust them. Nothing equals the importance of revealing our real selves so we can be known, healed, and loved.

This work prepares us to become mentors to other people who are beginning to deal with their traumatic past. In this workshop and in other places and times, we exhibit to others what we are learning for ourselves. We show how the discipline of the Twelve Steps is strengthening our walk with God. Sharing our experience, strength, and hope with others encourages their growth. Simultaneously we encourage others to discover the joys they have awaiting them.

We take turns being followers until we are ready to lead. We learn from others by the principles and practices that produced positive and healthy experiences for them. By our continued commitment to heal our character flaws, we will find others looking to us for comfort, direction, and wisdom.

For many of us, our participation in this study makes us want to bring together members of our biological families. This is because each of us has a deep need to participate as loving members of a healthy family system. We may be able to do this successfully with our own families, or we may discover another family of people who love us, whether they are relatives or not. The recovery process is a time for us to realize that we don't have to be without a loving family.

Your Story: Describe your present relationship with members of your family of origin. _____

_____

_____

WORKING WITH A RECOVERY PARTNER

The concern, support, and input of others is essential to the recovery process. One way to ensure this support is through working with a "recovery partner." A recovery partner is someone we can trust, someone who will help us recognize how denial keeps us from discovering the truth about ourselves. Working with a recovery partner makes it easier to identify our fears and resentments, as well as our self-defeating and addictive behavior.

Sharing with a recovery partner offers us an opportunity to experience a one-on-one relationship without the distractions found when groups meet together. For individuals who have felt betrayed in the past, this is an opportunity to rebuild trust. We have an opportunity to develop mutual trust by communicating privately with a recovery partner. We can reveal ourselves to another person without feeling intimidated by others in a group setting. This dynamic can cause a breakthrough in learning to trust in someone and in being willing to share openly about their life experiences.

CHOOSING A RECOVERY PARTNER

A recovery partner is similar to a mentor or sponsor. This person can be a role model for learning how to enjoy a better quality of life through the love of God and the wisdom of the program. It is important to choose someone who displays qualities you value and respect. These qualities can include:

- Belief in the Christian faith and a willingness to share his or her walk with God.

- Sincerity and honesty in sharing personal stories of recovery and how the Twelve Steps work in his or her life.

- Willingness to provide support and encouragement by listening and giving honest feedback without trying to force change.

- Ability to confront difficult issues and ask for accountability in keeping commitments.

- Openness of communication in all matters, even when discussing sensitive issues such as sexual abuse, violence, or other severe trauma-inducing subjects.

What other qualities would you like to have in a recovery partner? _____

_____

_____

When choosing a recovery partner, it is advisable to select an individual who:

- Shares common interests and experiences and displays positive results in recovery.

- Understands and identifies with addictive, compulsive, or obsessive behavior.

- Has patience and compassion and is willing to listen attentively and offer suggestions without giving advice.

- Is available to spend time together when it is necessary.

- Is the same sex and can relate to personal issues in a nonthreatening way.

What other qualities would you add? _____

_____

_____

Questions and expectations arise when choosing a recovery partner. Some of them are:

- **What about the fear of rejection?** The process of dealing with fear of rejection can occur when asking someone to be a recovery partner. Because the program encourages rigorous honesty, we should begin by honestly telling the other person about any discomfort we feel when seeking a recovery partnership. We should offer the other person freedom of choice in the decision, and then detach from the outcome by trusting that God's will prevails.

- **What happens when you are asked to be a partner and don't want to be?** This program can help us establish boundaries for ourselves. Boundaries include how we spend our time, express our feelings, and enter new relationships. Knowing when to say, "Thank you for asking, but that won't work for me," is all a part of setting boundaries. Setting boundaries can be an important step we take in simplifying our life, and does not require an explanation.

- **What about ending a recovery partnership?** Ending a recovery-partner relationship is part of learning when to select more appropriate support. It is also a reminder that one may not meet the needs of the recovery partner forever. Personal growth is a natural part of the process. The outcome may still be a very good friendship.

What do you fear most when looking for or working with a recovery partner?

_____

_____

BENEFITS OF A RECOVERY PARTNER

Many benefits result from working with a recovery partner, including the fulfillment of many biblical admonitions. Below is a list of some of the benefits along with related biblical references.

- Partners provide a non-threatening system of mutual accountability. For example, a partner can agree to call the other for support and prayer in abstaining from a harmful habit.

"Therefore confess your sins to each other and pray for each other so that you may be healed. The prayer of a righteous man is powerful and effective." (James 5:14–16)

- Partners minister to each other's specific area of need with directed prayer each time they meet. Openly sharing thoughts and feelings helps to clarify needs in problem areas. This contributes to one's freedom from the past. The focus is to live honestly in the present with realistic expectations.

"Pray continually; give thanks in all circumstances, for this is God's will for you in Christ Jesus." (1 Thess. 5:17)

- Partners encourage one another to progress from a state of physical, emotional, and spiritual sickness to wholeness of life. It is normal to feel discomfort when unhealthy familiar behaviors are being transformed. Healthy behavior is a result of doing God's will.

"...consider how we may spur one another on toward love and good deeds." (Heb. 10:24)

- Partners aid one another in applying biblical truths to personal and relationship needs. When partners openly share their faults with one another, honesty, trust, and healing occur. This also means we can appropriately quote Scripture to shed light on an experience. It is not appropriate to over-spiritualize and lose the vulnerability of the moment or lose the point of what is shared.

Jesus said, " 'If you hold to my teaching, you are really my disciples. Then you will know the truth, and the truth will set you free.' " (John 8:31–32)

What do you want most from a recovery partner? _____

_____

_____

MUTUAL AGREEMENT

A key part in establishing a relationship with a recovery partner is to agree on how the partners want to interact with one another. The agreement can establish what the expectations are between one another, and the length of time in which the agreement will be in effect. Times can be selected to evaluate the quality of the relationship. It is helpful to have an understanding of how the relationship or agreement can be ended.

Following is a preview of the agreement with brief explanations to clarify each statement and its value.

Focus on the Twelve Steps as a tool to enhance one's relationship with God and others.

- At times encouragement or confrontation is needed when one has stopped working the steps. If a partner is unavailable or can't answer a question, seek out other Twelve-Step fellow travelers to help in understanding how they use this discipline in their recovery. It is inappropriate to impose personal views on one's recovery partner, particularly regarding one's relationship with God.

Be available for phone calls or meeting in person.

- A key to success in recovery is making and keeping commitments. Making a commitment to being available may be something new, but it is an important part of the process. Healing and change are easier when someone is available to offer support and encouragement.

Share true feelings between each other.

- Rigorous honesty is important when sharing feelings. Healing is supported when partners tell the truth. Feelings require acknowledgment and appropriate expression without their being judged as right or wrong. Selective disclosure when talking about feelings may create doubt between partners.

Refrain from giving lengthy explanations when sharing.

- Sharing is not a lengthy or dramatic re-creation of personal stories. Referring to journal notes or workbook writing keeps the focus on the subject shared and helps to avoid intellectualizing.

Complete the homework assignment each week.

- Partners can provide support and encouragement to each other in completing the assignment. Sharing the results of homework writing often helps clarify the meaning of questions and is an opportunity to hear another perspective.

Spend a minimum of 15 minutes each day reading Scripture, praying, and meditating, including prayer for your recovery partner.

- Prayer is talking to God, meditation is listening to God. Spending time in prayer and meditation can be a vital part of the recovery process. This is a spiritual program founded upon seeking to know God's will and experiencing his grace.

Respect confidentiality and refrain from gossip.

- This program is built on trust. Fear of gossip may prevent some people from honestly sharing the pain of their lives. Healing will be hindered unless there is trust that personal matters between partners will remain confidential.

Accept discomfort as part of the healing process, and be willing to talk about it.

- Some meetings may be painful when memories of certain events or hurtful feelings are recalled. It is important to have a recovery partner available to show compassion and be supportive as we confront painful issues that cause us discomfort. It is best to admit the discomfort and deal with it. A recovery partner can help us face the issues without reverting to old coping methods.

Support one another by listening attentively and offering constructive feedback.

- Listening attentively and offering feedback enables us to explore options and possible courses of action. This can strengthen one another's ability to make healthy choices that provide good results. Feedback, however, must not be confused with unsolicited advice.

Refrain from spiritualizing or intellectualizing when sharing.

- Partners are not spiritual directors to each other nor are they sources of advice in areas more appropriately handled by clergy or a professional therapist. Instead, partners share their own experience, strength, and hope with one another. In spiritual matters, recovery partners share how God works in their lives without over-spiritualizing or preaching.

MUTUAL AGREEMENT
BETWEEN RECOVERY PARTNERS

I, _____, agree to enter a Recovery Partner agreement with _____, as a way to be supported and held accountable in dealing with behaviors that keep me from the best God has for me. I am seeking recovery from these ineffective patterns of behavior so that I may become more fully connected to God, myself, and others.

I will make a sincere effort to:

❑ Focus on the Twelve Steps as a tool to enhance my relationship with God and others.

❑ Be available for phone calls or meetings in person.

❑ Share my true feelings with my recovery partner.

❑ Refrain from giving lengthy explanations when sharing.

❑ Complete the homework assignment each week.

❑ Spend a minimum of 15 minutes each day reading Scripture, praying and meditating, including specific prayer for my recovery partner.

❑ Accept discomfort as part of the healing process, and be willing to talk about it.

❑ Support one another by listening attentively and offering my constructive feedback.

❑ Refrain from spiritualizing or intellectualizing when sharing.

The term of this agreement is from _____ to _____.

We agree to meet _____ (weekly, monthly, etc.) outside the weekly meetings, and spend time reviewing the progress and compatibility of this relationship. If for any reason either partner feels this relationship does not serve his/her recovery needs, the agreement can be ended by notifying the other partner.

_____   _____
Signed   Partner

COMMON BEHAVIOR CHARACTERISTICS

Adults who were reared in dysfunctional homes share certain common behavior characteristics. This is especially true when their caretakers were chemically dependent or emotionally repressed individuals. The behaviors reveal an underlying structure of disorder that is damaging to those involved. Although the general population displays many of the behaviors, individuals from dysfunctional families tend to have a higher incidence of these characteristics. This list is intended to help you recognize areas of your life in which dysfunctional behavior characteristics are present. Examples are given to help you identify some of your thoughts, feelings, and behaviors.

1. We have feelings of low self-esteem that cause us to judge ourselves and others without mercy. We cover up or compensate by trying to be perfect, take responsibility for others, attempt to control the outcome of unpredictable events, get angry when things don't go our way, or gossip instead of confronting an issue. For example:

- I'm inclined to talk about my family and extended family. I often recite all of their faults and shortcomings to others.

- When I am alone with my own thoughts I tend to criticize myself. Sometimes I feel stupid, inadequate, ugly, or worthless.

- I don't feel important. I try to help others and hope they will notice me.

- I gossip and complain about those who make me feel powerless.

I compensate for my feelings of low self-esteem by _____

_____

2. We tend to isolate ourselves and to feel uneasy around other people, especially authority figures. For example:

- I like to blend into the scenery at work. I especially don't want the boss to notice me.

- I feel uncomfortable in most conversations, especially when the focus is on me.

- When I speak with someone in authority, I have trouble expressing myself.

- I isolate myself because it's easier than dealing with others.

NOTE: The meeting format for Week Four is in Appendix One on page 241.

I isolate myself from other people by _____

_____

When I am around authority figures I usually _____

_____

3. We are approval seekers and will do anything to make people like us. We are extremely loyal even in the face of evidence that suggests loyalty is undeserved. For example:

- I offer to do favors for people even before they ask.

- I worry about what others are thinking and saying about me. When people stop talking as I approach, I assume they're talking about me.

- Although I may not like my boss or friends, I am loyal because I fear being rejected.

- I find it hard to admit that I came from a dysfunctional home. I feel guilty for admitting that my parents were less than perfect.

The ways I seek approval from my family or friends include _____

_____

I suspect my loyalty toward _____ is inappropriate because _____

_____

4. We are intimidated by angry people and personal criticism. This causes us to feel anxious and overly sensitive. For example:

- I find it nearly impossible to listen to a "fire and brimstone" sermon.

- When someone with strong opinions speaks to me, I rarely share my true feelings. Instead, I say what I think the other person wants to hear.

- I may harbor a secret desire to retaliate against the angry and opinionated people who threaten my peace.

- I panic when someone points out a mistake or a problem with my work.

My first recollection of being intimidated by an angry person is when_____

_____

I respond to personal criticism by _____

_____

5. We habitually choose to have relationships with emotionally unavailable people with addictive personalities. We are usually less attracted to healthy, caring people. For example:

- I am in a relationship with someone who seems uncaring. I sense that my problems don't matter.

- Life is always a crisis. I wonder what it would be like to live a normal life.

- Others and not myself seem to set the agenda for my life.

- I sometimes feel that I deserve to "give in" to temptation, especially after I've suffered and done so much for others.

The people in my life with addictive/compulsive personality styles (e.g., alcoholic, workaholic, gambler, overeater, religious fanatic, perfectionist) are _____

_____

The relationships from which I receive the most nurture and support are _____

_____

6. We live life as victims and are attracted to other victims in our love and friendship relationships. We confuse love with pity and tend to "love" people we can pity and rescue. For example:

- I seem to get the short end of every stick, and I agree with the saying, "No good deed goes unpunished."

- I almost feel good about myself when I am doing something for others. However, I've learned from experience that they won't appreciate it.

- My friends tell me that I am a good listener, but I resent how they lose interest when I share.

- I spend a lot of my time fixing other people's problems.

The last time I noticed that I was "being used" by someone was when_____

_____

I try to rescue others by doing things like _____

_____

7. We are either overly responsible or very irresponsible. We try to solve others' problems or expect others to be responsible for us. This enables us to avoid looking closely at our own behavior. For example:

- I am usually called when family members have a problem.

- No one at my job or church cares as much or works as hard as I do.

- When things fail at home or at work, I feel that I have somehow failed.

OR

- Others don't understand how sick I am, and I'm expected to do too much.

- I'm just waiting for the right opportunity to become reinvolved in life.

- I'm waiting for God to make positive changes in my life.

I feel overly responsible when _____

_____

I feel very irresponsible when_____

_____

8. We feel guilty when we stand up for ourselves or act assertively. We give in to others instead of taking care of ourselves. For example:

- After I stand up for myself, I feel guilty and think maybe I was wrong.

- When I feel safe with a close friend or family member, I share all my resentments about the pushy people in my life.

- I feel sick when I'm told that certain people are wanting to see me or talk to me.

- I store a great deal of anger inside instead of releasing it properly. I sometimes scream, slam doors, or break things when no one is around.

Recently I was afraid to express my true feelings and I gave in to_____

when _____

9. We deny, minimize, or repress our feelings from our traumatic childhoods. We have difficulty expressing our feelings and are unaware of the impact this has on our lives. For example:

- There are portions of my childhood that I simply cannot remember.

- I sometimes react with overwhelming panic, anxiety, or fear in certain situations, and I have no idea why.

- I find it hard to get really excited about things. Other people are annoyed when I don't share their excitement.

- When I start to feel too much anxiety or fear or when I hear the committee in my head, I look for something to distract me or kill the pain.

I deny, minimize, or repress my feelings when _____

_____

10. We are dependent personalities who are terrified of rejection or abandonment. We tend to stay in jobs or relationships that are harmful to us. Our fears can either stop us from ending hurtful relationships or prevent us from entering healthy, rewarding ones. For example:

- When someone close to me is silent or emotionally absent, I panic and fear the worst.

- If my superiors don't seem to recognize my work, I assume that they are displeased and ready to let me go.

- When I disagree with a friend or companion, I later fear that I have irreparably damaged the relationship. I may even call several times to smooth things over or apologize.

- I spend time daydreaming about what it would be like to have a different job, spouse, friends, etc.

I fear rejection or abandonment the most in my relationship with _____

_____

I currently deal with this fear by _____

_____

11. Denial, isolation, control, and misplaced guilt are symptoms of family dysfunction. Because of these behaviors, we feel hopeless and helpless. For example:

- I just wish that people would leave me alone.

- I try to manage my own life, but circumstance and other people are always invading my plan.

- I work hard to reveal little about myself, or I try to manage how people think of me.

- I don't have much hope that things will change. Good things happen to others, but not me. I seem to be cursed, or something.

- Sometimes I can't wait to go home, close the door, and disconnect from reality.

The results of my family's dysfunction are seen in my life when I _____

_____

12. We have difficulty with intimate relationships. We feel insecure and lack trust in others. We don't have clearly defined boundaries and become enmeshed with our partner's needs and emotions. For example:

· If someone close to me is angry, I immediately feel threatened, even if the anger is toward another person or outside force.

· I can have sex with my spouse, but I sometimes find it difficult to be really close or romantic.

· I often belittle my looks (if only to myself) or doubt my attractiveness.

· I may try to change my spouse or companion's mood by suggesting some pleasurable activity.

My present difficulties with intimate relationships are _____

_____

I have difficulty trusting _____ because _____

_____

13. We have difficulty following projects through from beginning to end. For example:

· I finish most projects at the last minute.

· My desk is full of great projects that I *was* excited about but never handled.

· I have at least one room (or more) in my house that I hope no one ever sees.

· I feel guilty when I think of all the time and resources I've wasted on half-baked ideas or schemes.

When I lack motivation or procrastinate, I feel_____

_____

The current projects I'm not completing are _____

_____

14. We have a strong need to be in control. We overreact to change over which we have no control. For example:

· I want to know what my spouse or children are doing. I may even search their private belongings.

· If other people work for me, I find it hard to let them express their creativity. I want things done my way.

• When serious things happen that are beyond my control, I panic and take out my frustration on others. Or I take control through a flurry of activity.

• I find it very hard to relax or sleep. People sometimes tell me that I am "high-strung."

When I am not in control I fear _____

_____

When I am not in control I feel _____

_____

15. We tend to be impulsive. We take action before considering alternative behaviors or possible consequences. For example:

• I settle for less than what I really want, because I find it hard to decide.

• I sometimes write letters that I later wish I could get back.

• I go places and do things without much planning. I have made many "mistakes" in life.

• I make commitments that I later regret. I may even have my spouse or children call and cancel my commitments.

My impulsiveness caused me to make a poor decision when I _____

_____

PREPARING FOR COMMUNITY

Which three characteristics would you like to share with others? _____

_____

What is your overall reaction to reading the characteristics? To what degree do they apply to you? _____

_____

In what areas do you see yourself as overly responsible or very irresponsible? ____

_____

Which characteristic do you most closely relate to? How does this characteristic present itself in your life? _____

_____

We admitted we were powerless over the effects of our separation
from God—that our lives had become unmanageable.
. . .
I know that nothing good lives in me, that is, in my sinful nature. For I have
the desire to do what is good, but I cannot carry it out.
(ROM. 7:18)

UNDERSTANDING STEP ONE

When we were young, we were sometimes tickled by those who were bigger than us. They would often tickle us so hard and long that we lost control. We would gasp and cry for them to stop, and we would scream, "I quit, I give up, please stop!" Sometimes they stopped when we cried and sometimes they stopped only when someone older or bigger came to our rescue.

Step One is like this episode from childhood. Our own life and behavior is like the cruel tickler who inflicts pain and discomfort. We have done this to ourselves. We took control to protect ourselves, but results have frequently ended in chaos. And now we don't want to give up control and release ourselves from the torment. In Step One we admit that we can't stand it anymore. We plead for release. We cry, "I quit!"

WORKING STEP ONE

Step One is an opportunity to face reality and admit that our life isn't working with us in control. We embrace our powerlessness, we stop pretending. In a sense, we stop the juggling act that we have performed for so long. We admit that we can't continue the illusion of control. If it means that all the balls fall to the ground, then so be it. We are so tired of juggling our lives, we are ready to accept whatever comes.

PREPARING FOR STEP ONE

The way we manage our own lives brings us to the end of our rope. We hit bottom. Our ways and our efforts fail us. At this point, Step One provides needed direction for our unmanageability. We prepare ourselves by realizing that Step One is the first step in a spiritual journey toward wholeness. This step stops us. It puts a halt to our own efforts and gives us permission to quit.

NOTE: The meeting format for Weeks Five through Twenty-Nine are in Appendex One on page 243.

2nd Corin 11:30

PRAYER FOR STEP ONE

Today, I ask for help with my recovery. I feel a little lost and am very unsure of myself. Denial has kept me from seeing how powerless I am and how unmanageable my life has become. I need to learn and remember that I cannot manage my life or the lives of others. I also need to remember that the best thing I can do right now is to let go. I choose to let go—I admit that I am powerless and that my life is unmanageable.

The ideas presented in Step One are overwhelming to most of us until we begin to see our lives as they really are. It is threatening to imagine that we could be powerless, and that our lives could be unmanageable. Our life experiences, however, remind us that our behavior does not always produce peace and serenity. Our background, if affected by alcohol or other types of family dysfunction, undermines our best plans, desires, and dreams. Often, our troubled background has caused us to lose touch with God and ourselves. Our lives are full of unwelcome behaviors and overwhelming emotions.

We may have been taught to believe that we only have to accept Christ as our Lord and Savior for our lives to be complete and satisfying. This may have been the magic we relied upon to prepare us for the hereafter. Our proclamation that "I am born anew; the past is washed clean; I am a new creature; Christ has totally changed me" is true. Our Spirits are born anew, but since we have a lifetime of habits and wounds, we need more than salvation. We need transformation—the hard work of change. To over-spiritualize the initial work of salvation may be to deny the actual condition of our lives.

The fact that we still feel pain from our past is not a sign of a failed relationship with God. The presence of pain does not lessen the impact of salvation in our lives. This is simply a signal we need to begin the process of healing by daily working the steps with God's help. God will bring the healing and make the necessary changes. To admit to pains and problems may seem a contradiction of our strong claim to salvation, but it is not. The Bible is full of accounts of men and women who struggled continually to overcome past mistakes and life's many temptations.

The idea that there are areas of our lives over which we are powerless is a new idea for us. It is much easier for us to feel that we have power and are in control. Paul the Apostle, in his letter to the Church of Rome, describes the powerlessness and unmanageability of his life. He writes of his continued sinful behavior as proof of his separation from God (Rom. 7:14). Yet his admission does not interfere with his commitment to do God's will. Without knowing the details of Paul's background, we can only assume from his comments that self-will was a problem. Paul's will got in the way of God's will. Because of our background, we function in much the same way as Paul did, allowing our self-will to work against us and frustrate God's plan for us.

We live in a culture that places a high value on individual accomplishment. Most of us, from the time we were small children, were bombarded by the ideal of high achievement. Being competitive in school, sports, and business is viewed as important in our society. We are taught that if we compete hard enough we will be "winners" and, therefore, good people. If, however, we don't measure up to what is expected of us and are losers, we believe we are failures. Due to the absence of good role models during childhood, many of us are confused. We don't know where we fit in. We continue to allow our worth and self-esteem to be determined by what we do and what others think of us, and not by who we are in Christ. Looking back at our past, we may continue to classify ourselves as losers. We may condition ourselves to fail. Our low self-esteem keeps us from becoming winners and causes extreme stress and anxiety.

As we mature, matters get worse. The stressful lives we lead give us no satisfaction, and the stress compounds our problems. Our fears and insecurities increase, creating a sense of panic. Some of us revert to abusing mood-altering substances such as drugs, alcohol, or food to relieve our tension. In more subtle ways, we may bury ourselves in church activities, work, relationships, or other addictive/compulsive behaviors to try to combat the anxieties that seem to overwhelm us. When we come to grips with ourselves and realize that our lives are just one big roller-coaster ride, we are ready for Step One. We have no alternative but to admit that we are powerless and that our lives have become unmanageable. When we begin to recognize the seriousness of our condition, it is important that we seek help.

Step One forms the foundation for working the other steps. In this vital encounter with the circumstances of our lives, we admit our powerlessness and accept the unmanageability of our lives. Surrendering to this idea is not an easy thing to do. Although our behavior has caused us nothing but stress and pain, it is difficult to let go and trust that things will work out well. We may experience confusion, drowsiness, sadness, sleeplessness, or turmoil. These are normal responses to the severe inner struggles we are experiencing. It is important to remember that surrender requires great mental and emotional energy as well as determination. Do not give up. A new life of freedom awaits us.

PERSONAL REFLECTION

In Step One, we come to grips with the reality of our lives. Perhaps for the first time, we finally admit defeat and recognize that we need help. In looking at Step One, we see it has two distinct parts. The first part is the admission that we have obsessive traits. Those traits appear in the way we try to manipulate the affairs of our lives to ease the inner pain of separateness from God. We are in the grip of an addictive process that has rendered us powerless over our behavior. The second part is the admission that our lives have been, and will continue to be, unmanageable if we insist on living by our own will.

1. What is keeping you from recognizing your powerlessness and your life's unmanageability? _____

_____

_____

> *I am worn out from groaning; all night long I flood my bed with weeping and drench my couch with tears. My eyes grow weak with sorrow; they fail because of all my foes.*
> PS. 6:6–7

2. What area of your life is causing you the most sadness? _____

_____

_____

Our pride cries out against the idea of powerlessness and giving up control. We are accustomed to accepting full responsibility for all that happens in our lives and in the lives of others. Having grown up in a dysfunctional environment, it is natural for us to react. Some of us become overly responsible while others withdraw and become very irresponsible. Until we reach an intolerable threshold of pain, we will be unable to take the first step toward liberation and renewed strength. We must realize that we are powerless before we can totally surrender.

3. What events in your life caused you to realize the extent of your pain? _____

_____

_____

HELPFUL
HINT
• • •
Read Meditation for
Deuteronomy
30:19–20, page 5,
*Meditations for The
Twelve Steps—A
Spiritual Journey*

> *This day I call heaven and earth as witnesses against you that I have set before you life and death, blessings and curses. Now choose life, so that you and your children may live and that you may love the Lord your God, listen to his voice, and hold fast to him.*
> DEUT. 30:19–20

4. Pain is a signal to act out your addiction, obsession, or compulsion. Now pain can be a signal to acknowledge your powerlessness and to "choose life." What specific pain is your loudest signal? _____

_____

_____

As we begin to accept the reality of our condition, we naturally [look]
for answers. We feel like timid spiritual beginners and wonder [why the]
life we are seeking has escaped us. Friends may tell us, "Read you[r Bible]
about it." Some may suggest we talk with our minister. No m[atter what]
outside sources we seek, there will be no relief for us until we, by o[ur]
own minds and hearts,(acknowledge our powerlessness.)Then, and [only then,]
we begin to see that Step One is the beginning of a way out.

> **The man who thinks he knows something does not**
> **yet know as he ought to know.**
> 1 COR. 8:2

5. We think that life is working when we rely on our old survival technique[s. How]
has this blocked you from seeing your real problems? _____ ___

_____

_____

Step One is an ongoing commitment.(We must remember that our damaging traits, habits, and behaviors are a part of us.)They are unconscious reactions to the stresses of life. We must watch our behavior for the appearance of destructive tendencies. As we notice self-defeating behaviors and reactions surface, we can admit our powerlessness and seek God's help. God will then open new courses of action for us.

6. In what area of your life do you experience the strongest need to be in control? _____

_____

_____

7. What are the results of your self-defeating habits? _____

_____

_____

> **That day…they took him along…in the boat. A furious squall came**
> **up, and the waves broke over the boat…Jesus was…sleeping on a**
> **cushion. The disciples…said to him, "…don't you care if we**
> **drown?" He…said to the waves, "Quiet! Be still!" Then the wind**
> **died down and it was…calm. He said to his disciples, "Why are**
> **you so afraid? Do you still have no faith?"**
> MARK 4:35–40

The Apostles felt fear and doubt because of their powerlessness. What do you fear the most? What causes you to doubt? _____

_____

_____

HELPFUL HINT

...

Read "The Beatitudes," page 61, *Prayers for The Twelve Steps—A Spiritual Journey*

The second part of Step One, admitting that our lives are unmanageable, is as difficult as acknowledging that we are powerless. We can become more observant of the thoughts and behaviors we still rely upon from our past as a way to hide the truth about ourselves today. We need to be totally honest, drop the disguises, and see things as they really are. When we stop finding excuses for our behavior, we will have taken the first step toward achieving the humility we need to accept spiritual guidance. It is through this spiritual guidance that we can begin to rebuild ourselves and our lives.

9. In what areas of your life do you experience the greatest sense of unmanageability? _____

_____

_____

10. Cite specific situations of how you find excuses for your behavior. _____

_____

_____

> *"I am the true vine and my Father is the gardener. He cuts off every branch in me that bears no fruit, while every branch that does bear fruit he trims clean so that it will be even more fruitful."*
> JOHN 15:1-2

11. Which ineffective behaviors need to be eliminated? _____

_____

_____

A physical disease can only begin to be healed when we acknowledge its presence. In a similar way, the spiritual healing of our obsessive/compulsive behavior begins when we acknowledge the problem behavior. In Mark 10:51, it was obvious to others that Bartimaeus was blind. However, he openly asked Christ to heal his blindness. Until we realize this truth, our progress toward recovery will be blocked. Our healing begins when we are willing to acknowledge our problems and take the necessary steps to resolve them.

12. What specific behavior is a problem you have been avoiding? Or what behavior are you defending or excusing? How do you do this? _____

_____

_____

> *When he came to his senses, he said, "How many of my*
> *father's hired men have food to spare, and here*
> *I am starving to death!"*
> LUKE 15:17

13. The prodigal son's decision to live a self-centered life rendered him powerless and caused his life to be unmanageable. In what ways are you like him? ___

_____

_____

As we progress through the steps, we will discover that true and lasting change does not happen by trying to alter our life conditions. Although it is tempting to think so, outside adjustments cannot correct inside problems. Extraordinary healing requires surrendering the belief that we can heal our lives by manipulating our environment. Our willingness to work the steps will enable us to begin our true healing, which starts on the inside.

14. In the past, how have you tried to alter your life's conditions by manipulating your environment? _____

_____

_____

> *"I know that nothing good lives in me, that is, in my sinful nature.*
> *For I have the desire to do what is good, but I cannot carry it out.*
> *For what I do is not the good I want to do; no, the evil I do not*
> *want to do—this I keep on doing. Now if I do what I do not want to*
> *do, it is no longer I who do it, but it is sin living in me that does it."*
> ROM. 7:18-20

15. Can you relate to the above verse? In what part of your life do you feel this tug of war the most?_____

_____

_____

As we grow in faith and progress in our recovery, we become aware that we are not alone. Our Lord said he will not leave us comfortless for he has sent his Holy Spirit. In time, we will come to know his constant presence. For now, each day is a new opportunity to admit our powerlessness and the unmanageability of people, events, and things in our lives.

16. Have you felt any comfort or help from God while accepting the powerlessness and unmanageability of your life? Explain. _____

_____

_____

HELPFUL
HINT
...
Read Recovery Note
for 2 Corinthians
11:30 and 12:1–10,
page 1295,
Life Recovery Bible

> *But he said to me, "My grace is sufficient for you, for my power is*
> *made perfect in weakness." Therefore I will boast all the more*
> *gladly about my weaknesses, so that Christ's power may rest on me.*
> *That is why, for Christ's sake, I delight in weaknesses*
> *in insults, in hardships, in persecutions, in difficulties*
> *For when I am weak, then I am strong.*
> 2 COR. 12:9-10

17. What does "for when I am weak, then I am strong" mean to you? _____

_____

_____

> *He who trusts in himself is a fool, but he who walks*
> *in wisdom is kept safe.*
> PROV. 28:26

18. Why do you suppose trusting yourself is not a wise thing to do? _____

_____

_____

PREPARING FOR COMMUNITY

19. Which three questions from this step would you like to share with others?

_____

_____

20. What could someone else do to encourage you in your Step One work and in your recovery? _____

_____

_____

21. What can you do, specifically, to be of service and encouragement to others in recovery? _____

_____

_____

Powerless: In Step One we discover that recovery begins with an admission that we are powerless. We admit that we do not have the power on our own to live life as God intends.

Unmanageable: We have tried to manage our lives and the lives of others. However, our management has always met with failure. In Step One we admit that we cannot control or manage our lives any longer.

Dysfunction: If something is functioning normally we understand that it is running the way it is supposed to run. However, *dys*function implies that the function is "impaired" or "abnormal." The Greek prefix *dys* implies "unlucky" or "dangerous." Those of us in recovery understand all too well that our lives have fit these descriptions. We have not been living life as God intended. The functioning of our lives has been impaired, abnormal, unlucky, and even dangerous. Our lives have been *dys*functional.

_____

_____

_____

_____

_____

_____

_____

_____

GROUP ACTIVITIES

ACTIVITY #1: "In the Dark"

Supplies Needed: Paper and pens.

Objective: To experience the powerlessness and unmanageability of trying to write or draw something in the dark.

❑ Make preparations to draw or write something (e.g., a self-portrait, a drawing of a favorite pet, or a letter to self).

❑ Turn off the lights so that it is completely dark and begin. Allow about five minutes. If darkness is not possible, ask people to close their eyes—no cheating.

❑ When the time is up each person shares his or her work—one at a time. To create suspense and prolong the fun, keep the work face down until it's your turn to share.

❑ Finally, discuss how this exercise in the dark is similar to feelings of powerlessness and unmanageability.

ACTIVITY #2: "A Portrait of Unmanageability!"

Supplies Needed: Plain white paper, colored pencils or crayons, tables or clipboards, and imagination.

Objective: To artistically express unmanageability through drawing.

❑ Draw a picture representing the unmanageability of your life (e.g., a furnace burning up money to demonstrate financial unmanageability, or several monsters circling your head to represent your fears). Imagination and creativity are the important elements.

❑ At the end of the exercise, show and explain your picture to the group.

ACTIVITY #3: "Prayers for Step One"

Supplies Needed: Paper and pens.

Objective: To write a Step One prayer and share the prayer with the group.

❑ Begin by writing a Step One prayer. It is helpful to recall Step One themes from the chapter. Stay away from themes or concepts that are related to future steps. For example, write about powerlessness and unmanageability rather than faith or amends.

❑ Assume a prayerful mood while each participant reads his or her own prayer. To create a soft atmosphere, lights could be turned off and each participant could be given a candle.

The following is an example of a Step One prayer:

To be honest, I'm not sure who I'm praying to.
Maybe I'm talking to myself, but...
To be honest, I can't take any more.
My life is a failure, I feel like a...
To be honest, I wanta die, I wanta quit,
I wanta quit hurting me, I wanta quit hurting them.
To be honest, I don't know what to do.
For the first time, I'm really lost...
To be honest, I don't know if anyone hears me,
But if someone hears, please come find me.

(Taken from *Prayers for The Twelve Steps—A Spiritual Journey,* pages 8–9)

STEP TWO

*Came to believe that a power greater than ourselves
could restore us to sanity.*

• • •

For it is God who works in you to will and to act according to his good purpose.
(PHIL. 2:13)

UNDERSTANDING STEP TWO

"I looked at the white, turbulent waters of the river and melted inside. Any courage I had mustered seeped through my sweating pores. My legs turned to spaghetti at the thought of taking the inflated raft down the rapids—all in the name of fun. Then the river guide, who would steer and command our raft, began to speak. He sounded so sure of himself, so confident that everything would be fine. He gave us instructions, taught us the commands, made us laugh, and even put me at ease. It was crazy, I guess, but I trusted him to make this insane river ride a safe and enjoyable experience."

Step Two is about faith—trust and believing. Faith isn't intellectualized—it just is. Faith isn't manufactured—it's from God. Faith isn't earned—it's a gift. Faith isn't optional—it's a must. Many turbulent and troubled waters await us in our recovery. God knows that, and he prepares us by placing faith in our hearts. When we finally look to God, we will already have the faith to believe he is there.

WORKING STEP TWO

Step One, if worked properly, leaves us feeling empty. We have admitted our own powerlessness and the unmanageability of our lives. So we are left saying, "If I am powerless and cannot manage my life, who can?" God can! God begins to show us his ability by putting a simple seed of faith in our hearts. That seed of faith is not great. It is simply a growing confidence that someone else, far greater than ourselves, will take charge. Step Two helps us acknowledge the seed of faith that God has given us. This begins the process of trusting that a power greater than ourselves is at work in our lives.

PREPARING FOR STEP TWO

We prepare for Step Two by acknowledging that we don't know everything about our Higher Power. Many of us have a distorted view of God. Although we are not quick to admit it, we may believe that God is like our abusive or absent parents or significant others. We may believe that God doesn't care how we feel, that he is cruel and waiting to judge us. We may have been threatened with God's

43

punishment all our lives. *"The distorted images that parents place in our hearts and minds carry directly over to our image of God. We grow up feeling that God sees us as our parents did. And so, we grow up seeing ourselves and our God through distorted eyes."*[1] Preparing for Step Two requires that we set aside our old images and mistaken beliefs about God. For now we can simply hold on to the words of AA's Second Tradition, "...there is but one ultimate authority—a loving God..."

PRAYER FOR STEP TWO

I pray for an open mind so I may come to believe in a power greater than myself. I pray for humility and the continued opportunity to increase my faith. I don't want to be crazy any more.

(Taken from *Prayers for The Twelve Steps—A Spiritual Journey*, page 10)

With the help of Step One we came to grips with the fact that we are powerless and our lives are unmanageable. Our next step is to acknowledge the existence of a power greater than ourselves. Believing in God does not always mean that we accept his power. As Christians, we know God, but do not necessarily invite his power into our lives. In Step Two, we have an opportunity to experience God in a different light. Jesus said in John 14:26 that the Holy Spirit would be sent in his name to teach us and remind us of all he has said. In Step Two, we begin to reestablish our relationship, or, establish a relationship with God for the first time. This step gives us an opportunity to experience faith in a power greater than ourselves. This connection will grow and become a vital part of our daily lives.

For many of us, this step presents major obstacles. Since we find it hard to trust others, the loneliness of our present condition causes us to fall back on our own resources. We may even doubt that God can heal us or even be interested in doing so. Unless we let go of our distrust and begin to lean on God, we will continue to operate in an insane manner. The chaos and confusion of our lives will only increase.

Depending on our religious background, some of us may have been taught that God is an authority to be feared. We never saw him as a loving God. As children, we were anxious and feared doing something wrong. Sometimes the threat of being punished by God was used by adults to control our childish behavior. Our fear of displeasing God magnified our growing sense of guilt and shame. As adults, we continue to fear people in authority and are often overcome by guilt and shame for simple misdeeds.

---

[1] Seiden, Jerry, *Divine or Distorted? God as We Understand God* (San Diego, CA: RPI Publishing, Inc., 1993), p. 8.

We still may be harboring childhood anger at God because he often disappointed us. Due to the severity of our experiences, some of us rejected God because he did not relieve our pain. Despite our belief that God is with us, in moments of fear we sometimes doubt his presence. Even those who are dealing with their problems and are in contact with their Higher Power experience periodic moments of doubt and fear. In Step Two, our goal is to believe that God, a power greater than ourselves, can guide us in our journey toward peace and healing.

For some of us, belief in self-will and our ability to manage our own lives is all we have. We perceive God as a crutch for children and weak-willed individuals who are incapable of managing their own lives. As we begin to see God's true nature, a weight is lifted from our shoulders. We begin to view life from a different perspective.

One of the great paradoxes of Christianity is that man is never completely free until he totally yields to God. In John 8:32, Jesus made a promise when he said, *"You shall know the truth and the truth shall make you free."* In this step, we begin to recognize that God does, in fact, have the power and intention to alter the course of our lives. In the Scriptures, we are assured of God's presence within us. We are shown that through him all things are possible. If we have accepted the truth regarding our condition and have come to believe in our Higher Power, we are well on our way to true spiritual freedom.

Step Two is often referred to as "The Hope Step." It gives us new hope as we begin to see that help is available to us. We must simply reach out and accept what our Higher Power has to offer. It is here that we form the foundation for growth of our spiritual life, which will help us become the person we want to be. All we need to do is be willing to believe that a power greater than ourselves is waiting to be our personal salvation. What follows as we proceed through the steps is a process that will bring this power into our lives and enable us to grow in love, health, and grace.

PERSONAL REFLECTION

Coming to believe in a power greater than ourselves requires faith. In the past, we have placed our faith in our own abilities to run our lives, and that faith has proven worthless. It was misplaced and never did for us what we thought it would. Now we need to actively place our faith in God. At first, it may seem unrealistic to place our faith in a power we cannot see or touch. Yet the very existence of our universe in all its glory gives ample evidence of the true power, love, and majesty of the God we seek.

1. List some of the experiences that caused you to lose faith in God. _____

_____

_____

2. Faith is the evidence and substance of things hoped for yet not seen. What do you hope for? _____

_____

_____

HELPFUL
HINT
· · ·
Read Step Two
Devotional on "Hope
in Faith" from
Hebrews 11:1-10,
page 1391, *Life
Recovery Bible*

> *Immediately Jesus made the disciples get into the boat and go on ahead of him to the other side...but the boat was...buffeted by the waves... During the fourth watch of the night Jesus went out to them, walking on the lake. ...the disciples saw him walking on the lake..."Lord, if it's you," Peter replied, "tell me to come to you on the water." "Come," he said. Then Peter got down out of the boat and walked on the water to Jesus. But when he saw the wind, he was afraid and, beginning to sink, cried out, "Lord, save me!" Immediately Jesus reached out his hand and caught him. "You of little faith," he said, "why did you doubt?" And when they climbed into the boat, the wind died down. Then those who were in the boat worshiped him, saying, "Truly you are the Son of God."*
>
> MATT. 14:22–32

3. How do you relate to Peter's experience? _____

_____

_____

Faith grows through practice. Each time we sense faith and act upon it, our faith becomes stronger. Every time we ask our Higher Power for help and receive it, our faith is strengthened. We will finally accept the fact that God is dependable and will never leave us. All we need to do is ask for help and trust in his power.

> *He replied, "Because you have so little faith. I tell you the truth, if you have faith as small as a mustard seed, you can say to this mountain, 'Move from here to there' and it will move. Nothing will be impossible for you."*
>
> MATT. 17:20

4. Mustard-seed faith is like a glimmer of hope mixed with confidence that God will take care of a dilemma in our lives. In what area of your life is God giving you "mustard-seed faith?" _____

_____

_____

> *"If you can?" said Jesus. "Everything is possible for him who believes." Immediately the boy's father exclaimed, "I do believe; help me overcome my unbelief!"*
> MARK 9:23–24

5. What is keeping you from truly believing that a power greater than yourself can restore you to sanity? _____

_____

_____

One great secret of learning to have faith is found in the joyful revelation that the Spirit of God is always within us. God wants to share an intimate relationship with us. God declares that he will never leave us or forsake us. He will be as close to us as we allow him to be.

> *The Lord is close to the brokenhearted and saves those who are crushed in spirit. A righteous man may have many troubles, but the Lord delivers him from them all; he protects all his bones, not one of them will be broken. Evil will slay the wicked; the foe of the righteous will be condemned. The Lord redeems his servants; no one who takes refuge in him will be condemned.*
> PS. 34:18–22

6. Jesus Christ has the power to mend your crushed and broken spirit. What can you do to open yourself to Christ's power? _____

_____

_____

We begin to trust our Higher Power as we develop a closer relationship with Jesus Christ. We also begin to rely on him to help us become aware of the extent of our disabling condition. Step Two implies that we are insane. A common definition of insanity in the program is doing the same thing over and over and expecting different results each time. In this sense, we can see our behavior as insane. We still may be blaming everyone and everything for our condition instead of taking responsibility for our own behavior. Or we may still be struggling to control others in order to improve our own lives.

7. In what ways do you see your behavior as insane? _____

_____

_____

> *Indeed, in our hearts we felt the sentence of death. But this happened that we might not rely on ourselves but on God, who raises the dead.*
>
> 2 COR. 1:9

8. In what way have you felt "the sentence of death" in your life? _____

_____

_____

Our traumatic childhood experiences caused us to become defiant, indifferent, resentful, self-deluded, and self-centered. Our adult lives need to be restored to a more balanced state. We can find that balance if we are willing to believe that God's Holy Spirit is a power greater than ourselves and that he can restore us to sanity. When we attempt to do it alone, we often deceive ourselves by looking to outside sources for the causes of our problems. With the help of Christ, these deceitful behaviors can be healed from the inside out.

> *For it is God who works in you to will and to act according to his good purpose.*
>
> PHIL. 2:13

9. In what ways do you see God at work restoring you to sanity? _____

_____

_____

One way God helps us see our condition clearly is to bring us into contact with others who share experiences similar to ours. It becomes evident, when sharing our stories in meetings and through fellowship, that each of us can maintain "emotional sobriety" only one day at a time. Also, God helps us realize that actions destructive to ourselves or to others are not acceptable. As we become more dependent on God's power, the quality of our lives will improve.

10. What can you do to maintain your "emotional sobriety?" _____

_____

_____

HELPFUL HINT

• • •

Read "Possibilities Prayer," page 63, *Prayers for The Twelve Steps—A Spiritual Journey*

> *Not that we are competent in ourselves to claim anything for ourselves, but our competence comes from God.*
>
> 2 COR. 3:5

11. In what ways do you hope your relationship with God will improve your ability to deal with daily life? _____

_____

_____

When we started this program, we may have been expecting instant results. From our childhood, we remember feeling anger or confusion when things didn't happen "right now." In this program, sudden change is the exception, not the rule. It requires patience and perseverance to achieve the recovery we seek. Each of us is unique, and recovery begins for each of us at different stages in the steps. Some of us may experience instant relief, whereas others may not begin to feel stronger until later in the program. There is no rule or guideline. Progress occurs at the most appropriate time.

12. What is your reaction to the fact that recovery requires patience and understanding, that it doesn't happen instantly? _____

_____

_____

> *Do you not know? Have you not heard? The Lord is the everlasting God, the Creator of the ends of the earth. He will not grow tired or weary, and his understanding no one can fathom. He gives strength to the weary and increases the power of the weak. Even youths grow tired and weary, and young men stumble and fall; but those who hope in the Lord will renew their strength. They will soar on wings like eagles; they will run and not grow weary, they will walk and not be faint.*
> ISA. 40:28–31

13. In what areas of your life have you experienced God's strength replacing your powerlessness? _____

_____

_____

Step Two suggests a restoration to sanity. Humility is required to allow this state of mind to unfold. For most of us, lack of humility contributed to our present situation. Humility is a spiritual virtue that we develop with God's help. Developing humility is a recurrent theme of the program. We become humble as we are slowly able to relinquish our pride, self-will, and defiance. In Philippians 2:5

we are told, *"Your attitude should be the same as that of Christ Jesus."* And Jesus' attitude was one of obedience to do his Father's will, to submit to his Father's plan and power.

14. In what areas of your life do you demonstrate self-will or defiance toward God? _____

_____

_____

15. In what aspects of your life do you need to be more gentle? _____

_____

_____

> *For I am convinced that neither death nor life, neither angels nor demons, ...neither height nor depth, nor anything else in all creation, will be able to separate us from the love of God that is in Christ Jesus our Lord.*
> ROM. 8:38–39

16. What is the nature of your present relationship with Christ? How can it be improved? _____

_____

_____

When we become ready to accept our powerlessness and unmanageability (Step One), and when we trust our Higher Power, Jesus Christ, to restore us to sanity (Step Two), we will be ready to make a decision to turn our lives over to the care of God (Step Three). There is no need to rush the process of working the steps. The important thing is to heed the Bible's admonition that *"the hour has come for you to wake up from your slumber"* (Rom. 13:11). We move forward in faith so we will be able to proceed with the remaining steps. The faith we develop now in Step Two is our most important building block in recovery. Our success in the program depends upon our relationship with God. We must believe he is able to help us.

17. List areas in Step One or Step Two where you still struggle with the program. _____

_____

_____

18. What do you think you need to do to remedy this problem? (For example: maybe you need to share your difficulty with a friend and ask for prayer, support, or counsel.) _____

_____

_____

> *So do not fear for I am with you; do not be dismayed, for I am your God. I will strengthen and help you; I will uphold you with my righteous right hand.*
> ISA. 41:10

19. What help do you want from the Lord as you begin to look to him for strength? _____

_____

_____

> *For God so loved the world that he gave his one and only Son, that whoever believes in him shall not perish but have eternal life. For God did not send his Son into the world to condemn the world, but to save the world through him.*
> JOHN 3:16-17

HELPFUL
HINT
• • •
Read Meditation for
John 3:16–17, page
27, *Meditations for The
Twelve Steps—A
Spiritual Journey*

20. Are you able to accept God's love for you? Why or why not? _____

_____

_____

PREPARING FOR COMMUNITY

21. Which three questions from this step would you like to share with others?

_____

_____

22. Describe your relationship with God during childhood._____

_____

_____

23. What current events in your life interfere with your relationship with God?

_____

_____

KEY IDEAS

Higher Power: Because Step One has helped us understand our powerlessness, we need a power beyond ourselves to help and heal us. God is so great and merciful that he does not require that we name him precisely. God is even willing to be anonymous for a time. Remember how God led the Three Wise Men from the East to Christ? The Wise Men did not know the God of Israel or Jesus. They worshiped the stars. So God used a star to lure them. In a similar way, God leads many to himself through the idea of a "Higher Power" in Twelve Step programs. In Step Two we need to come to believe that there is a loving Higher Power who is willing to help us.

Belief: Belief in something or someone is more than acknowledging that something or someone exists. For example, the Bible says that the demons in hell believe that God exists, yet that belief doesn't save them (James 2:19). Belief that saves implies trust and commitment. It is one thing to believe that a chair will hold my weight. It is another thing to sit in it. When I sit in the chair, I truly believe in it. In Step Two we come to believe that a power greater than ourselves can restore us to sanity. We do more than acknowledge God's existence—we begin to exercise trust in him to hold us.

NOTES

_____

_____

_____

_____

_____

_____

_____

_____

_____

_____

GROUP ACTIVITIES

ACTIVITY #1: *"How I'm Feeling"*

Objective: To identify feelings. An important part of recovery is to be honest about our feelings.

❑ Take a moment to evaluate your strongest feeling right now.

❑ Depict the feeling in a creative way by drawing just a face. It can be as simple as the common "happy face" type drawing or as elaborate as time allows.

❑ At the end of the exercise share the drawings and explain them to the family group.

ACTIVITY #2: *"Jesus, Help Me!"*

Objective: To identify with one of the three needy persons in Mark 5 who recognize Christ as their Higher Power.

❑ Close your eyes and position yourselves in a comfortable posture for meditation. Select someone to read all of Mark 5.

❑ Listen carefully to the reading of Mark 5 and visualize the stories.

❑ After the reading, identify the three needy people from the chapter (e.g., the demon-possessed man, the sick woman, and the dead girl [or her father]).

❑ Share who you most identified with in the chapter, and why. Identify why a Higher Power was so important for your character, and share how you relate to that kind of desperate need.

ACTIVITY #3: *"Who Am I?"*

Supplies Needed: Pieces of paper and tape or pins.

Objective: To experience relying on another person for help. Family group members will have the name of a famous person on their back, and others will give them "yes" or "no" hints to help them figure out whose name they have. Those who are providing clues represent a greater power because they are able to see what the other person cannot.

❑ In advance, place the names of famous persons (persons familiar to all) on pieces of paper. Use one name per piece of paper and have one piece of paper for each family group member.

❑ When the activity begins, pin or tape a name on the back of all the family group members. Be sure that they do not see the name intended for their backs.

❑ When everyone has a name, begin asking for clues to determine the identity of the specific person. They may only ask questions that require a "yes" or "no" response. For example, someone might ask, "Am I male?" or "Was I a president?" or "Am I still alive?," etc.

❑ The activity is over when all persons have been identified. The group facilitator may choose to award a fun prize to the winner and a booby prize to the last one done.

A WORD ABOUT LEAVING YOUR FAMILY GROUP

Most of us are free to do as we please. When we want to go, we go; when we want to stay, we stay. Participating with your family group has possibly raised some questions as to the compatibility of members in your group and made you feel like you didn't want to stay with your family. If you are experiencing pain, frustration, or discomfort from working the step material, you may feel discouraged and fearful. You may have fallen behind, and are finding it difficult to complete the work. If you have not developed a close bond with your family members, you may consider quitting.

If any of these feelings and thoughts are present, we strongly suggest that you:

❑ Take a risk; reach out to your family group (or an individual member) and share your true feelings and fears.

❑ Take time to consider your options; ask for help from the Lord, and make the decision that will be best for you.

When you make your final decision, inform your family members. Allow them to preserve the dignity of their experience. Do not be concerned about their reaction. It is important for you to express your needs and wants, and realize that other people are there to be supportive. This is a healthy way to complete the relationship, and will help to minimize any feelings of abandonment that may result from your decision to leave.

STEP THREE

**Made a decision to turn our will and our lives over
to the care of God as we understood him.**

. . .

*Therefore, I urge you, brothers, in view of God's mercy, to offer your bodies as
living sacrifices, holy and pleasing to God—which is your spiritual worship.*

(R O M . 1 2 : 1)

UNDERSTANDING STEP THREE

Imagine the insanity of trying to perform surgery on ourselves. At the first hint
of pain from the scalpel, we would stop. Healing would never happen. It is just
as insane to think that we can manage our own recovery. We must put our lives
into the hands of our Higher Power. God alone knows the extent of our disease.
God alone knows what is needed for healing. And God alone has our best interest
at heart.

In Step Three we decide to turn the scalpel over to God. We decide to ask
him to take control of our will and our lives. We have admitted our powerlessness
and inability to manage our lives. We also have come to believe that God can heal
us, and now, we decide to turn our will and our lives over to God's care.

WORKING STEP THREE

We work Step Three by going through a decision-making process. Think of other
big decisions that we have made in our lives. For example, when making a
decision about buying a house, we consider such things about the house as cost,
location, condition, etc. We also take into consideration things about ourselves
such as our ability to pay, housing needs, personal preferences, etc. Finally, when
all things have been weighed, we make a decision. In a similar way we work Step
Three. We consider how well the present management of our lives is going. We
consider our needs, God's ability, the future. We take time to contemplate the
changes. And finally, we make a decision that God is the only one able to manage
our lives, that his will for us is best.

PREPARING FOR STEP THREE

We prepare for Step Three by thoroughly doing Steps One and Two. If we are
not convinced that we are powerless and that our lives are unmanageable, we are
not ready for Step Three. This step will be difficult if we have not come to believe
that God can restore us to sanity and is able to care for us. We also prepare for
Step Three by fully accepting our powerlessness and our inability to manage our

lives. We prepare by allowing God to plant seeds of faith in our hearts. When those things are in place, Step Three comes easily.

PRAYER FOR STEP THREE

Lord,
I am learning that there is an awful lot I can't do.
I can't control life the way I am used to.
I can't make people be what I want.
I can't stop the pain inside me.
I can't even fully submit to your plan yet—I'm still too frightened of you.
But I know that there is one thing I can do right now.
I can make a decision to turn my will and my life over to you.
Making the decision doesn't mean I have to make it happen.
Making the decision doesn't mean I understand you or your plan.
Making the decision doesn't even mean I'm entirely willing, but it does mean that I know your way and will is right.
Lord, turn my simple decision into reality.

(Taken from *Prayers for The Twelve Steps—A Spiritual Journey,* pages 12–13)

Step Three is the central theme of all the steps. It is the point at which we make a decision to turn our will and our lives over to the care of God. Step Three is an important cornerstone for building an effective and peaceful life. In Steps One and Two we established the basis for turning our lives over to the care of God. The commitment we now make in Step Three must be repeated more than once. Actually, we are just beginning to turn things over to God. Repeated working of the first three steps helps to build a solid foundation for working the total program.

Many of us come to this program with strong negative perceptions about the world in which we live. Those perceptions may be based on hurtful childhood experiences, misguided academic training, or simply the accumulated lessons of our lives. Because of past experiences, we may have perceived God to be unloving and judgmental. If we have experienced extreme violence as children, we may find it hard to trust anyone or anything—even God. Whatever the source, our recovery is hindered if our beliefs make it difficult to let go of our fear and surrender our lives to God. In Step Three, we decide to take the leap of faith and put our lives in his hands.

Biblical figures often resisted following God's will. The Bible illustrates some examples of doing God's will when it didn't make any sense. Yet, the end result showed it was wise to follow God's guidance. Such acts of faith are exemplified by Moses as he led the nation of Israel into the wilderness and by Abraham's willingness to sacrifice his son Isaac. Also, despite criticism of his contemporaries, Noah built the ark. The essence of these actions is summarized in Hebrews 11:6:

"And without faith it is impossible to please God, because anyone who comes to him must believe that he exists and that he rewards those who earnestly seek him."

Until now, our inaccurate perceptions of reality have led us into many compulsive/obsessive behaviors. Admitting our responsibility for these dysfunctions is often too difficult. It implies that we have not been "good people." Denial is our only recourse. Our denial acts as a shield against confronting ourselves as we really are. When denial is at work, it is like a shuttered window, closing out the sunlight. In Step Three, we begin the process of opening the shutters and allowing God's light to enter. God's word is a source of light with which we can examine our behavior and understand reality.

Step Three is an affirmative step. It is time to make a decision. In the first two steps, we became aware of our condition and accepted the idea of a power greater than ourselves. Although we began to know and trust God, we may find it difficult to give God total control of our lives. However, if the alternative is to face the loss of people or things vital to our lives, such as family, job, health, or sanity, God's guidance might be easier to accept. Our lives may have many beautiful and rewarding relationships that are being ruined by our addictive/compulsive behavior. We must not be discouraged by these discoveries. Instead, we can allow these discoveries to prompt our surrender to God.

As we begin to allow God's will to act in our lives, our self-destructive tendencies become fewer and much less distracting. Often, the confusion and grief we cause ourselves and others prevent us from successfully working and practicing the steps. Making the decision to begin this journey is an act of great importance and should not be made in a time of emotional upheaval. The key elements in Step Three are making the decision with a clear and rational mind, being committed to that decision, and, finally, trusting the outcome to God.

As we surrender our lives and stop carrying the burdens of our past, we will begin to feel better about ourselves. The more we learn to trust in the Lord, the more we will trust ourselves and extend that trust to others. Our decision to choose God's way will restore us to the fullness of life. As we free ourselves from our self-will, we in turn free ourselves from much of our negative behaviors, and we are able to deal more effectively with the daily routine of our lives. Our impatience and irritability disappear as we come to know God's love and yearn to share it with others. Our lives transform into a dynamic relationship with God. We become the persons he meant for us to be—full citizens in his kingdom.

PERSONAL REFLECTION

In Step Three, we acknowledge our need for God's guidance in our lives. We make the decision to surrender our lives to God's care. He becomes our new manager, and we accept life on his terms. God offers us a way to live that is free from the emotional pollution of our past, allowing us to enjoy new and wonderful experiences. Step Three provides us with an opportunity to turn away from behavior that fosters addiction, discouragement, sickness, and fear.

1.   What things in your life cause you to know that you must turn your will and your life over to the care of God? _____

_____

_____

HELPFUL
HINT
• • •
Read Meditation for
Proverbs 3:5–6, page
32, *Meditations for The
Twelve Steps—A
Spiritual Journey*

> *Trust in the Lord with all your heart and lean not on your own understanding; in all your ways acknowledge him, and he will make your paths straight.*
> PROV. 3:5–6

2. What attitudes or distortions stand in your way and hinder your trust in God (e.g., the belief that God is absent, uncaring, or cruel)? _____

_____

_____

> *Teach me to do your will, for you are my God; may your good Spirit lead me on level ground.*
> PS. 143:10–11

3. Describe a time when you felt that God's Spirit led you._____

_____

_____

Many of us begin the Step Three process by deciding to turn over only certain parts of our lives. We are willing to surrender the most difficult problems when we see they are making our lives unmanageable. We cling to other areas of our lives because we think we can manage them or because we think they are necessary for our survival. We eventually realize that we cannot barter with God. We must be prepared to surrender our entire will and every part of our lives to his care if we want to recover. When we are truly able to accept this fact, our journey to wholeness has begun.

4. Which parts of your life are you unwilling to turn over to God? Explain why.

_____

_____

_____

God doesn't do deals.

> *Therefore, I urge you, brothers, in view of God's mercy, to offer your bodies as living sacrifices, holy and pleasing to God—which is your spiritual worship.*
> ROM. 12:1

5. Turning control of your life over to God helps reduce stress. Why do you think this is true? _____

_____

_____

Step Three may make us feel we are losing our identity. We may think we are going to lose everything. Not knowing what is going to happen is frightening. Most of us have tried desperately to control our environment. Many of these behavior traits were developed during childhood and came about as a direct result of the circumstances in which we were raised. Deep within us may be a fearful childhood memory and a trembling child anxious about someone's anger, criticism, threats, or violence. As children, we tried to fix or take care of the people around us so they would not abandon us, leaving us with only broken promises and shattered dreams.

6. How do your childhood memories continue to frighten or otherwise affect you? _____

_____

_____

> *Yet to all who received him, to those who believed in his name, he gave the right to become children of God—children born not of natural descent, nor of human decision or a husband's will, but born of God.*
> JOHN 1:12–13

7. Describe your childhood relationship with God. _____

_____

_____

The conditions in which we were raised often kept us from ever trusting in God. Our prayers may have been unanswered, and we could not imagine how a loving God could be so cruel to us. Step Three is an opportunity to start over. As we work the Steps, we will get in touch with memories of childhood hurts. We also will begin to experience God's healing love, which transcends time, to repair the damage that has been done. Jesus told us that we must become like children to enter the Kingdom of God. This statement helps us recognize that a childlike state will enable us to regain our capacity to give and receive unconditional love. Thus, we can look forward to a return of childlike spontaneity, and a growing capacity to give and receive love and nurturing.

8. Step Three can be an opportunity to start over and mend your memories of childhood hurts. Which area from your childhood needs the most mending (e.g., trust, play, relationships, fear, emotions, faith, etc.)? Explain._____

_____

_____

> *"Come to me, all you who are weary and burdened, and I will give you rest. Take my yoke upon you and learn from me, for I am gentle and humble in heart, and you will find rest for your souls. For my yoke is easy and my burden is light."*
> MATT. 11:28–30

HELPFUL HINT
· · ·
Read "Prayers of Submission," Chapter Six, page 84–92, *Prayers for The Twelve Steps—A Spiritual Journey*

9. What burdens weigh heaviest on your heart? _____

_____

_____

Learning to trust in God and accept his support will enhance the quality of our lives. We will no longer feel the need to carry our burdens by ourselves. Much of the pain of our past is a result of feeling totally alone. Our need to control people and events kept us isolated, but as we trust and surrender, we will begin to relate better with others. With God's presence, our sense of self-esteem will improve, and we will begin to recognize that we are worthwhile human beings. Our capacity to receive and give love will increase, and we will come to place great value on fellowship and sharing.

10. How will you know when your self-esteem begins to improve? _____

_____

_____

> *It is better to take refuge in the Lord than to trust in man. It is better to take refuge in the Lord than to trust in princes.*
> PS. 118:8–9

11. Where has trusting in man failed you?_____

_____

_____

Christ exemplified the concept of "turning it over" by acceptance of his Father's will, which led to the Cross and the victory of resurrection. During his life on earth, Jesus' love for us led him into constant confrontations with the forces of evil. He was strong and steadfast in those confrontations because he placed his trust in his Heavenly Father. But Jesus had confrontations of a different nature: confrontations within himself. He struggled with doing God's will because it wasn't always the easy way. Even Jesus expressed his struggle in prayer, yet he always yielded to his Father's will because he knew it was best.

> *Going a little farther, he fell with his face to the ground and prayed, "My Father, if it is possible, may this cup be taken from me. Yet not as I will, but as you will."*
> MATT. 26:39

12. How does this incident in the life of Christ help you identify with the difficulty of Step Three?_____

_____

_____

13. In what ways do you relate to Christ's final willingness to surrender to his Father's will? _____

_____

_____

In this life, we too have crosses to bear. Some of us still may be experiencing the powerful impact of our history of disabling behavior. Whatever our addiction may be—drugs, destructive relationships, sex, alcohol, money, or food—we face the possibility of spiritual as well as physical death. As we turn away from these temptations, we accept God's offer to cast our burdens upon him. In the past our addictions or obsessive behaviors provided our escape from pain, but today, God offers himself as our escape.

14. What cross do you carry that forces you to turn to God for guidance?_____

_____

_____

> *I have been crucified with Christ and I no longer live, but Christ lives in me. The life I live in the body, I live by faith in the Son of God, who loved me and gave himself for me.*
> GAL. 2:20

15. In what ways do you experience Christ living in you? Explain how his presence helps you cope with your daily life. _____

_____

_____

When we develop a daily routine of working Step Three, a change will come over us. We will feel less responsible for everything and everybody. Peace and serenity will come to us in measures never before experienced. Our eyes will be opened, and we will become increasingly aware that God is guiding us. People around us may notice that we have become more confident and trustworthy.

> *Commit to the Lord whatever you do, and your plans will succeed.*
> PROV. 16:3

16. Have you seen any changes in yourself that can be attributed to working the steps? Explain. _____

_____

_____

No matter how far we progress in recovery, we must continually turn our lives over to the care of God and be vigilant. It is foolish for us not to anticipate relapses. We need only to recognize this, and to willingly work the program on a daily basis. It is especially important to continue to practice Step Three. Our willingness to trust in God ensures our victory.

17. How do you plan to practice Step Three in your daily routine of living? ___

_____

_____

> *I tell you the truth, anyone who has faith in me will do what I have been doing. He will do even greater things than these, because I am going to the Father. And I will do whatever you ask in my name, so that the Son may bring glory to the Father.*
> JOHN 14:12-13

18. Christ will help you surrender your will to God, but you must ask. Describe your prayer life and how it is a part of your recovery. _____

_____

_____

> *"For I know the plans I have for you," declares the Lord, "plans to prosper you and not to harm you, plans to give you hope and a future. Then you will call upon me and come and pray to me, and I will listen to you. You will seek me and find me when you seek me with all your heart. I will be found by you," declares the Lord.*
> JER. 29:11–14

HELPFUL HINT
...
Read Recovery Note for Jeremiah 29:11, page 813, *Life Recovery Bible*

19. What kind of loving attention do you hope to receive when you turn yourself over to God's care? _____

_____

_____

Countless thousands of people seeking to experience peace, serenity, and fellowship with the Lord have walked this same path. Our daily task is to continually ask God for guidance. We receive Christ and his guidance by personal invitation. Jesus said, *"Here I am! I stand at the door and knock. If anyone hears my voice and opens the door, I will come in and eat [fellowship] with him, and he with me."* (Rev. 3:20) All we need to do is open the door of our hearts to Christ. The following prayer can help us with our relationship with Christ and strengthen our daily walk:

Lord Jesus,
I turn my will and my life over to you.
Mold me and do with me as you will.
I trust you to guide my steps, and
I enter the world with hope that I may better do your will.
I ask for your forgiveness and acceptance.
I welcome your Holy Spirit's power, love, and guidance
in everything I do. Amen.

PREPARING FOR COMMUNITY

20. Which three questions from this step you would like to share with others?

_____

_____

21. Describe a situation during this week in which your self-will interfered with your recovery. _____

_____

_____

22. What could someone else do to encourage you in your Step Three work and in your recovery? _____

_____

_____

KEY IDEAS

Turn it Over: This phrase of surrender is a key idea for Step Three. Imagine turning over your car keys to someone else. Think of turning over a job or a responsibility to a more capable person. People who have been in the program for any length of time talk about turning over problems and daily troubles to their Higher Power. For those of us who are working Step Three for the first time, we are turning over our will and our lives to God's care. Whatever imagery you choose, let the meaning always be the same: the surrender of your will and life. Turn it over. Give God control.

Self-Will: Self-will is the determination within us all to control our own lives. Self-will in itself is not wrong; God has given us the power to choose. The problem with choice occurs when our will conflicts with God's. Our choices have brought us pain, hardships, addictions, compulsions, and self-defeating behaviors. God's will for our lives brings us hope, healing, and peace. His plans are good. Our self-will is best exercised in choosing surrender to God.

NOTES

_____

_____

_____

_____

_____

_____

_____

_____

As part of our spiritual walk with the Lord, it is helpful to maintain a log of our meaningful experiences with Christ. Following is an example of how to record these experiences during the spiritual journey toward wholeness.

Journal Entries

March 20—Things are going so bad lately, I decided to read from the book of Job. I noticed how Job's friends really weren't very good friends. Whenever he tried to express how he felt or what he was thinking, they put him down or shamed him. That's how I feel. So, I just quit talking to my old friends. For the first time, I really told God how I feel, and imagined I was speaking to Jesus. I pictured myself as one of the sinners he ate with. I think it was the first time I ever really prayed. Thanks for hearing me, God.

FOOTPRINTS

One night a man had a dream.
He dreamed he was walking along the beach with the Lord.
Across the sky flashed scenes from his life.
For each scene, he noticed two sets of footprints in the sand;
one belonged to him and the other to the Lord.
When the last scene of his life flashed before him,
he looked back at the footprints in the sand.
He noticed that many times along the path of his life
there was only one set of footprints.
He also noticed that it happened at the very lowest
and saddest times in his life.
This really bothered him, and he questioned the Lord about it.
"Lord, you said that once I decided to follow you,
you'd walk with me all the way.
But I have noticed that during the most troublesome times
in my life, there is only one set of footprints.
I don't understand why when I needed you most,
you would leave me."
The Lord replied, "My precious, precious child,
I love you and would never leave you.
During your times of trial and suffering,
when you see only one set of footprints,
it was then that I carried you."

GROUP ACTIVITIES

ACTIVITY #1: "How I See God"

Objective: To consider distortions of God through role playing. Many find it hard to turn their will and lives over to God because they see God through distortions formed in childhood. An important key to recovery is trust in God, but that is difficult for those who believe God is punishing, untrustworthy, or judgmental.

❑ Pick three people to role-play a situation in which a child is caught in the act of lying or some other misbehavior. The role-players will be the child, the father, and the mother. In the situation, the parents should act out the behaviors that create distortions of God. For example, the father might be excessively cruel and punishing; the mother might threaten the child with God's wrath and judgment.

❑ To involve more role-players, the parents might shame the child before siblings or take the child to the priest or pastor. Allow the real experiences of people from the group to surface, but remember to add in an element of humor lest the exercise become *too* real or oppressive.

❑ Spend some time discussing this problem and brainstorm on ways to overcome distortions of God.

ACTIVITY #2: "Heroes"

Objective: To identify people we admired, to recognize their qualities, to recall the ways they nurtured us, and to consider how they showed us God. This role-playing exercise is an opportunity to think about those people who were special in our lives and to realize that through them we saw God's goodness.

❑ Someone from the family group should share about a particular person he or she admired during childhood. The person should describe how that person showed God's goodness through his or her behavior.

❑ From the description of the person above, create a role-playing situation in which the admired person shows godly character and compassion. For example, a child might be caught in a lie, but instead of being severely punished or shamed, the child is shown mercy and lovingly encouraged to change.

❑ Discuss how Christ showed God's goodness through his treatment of sinners.

ACTIVITY #3: "Help! I'm falling!"

Objective: To experience the feeling of helplessly falling backward with the assurance that someone will catch you. This will illustrate the concept of surrender and trust in a Higher Power.

❑ Pair up with someone of relatively equal size and stature. In the exercise you will fall straight backward into the waiting arms of your partner. Someone who has done this before should explain and demonstrate the exercise.

❑ Alternate roles of the person who falls and the catcher.

STEP FOUR *truthful*

Made a searching and fearless moral inventory of ourselves.

• • •

Let us examine our ways and test them, and let us return to the Lord.
(LAM. 3:40)

UNDERSTANDING STEP FOUR

If we lived alone and were unable to see, we would be faced with a number of special needs. For example, we might find it difficult to clean our home thoroughly by ourselves. We might ask a sighted friend to come over and help. This friend would see areas in need of cleaning that we had missed. Our friend would point these problems out and then, we hope, help us clean them.

In Step Four we realize there are areas of our lives that need attention. We also realize that we cannot see all those areas. Denial has kept us blinded to the dirt in our corners. Low self-esteem has kept us ignorant about the beauty and worth of our lives. In this step, our Higher Power comes to us as a caring friend. God opens our eyes to the weaknesses in our lives that need changing and helps us to build on our strengths.

WORKING STEP FOUR

Just as any business would take inventory of its stock, we take inventory of our lives in Step Four. With clipboard in hand, we walk down the aisles of our lives and note areas of weakness and strength. When we come to relationships, we take stock of the resentments and grudges, but we also examine our loving and healthy relationships. When we come to our communication, we note the lies, but we also list the positive ways we share with others. In this process we can look to God for guidance. He knows the contents of our warehouse far better than we do.

PREPARING FOR STEP FOUR

We prepare for Step Four by recognizing the fact that, to some degree, denial has been operating in our lives. We prepare by asking God for the courage to face those areas that have been protected by denial. And we prepare for Step Four by planning to nurture ourselves during and after the inventory process. This nurturing can take a number of forms, but the goal is the same: to support ourselves to assure a thorough inventory and our continued progress. Our need for nurturing should not be under estimated. The Twelve-Step process is not easy, and Step Four is particularly demanding.

PRAYER FOR STEP FOUR

Dear God,

It is I who have made my life a mess. I have done it, but I cannot undo it. My mistakes are mine, and I will begin a searching and fearless moral inventory. I will write down my wrongs, but I will also include that which is good. I pray for the strength to complete the task.

(Taken from *Prayers for The Twelve Steps—A Spiritual Journey,* page 14)

Step Four begins the growth steps of our journey. Here, we examine our behavior and expand our understanding of ourselves. The adventure of self-discovery begins with Step Four and continues through Step Seven. During these next four steps, we will prepare a personal inventory, discuss it with others in the program, and invite God to remove our shortcomings. Being totally honest in preparing our inventory is vital to the self-discovery that forms the foundation of our recovery. It allows us to remove obstacles that have prevented us from knowing ourselves and truthfully acknowledging our deepest feelings about life.

Step Four helps us get in touch with our "shadow," that part of us that we have hidden away for so long—our repressed nature. In the process of making our inventory, we will develop and broaden our understanding of our behavior. We will see that our "shadow" is an integral part of our nature and must be accepted by us. This part of our nature hides our resentments, fears, and other repressed feelings. As we begin to see ourselves, we will learn to accept our whole character—the good and the bad. This acceptance will free us to discover survival behaviors that began in childhood. In the context of our turbulent early years, these behaviors were lifesaving. However, their continuation into our adulthood renders us dysfunctional.

Denial is a key survival skill that we learned early in childhood. It stunted our emotional growth by keeping us in a make-believe world. We often fantasized that our situation was better than it really was. Denial protected us from our feelings and helped us repress the pain of our family environment. Our shame and guilt caused us to be silent, rather than to be honest and face the fear of being ridiculed by others. This withdrawal hindered us from developing into mature, emotionally healthy adults. As our self-discovery unfolds, we begin to recognize the role that denial has played in our lives. This realization is the basis for our acceptance of the truth of our personal history.

Resentment and fear are two issues that need to be dealt with before we can begin the process of preparing our inventory. Our resentment toward people, places, and things that have injured us keeps us preoccupied and limits our ability to live in the present. Resentment results from hiding the bitter hurts that have tarnished our lives. It evokes anger, frustration, and depression. When our resentments are unresolved, we risk developing physical and mental illnesses.

Fear limits our ability to be rational. When fear is present, it is difficult to see situations in their true perspective. Fear is the root of other repressive and painful feelings. It prevents us from expressing ourselves honestly and stops us from responding in appropriate ways to threatening situations. So to change our behavior, we must first face and accept our fears. By acknowledging our fearful nature, we can expect a temporary loss of self-esteem; fortunately, this will return as we become more willing to rely on God.

Preparing our inventory requires that we look to God for guidance. We renewed our relationship with our Higher Power in Steps Two and Three, and now we ask God for help. We will look closely at our personal histories and acknowledge what we see in them. As the process unfolds, we will recognize the need for change. This task will be much easier if we just remember that God is with us. With God's help, we can courageously review our strengths and our weaknesses.

Step Four gives us the opportunity to recognize that certain skills, acquired in childhood, may be inappropriate in our adult lives. Blaming others for our misfortunes, denying responsibility for hurtful behavior, and resisting the truth are behavior patterns we must discard. These particular learned behaviors were developed early in life and have become character defects. We look at them now and feel troubled. Painful memories may return and we remember things that we thought were forgotten. Our willingness to be honest about what we uncover will give us the clarity of mind that is vital for our continued recovery.

Putting our thoughts on paper is valuable and necessary when completing Step Four. The process of writing focuses our wandering thoughts and allows us to concentrate on what is really happening. It often causes repressed feelings to surface and gives us a deeper understanding of ourselves and our behavior. Our fearless moral inventory provides insights regarding our strengths and weaknesses. Instead of judging ourselves, we need to accept whatever we discover, knowing that this discovery is merely another step toward a healthier life. We must be honest and thorough to complete Step Four successfully.

PERSONAL REFLECTION

Denial stems from our childhood environment, which we were unable to control. This was our way of dealing with the confusion, instability, and violence of the adults around us. We rationalized what was happening and invented acceptable reasons for their unacceptable behavior. By doing this, we ignored the chaos and denied the overwhelming problems. As we matured, our denial continued to protect us from the need to face reality and helped us hide behind our delusions and fantasies.

1. In what ways do you tend to hide from reality? _____

_____

_____

> *"The heart is deceitful above all things and beyond cure. Who can understand it? I the Lord search the heart and examine the mind, to reward a man according to his conduct, according to what his deeds deserve."*
> JER. 17:9–10

2. Describe an action or behavior that reminds you that you have a deceitful heart. _____

_____

_____

The power of denial is illustrated in the Bible when Peter denies Christ. Because of his great love for Christ, Peter thought it inconceivable that he could deny Christ. However, when Peter was confronted with the situation, it was easier for him to deny Christ than it was to admit being a follower and face the consequences of his behavior. When Peter realized what he had done, he was devastated. In much the same way, when we realize what denial has done to us, we experience feelings of self-hatred. It is now that denial needs to be acknowledged and resolved.

3. Explain ways in which denial causes you pain or embarrassment. _____

_____

_____

> *While Peter was below in the courtyard, one of the servant girls...saw Peter warming himself..."You also were with that Nazarene, Jesus," she said. But he denied it....and went out into the entryway. When the servant girl saw him there, she said again to those standing around, "this fellow is one of them."...He began to call down curses on himself, and swore... Immediately the rooster crowed... And he broke down and wept.*
> MARK 14:66–72

Denial was one of the many ways we protected ourselves as children. It has many faces and can be easily masked. It appears in different ways and operates in various fashions. Some recognizable forms are:

Simple Denial: To pretend that something does not exist when it really does (e.g., discounting physical symptoms that may suggest the presence of problems).

Minimizing: To acknowledge a problem, but refuse to see its severity (e.g., admitting to an overusage of prescription drugs when in fact there is overt addiction).

Blaming: To recognize the problem, then blame someone else for its cause (e.g., blaming others for your tendency to isolate).

Excusing: To offer excuses, alibis, justifications, and other explanations for our own or others' behavior (e.g., calling in sick for a partner when the actual cause of the absence is drunkenness).

Generalizing: To deal with problems on a general level which typically avoids personal and emotional awareness of the situation or conditions (e.g., sympathizing with a friend's unemployment when you know the underlying cause is irresponsibility).

Dodging: To change the subject to avoid threatening topics (e.g., talking about the weather when your spouse is discussing the overdrawn checkbook).

Attacking: To become angry and irritable when reference is made to the existing condition, thus avoiding the issue (e.g., arguing about work conditions when the boss addresses tardiness).

4. In what areas of your life do you suspect that denial is most active?_____

_____

_____

> *If anyone thinks he is something when he is nothing, he deceives himself. Each one should test his own actions. Then he can take pride in himself, without comparing himself to somebody else, for each one should carry his own load.*
> GAL. 6:3–5

HELPFUL HINT
...
Read Recovery Note for Galatians 6:1–3, page 1308, *Life Recovery Bible*

5. How does pride keep you from being honest with yourself? _____

_____

_____

Taking a personal inventory is similar to cleaning a closet. We take stock of what we have, examine what we want to save, and discard what is no longer useful or appropriate. It doesn't have to be done all at once, but it must be done eventually. If we take small sections at a time, the cleaning is more thorough and the long-term results are better. In the same way that clothes can trigger memories of the past, our inventory may provoke both positive and negative memories. We must remember that the past is only history. It is not the purpose of our inventory to dwell on the past. This reflection is only a tool to help us understand our current behavior patterns. Our main concern now is for our future. We can lessen our fears surrounding this task by approaching the inventory in this manner.

> *Let us examine our ways and test them,*
> *and let us return to the Lord.*
> LAM. 3:40

6. What anxieties do you have about memories of your past? _____

_____

_____

In Step Four, we will get in touch with many behaviors and attitudes that have been with us since childhood. Our growing awareness about the way we were raised will help us understand that our present behaviors are natural outgrowths of our early need to survive. As adults, we now can choose a different lifestyle for ourselves. We can learn to conduct ourselves in a way that is nurturing to us. As we look at our strengths and weaknesses, we will become aware of the areas of our lives that need to be strengthened. We also will see those areas in which we exhibit strength through our wise choices. We can use the inventory to decide which areas of our lives need changing, and which areas seem the way we want them to be.

7. Which of your behaviors are most damaging to your life? Explain. _____

_____

_____

> *Search me, O God, and know my heart; test me and know my*
> *anxious thoughts. See if there is any offensive way in me,*
> *and lead me in the way everlasting.*
> PS. 139:23–24

8. What obstacles keep you from asking God to search you and know your heart?

_____

_____

Our next task is to look at resentment and recognize how damaging it is to us. It is the number one offender and often the major cause of spiritual disease. As we list our resentments, we see how they have affected our self-esteem, our well-being, and our personal relationships. Holding on to resentment causes stress, anxiety, and uncontrollable feelings of anger. If these are unresolved, serious emotional and physical consequences will develop. If we allow our resentments to prevail, serious depression can develop and ultimately destroy our lives.

9. List your major resentment. How is it interfering with your life? _____

_____

_____

> *My dear brothers, take note of this: Everyone should be quick to listen, slow to speak and slow to become angry, for man's anger does not bring about the righteous life that God desires. Therefore, get rid of all moral filth and the evil that is so prevalent, and humbly accept the word planted in you, which can save you.*
> JAMES 1:19–21

10. List situations where you became angry because of your resentments. _____

_____

_____

The second most destructive offender is fear. It is the emotion we most strongly feel when we begin to look at ourselves. When fear is present, our need to deny, ignore, and avoid reality is increased. Our unrealistic perspective becomes greatly exaggerated and intensifies our emotional responses. Fear can cause us tremendous pain. It attacks us physically and causes feelings that range from apprehension to panic. When fear is present, we may become nervous, nauseated, or disoriented. As we inventory our fears, we may discover that they are a direct result of our inability to make decisions. Or we may believe that if we could make the right decisions, things would be different. And some of the most troubling decisions directly relate to the boundaries we know must be established. Fear is the first response we feel when we aren't in control of our lives. It is the opposite of faith. When we fear, we feel loss of control and we doubt God's ability to help.

11. List your major fear. How is it interfering with your life?_____

_____

_____

> *There is no fear in love. But perfect love drives out fear, because fear has to do with punishment. The man who fears is not made perfect in love.*
> 1 JOHN 4:18

12. What fears surface when you realize God knows all your faults? _____

_____

_____

Facing our resentments and fears requires a great deal of courage. Our past tendency has been to shut down our feelings. Now we begin to look at areas of our lives that we have never explored before. It is important to realize that God is with us and will help us every step of our way. With God's help and understanding, the pain will diminish.

HELPFUL
HINT
...
Read Meditation for 2
Corinthians 13:5–6,
page 54, *Meditations
for The Twelve
Steps—A Spiritual
Journey*

> *Examine yourselves to see whether you are in the faith; test yourselves. Do you not realize that Christ Jesus is in you—unless, of course, you fail the test? And I trust that you will discover that we have not failed the test.*
> 2 COR. 13:5–6

13. In what ways do you know that you have faith in Christ? _____

_____

_____

As part of preparing our Step Four inventory, we will look at our character traits and examine our strengths and weaknesses. Our strengths appear in behavior that has positive effects on us as well as on others. Our weaknesses are revealed in behavior that is destructive to ourselves and others. Before we can correct our problem areas, we need to acknowledge and examine both. Understanding begins when we discover how we became the people we are—how we formulated the ideas, beliefs, and attitudes that govern how we act. This doesn't require years of therapy. It involves only an honest consideration of the forces, influences, and needs that developed our survival skills and molded our current character traits.

14. What do you believe is your major strength? How does it support you? _____

_____

_____

15. What do you believe is your major weakness? How does it hurt you? _____

_____

_____

> *Get rid of all bitterness, rage and anger, brawling and slander,*
> *along with every form of malice.*
> EPH. 4:31

16. Toward whom or what do you feel bitterness, anger, rage, and other forms of malice? _____

_____

_____

When preparing our inventory, we may encounter some difficulties. If we are blocked at some point, denial may be operating. We need to stop for a moment, reflect on what we are attempting to do, and analyze our feelings. We must also ask God for help. In times like this, God's presence means a great deal to us, and we must be willing to look to him for support.

17. Identify and explain any resistance to making your inventory. _____

_____

_____

> *I remember my affliction and my wandering, the bitterness and the*
> *gall. I well remember them, and my soul is downcast within me. Yet*
> *this I call to mind and therefore I have hope: Because of the Lord's*
> *great love we are not consumed, for his compassions never fail.*
> LAM. 3:19-22

18. Which past hurts or failures cause you to feel depressed? _____

_____

_____

> *Blessed is the man who perseveres under trial, because when he has*
> *stood the test, he will receive the crown of life that God has prom-*
> *ised to those who love him.*
> JAMES 1:12

19. What things can you do to keep yourself focused on your Step Four inventory? (For example: keep a daily routine, allow time for thought and reflection, work with a partner, read Step Four materials, etc.)_____

_____

_____

The inventory we are preparing is for our own benefit, not the benefit of others. It will help us make a major breakthrough in our self-acceptance and lead us further along the road to recovery. As we go to Steps Five, Six, and Seven, the process continues to unfold as we acknowledge the truth about ourselves, discuss it with others, and, finally, ask God to remove our shortcomings. For now, our goal is to concentrate on making an honest and thorough inventory. If done properly and sincerely, our Step Four work will help us break free from the bondage of our past.

HELPFUL
HINT
· · ·
Read "I Need to Take
a Trip," pages 14–15,
*Prayers for The Twelve
Steps—A Spiritual
Journey*

> *Put to death, therefore, whatever belongs to your earthly nature: sexual immorality, impurity, lust, evil desires and greed, which is idolatry. Because of these, the wrath of God is coming. You used to walk in these ways, in the life you once lived. But now you must rid yourselves of all such things as these: anger, rage, malice, slander, and filthy language from your lips.*
>
> COL. 3:5–8

20. Ridding ourselves of unwanted behavior is impossible without God's help. In your own words, invite God's help._____

_____

_____

PREPARING FOR COMMUNITY

21. Which three questions from this step would you like to share with others?

_____

_____

22. What kind of support do you want from your family group members to help you complete your Step Four work?_____

_____

_____

23. Step Four is a difficult step. Describe any resistance, or discouragements you may be experiencing. _____

_____

_____

Moral Inventory: A moral inventory is a list of our weaknesses and our strengths. In this text the weaknesses are also referred to as wrongs, character defects, faults, and shortcomings. This inventory is something we prayerfully accomplish with God's help. It is for our benefit.

Survival Skills: Survival skills are those familiar defenses that we developed to protect ourselves from the chaos of our childhood homes. These early childhood survival skills followed us into adult life and added to our struggles.

Denial: Denial is a key survival skill. We protect ourselves by not admitting that anything is wrong. We ignore the real problems by replacing them with a host of elaborate explanations, rationalizations, and distractions such as minimizing, blaming, excusing, generalizing, dodging, attacking, etc.

Resentment: Resentment is a major roadblock to recovery that must be removed. Resentment is the bitterness and anger we feel toward those whom we perceive as threats to our security or well-being or those who have caused us harm. If not removed, our resentments hinder our progress and growth.

Fear: Fear is often our first response to anything new. We meet change with fear because we feel threatened by so many things. Fear creates a physical response that begins with the release of adrenaline and ends up with the whole body on alert. This alerted state often leads to persistent and unwanted tension and can develop into stress-related illness.

Shadow: Although "shadow" may sound odd or like unfamiliar Christian terminology, the idea of a battle between light and dark is a biblical truth. When St. John speaks of Christ's coming, he describes Christ as light. The idea of darkness and shadow illustrates the evil side of this world and the corrupt nature in ourselves. "Shadow" refers to the darkness we carry within us. Just as our shadow follows our every move, our dark side or fallen nature is always with us. Our shadow is most evident when contrasted with the light of day. Our old, fallen nature is very noticeable when we stand beside God's light, the Bible. Take time to read John 1:1–9, Romans 7:7–25, and 1 John 1:5–7.

IMPORTANT GUIDELINES
IN PREPARING YOUR INVENTORY

The materials offered in this Step Four Inventory Guide are different from the inventory guides used in other Twelve-Step programs. They emphasize those feelings and behaviors most commonly seen in individuals from homes where substance abuse or other damage-inducing behavior was prevalent. When preparing your inventory, choose the traits that specifically apply to you. Don't tackle them all at once. For now, only work on the ones that you feel comfortable doing. Come back to the difficult ones later. Focus on recent events and record words and actions as accurately as possible. Take your time. It's better to be thorough with some than incomplete with all.

The inventory begins with resentment and fear, followed by a series of feelings and behaviors to be examined. This process prepares you for Step Five. You are the primary beneficiary of your honesty and thoroughness in this inventory. It is important to refrain from generalizing. Be as specific as possible.

Following the section on character weaknesses there is an opportunity to list your character strengths. This chapter also includes an "Additional Inventory" for you to record your weaknesses and strengths that were not listed in the text.

NOTE: Step Ten includes a special inventory to measure the progress you have made since your initial inventory in Step Four.

Resentment is an underlying cause of many forms of spiritual disease. Our mental and physical ills are frequently the direct result of this unhealthy condition. No doubt others have harmed us, and we have a legitimate right to feel resentful. However, resentment doesn't punish anyone but ourselves. We can't hold resentments and find healing at the same time. It' s best released by asking God for the strength to forgive the offender. Learning to deal with resentment in a healthy way is an important part of our recovery process.

When we resent, we may be:

Feeling injured	Feeling left out	Experiencing low self-worth
Feeling violated	Retaliating	Angry or bitter

List situations where resentment is a problem for you.

Example: **I resent** my boss **because** he doesn't care to hear my explanation of why I am depressed. **This affects** my self-esteem. **This activates** unexpressed anger. **This makes me feel** even more depressed.

I resent _____

_____

_____

I resent _____

_____

_____

I resent _____

_____

_____

I resent _____

_____

_____

Self-Evaluation: On a scale from one to ten, how much does resentment negatively affect your life? Number one indicates that it has little negative effect. Number ten indicates that it has great negative effect. Circle where you are today.

| 1 | 2 | 3 | 4 | 5 | 6 | 7 | 8 | 9 | 10 |

FEAR

Fear is an underlying cause of many forms of spiritual disease. It is the first response we feel when we aren't in control of a situation. A wide range of mental and physical ills are frequently the direct result of this unwholesome emotion. Fear often prevents us from seeing options to effectively resolve the issues causing the fear. Learning to acknowledge fear in a healthy way is an important part of our recovery process.

When we fear, we may be:

Feeling threatened	Resisting change	Experiencing rejection
Fighting for survival	Facing our mortality	Anticipating loss

List situations where fear is a problem for you.

Example: **I fear** my spouse **because** I feel that I am never able to please him/her. **This affects** my self-esteem and sexuality. **This activates** my fear of abandonment. **This makes me feel** worthless and angry.

I fear _____

_____

_____

I fear _____

_____

_____

I fear _____

_____

_____

I fear _____

_____

_____

Self-Evaluation: On a scale from one to ten, how much does fear negatively affect your life? Number one indicates that it has little negative effect. Number ten indicates that it has great negative effect. Circle where you are today.

1	2	3	4	5	6	7	8	9	10

REPRESSED OR INAPPROPRIATELY EXPRESSED ANGER

Anger is a major source of many problems in the lives of adults who were reared in chaotic homes. It is a feeling that we often suppress, because admitting it makes us uncomfortable. In our chaotic homes, the turmoil was so intense that we either denied our anger or expressed it inappropriately. We felt it was safer to protect ourselves and simply hoped our feelings would go away. We were not aware that repressed anger could lead to serious resentment and depression. It causes physical complications that can develop into stress-related illnesses. Denying anger or expressing it inappropriately causes problems in relationships because we cannot be truthful about our feelings and must always be pretending.

When we repress or inappropriately express anger, we may experience:

Resentment	Depression	Anxiety
Self-Pity	Jealousy	Stress

List situations where anger is a problem for you.

Example: **I inappropriately express anger** toward my son **because** I am embarrassed by his behavior. **This affects** my self-worth. **This activates** my fear of rejection. **This makes me feel** incompetent as a parent.

I repress/inappropriately express anger_____

_____

_____

I repress/inappropriately express anger_____

_____

_____

I repress/inappropriately express anger_____

_____

_____

I repress/inappropriately express anger_____

_____

_____

Self-Evaluation: On a scale from one to ten, how much does anger negatively affect your life? Number one indicates that it has little negative effect. Number ten indicates that it has great negative effect. Circle where you are today.

1	2	3	4	5	6	7	8	9	10

APPROVAL SEEKING

Many of us fear disapproval and criticism. As children, we desperately wanted to receive approval from our parents, grandparents, siblings, and significant others. This rarely occurred for most of us. As a result, we constantly sought validation. This continued into adulthood and seriously affected the way we pattern our lives and thinking around the needs of others. Rather than look for approval in a positive way, we seek validation in order to feel better about ourselves and get people to like us. This keeps us out of touch with our own feelings and desires, and prevents us from discovering our own wants and needs. We look for reactions in others, and attempt to manage their impression of us. We constantly strive to please everyone and often stay in relationships that are destructive to us.

When we need approval from others, we may be:

People pleasing   Feeling unworthy   Fearing failure
Ignoring our own needs   Fearing criticism   Lacking confidence

List situations where approval seeking is a problem for you.

Example: **I seek approval** from my friends **because** I want to feel better about myself. **This affects** my relationship with my friends. **This activates** my fear of rejection. **This makes me feel** like I'm not important to anyone.

I seek approval _____

_____

_____

I seek approval _____

_____

_____

I seek approval _____

_____

_____

Self-Evaluation: On a scale from one to ten, how much does approval seeking negatively affect your life? Number one indicates that it has little negative effect. Number ten indicates that it has great negative effect. Circle where you are today.

| 1 | 2 | 3 | 4 | 5 | 6 | 7 | 8 | 9 | 10 |

As children, we frequently assumed the responsibility for concerns and problems of others that were far beyond our capability to handle. As a result, we were deprived of a normal childhood. The unrealistic demands placed on us, and the praise we received for being "little adults," made us believe we had Godlike powers. Taking care of others boosted our self-esteem and made us feel indispensable. It gave purpose to our lives. As caretakers, we are most comfortable with chaotic situations where others assure us that we are needed. Although we often resent others for taking and not giving, we are unable to allow others to care for us. We don't experience the joy of taking care of ourselves.

As caretakers, we may:

Be co-dependent	Lose our identity	Ignore our own needs
Rescue people	Feel very responsible	Feel indispensable

List situations where caretaking is a problem for you.

Example: **I take care of** my boyfriend's financial problems **because** I want him to love me more. **This affects** available funds for my own financial needs. **This activates** my resentment and tendency to withdraw. **This makes me feel** very lonely.

I take care of _____

_____

_____

I take care of _____

_____

_____

I take care of _____

_____

_____

Self-Evaluation: On a scale from one to ten, how much does caretaking negatively affect your life? Number one indicates that it has little negative effect. Number ten indicates that it has great negative effect. Circle where you are today.

1	2	3	4	5	6	7	8	9	10

CONTROL

As children, we had little or no control over our environment or the events that took place in our lives. As adults, we have extraordinary needs to control our feelings and behavior, and we try to control the feelings and behavior of others. We become rigid and unable to have spontaneity in our lives. We trust only ourselves to complete a task or to handle a situation. We manipulate others in order to gain their approval and keep a balance of control that makes us feel safe. We fear that our lives will deteriorate if we give up our management position. We become stressed and anxious when our authority is threatened.

Due to our need to be in control, we may:

Overreact to change	Be judgmental and rigid	Fear failure
Lack trust	Manipulate others	Be intolerant

List situations where control is a problem for you.

Example: **I attempt to control** my nineteen-year-old son **because** I am afraid of losing him. **This affects** my communication with him. **This activates** my fear of abandonment. **This makes me feel** very frightened and powerless.

I attempt to control _____

_____

_____

I attempt to control _____

_____

_____

I attempt to control _____

_____

_____

I attempt to control _____

_____

_____

Self-Evaluation: On a scale from one to ten, how much does control negatively affect your life? Number one indicates that it has little negative effect. Number ten indicates that it has great negative effect. Circle where you are today.

1	2	3	4	5	6	7	8	9	10

Fear of abandonment is a reaction to stress that we developed in early childhood. As children, we observed unpredictable behavior from responsible adults. We never knew from one day to the next if our parents would be there for us. Many of us were abandoned either physically or emotionally. As our parents' addictions increased in severity, their inability to parent also increased. As children, we simply were not important. As adults, we are inclined to choose partners with whom we can repeat this pattern. We try to be perfect by meeting all our partner's needs in order to avoid experiencing the pain of abandonment. Our need to reduce the possibility of abandonment takes precedence over dealing with issues or conflicts. This behavior produces a tense environment with poor communication.

When we fear abandonment, we may:

Feel insecure	Worry excessively	Become co-dependent
Become caretakers	Feel rejected	Avoid being alone

List situations where fear of abandonment is a problem for you.

Example: **I fear abandonment** by my husband **because** he doesn't pay much attention to me. **This affects** my peace of mind. **This activates** my caretaking and manipulation of him. **This makes me feel** very frightened and vulnerable.

I fear abandonment _____

_____

_____

I fear abandonment _____

_____

_____

I fear abandonment _____

_____

_____

Self-Evaluation: On a scale from one to ten, how much does fear of abandonment negatively affect your life? Number one indicates that it has little negative effect. Number ten indicates that it has great negative effect. Circle where you are today.

1	2	3	4	5	6	7	8	9	10

FEAR OF AUTHORITY FIGURES

Fear of people in roles of authority can be a result of our parents' unrealistic expectations of us—wanting us to be more than we were able to be. We see people in authority as having unrealistic expectations of us and thus, we fear we cannot meet their expectations. We are unable to deal with people whom we perceive as being in positions of power. Simple assertiveness displayed by others is often misinterpreted by us as anger. This can cause us to feel intimidated and to become oversensitive. No matter how competent we are, we compare ourselves to others and conclude that we are inadequate. As a result, we constantly compromise our integrity in order to avoid confrontation or criticism.

Fear of authority figures may cause us to:

Compare ourselves to others	Take things personally	Fear rejection
React rather than act	Feel inadequate	Be arrogant

List situations where fear of authority figures is a problem for you.

Example: **I fear** my boss **because** I don't want her to know how incompetent I feel. **This affects** my actions when I am around her. **This activates** my need to isolate—I try to be unnoticed. **This makes me feel** childish and immature.

I fear _____

_____

_____

I fear _____

_____

_____

I fear _____

_____

_____

Self-Evaluation: On a scale from one to ten, how much does fear of authority figures negatively affect your life? Number one indicates that it has little negative effect. Number ten indicates that it has great negative effect. Circle where you are today.

| 1 | 2 | 3 | 4 | 5 | 6 | 7 | 8 | 9 | 10 |

Many of us have difficulty expressing our feelings or even realizing that we have them. We harbor deep emotional pain and a sense of guilt and shame. As children, our feelings were met with disapproval, anger, and rejection. For survival purposes, we learned to hide our feelings or repress them entirely. As adults, we are not in touch with our feelings. We can only allow ourselves to have "acceptable" feelings to stay "safe." Our true nature is distorted so we can protect ourselves from the reality of what is truly happening. Distorted and repressed feelings cause resentment, anger, and depression, which often lead to physical illness.

When we have frozen feelings, we may:

Be unaware of our feelings	Be depressed	Have distorted feelings
Struggle with relationships	Become ill	Withhold conversation

List situations where frozen feelings are a problem for you.

EXAMPLE: **I repress my feelings** toward my spouse **because** I don't want to be hurt. **This affects** my actions and limits my ability to communicate with my spouse. **This activates** my need to isolate and causes me to be accused of being insensitive and unaffectionate. **This makes me feel** very isolated and lonely.

I repress my feelings _____

_____

_____

I repress my feelings _____

_____

_____

I repress my feelings _____

_____

_____

Self-Evaluation: On a scale from one to ten, how much do frozen feelings negatively affect your life? Number one indicates that they have little negative effect. Number ten indicates that they have great negative effect. Circle where you are today.

1	2	3	4	5	6	7	8	9	10

ISOLATION

We usually find it safer to withdraw from surroundings that are uncomfortable for us. By isolating ourselves, we prevent others from seeing us as we really are. We tell ourselves that we are not worthy and, therefore, do not deserve love, attention, or acceptance. We also tell ourselves that we cannot be punished or hurt if we don't express our feelings. Rather than take risks, we choose to hide, thereby eliminating the need to face an uncertain outcome.

When we isolate ourselves, we may:

Fear rejection   Feel defeated   Procrastinate
Be timid and shy   Be lonely   See ourselves as different

List situations where isolation is a problem.

Example: **I isolate** from my spouse **because** he/she is so negative toward me. **This affects** my self-esteem. **This activates** my negative self-talk and anger. **This makes me feel** worthless and stupid.

I isolate_____

_____

_____

I isolate_____

_____

_____

I isolate_____

_____

_____

I isolate_____

_____

_____

Self-Evaluation: On a scale from one to ten, how much does isolation negatively affect your life? Number one indicates that it has little negative effect. Number ten indicates that it has great negative effect. Circle where you are today.

| 1 | 2 | 3 | 4 | 5 | 6 | 7 | 8 | 9 | 10 |

Low self-esteem is rooted in our early childhood. During this time we were rarely encouraged to believe that we were adequate or important. Because of constant criticism, we believed that we were "bad" and the cause of many family problems. To feel accepted, we tried harder to please. The harder we tried, the more frustrated we became. Low self-esteem affects our ability to set and achieve goals. We are afraid to take risks. We feel responsible for things that go wrong, and when something goes right, we do not give ourselves credit. Instead, we feel undeserving and believe it is not going to last.

When we experience low self-esteem, we may:

Rescue or please others	Isolate from others	Be non-assertive
Have negative self-image	Appear inadequate	Fear failure

List situations where low self-esteem is a problem for you.

Example: **I feel low self-esteem** when I'm asked to speak in front of others **because** I believe everyone knows how worthless and unimportant I feel inside. **This affects** my ability to speak intelligently. I mumble, make excuses, and apologize for myself. **This activates** self-hatred and negative self-talk. I want to go hide afterward. **This makes me feel** hopeless.

I feel low self-esteem _____

_____

_____

I feel low self-esteem _____

_____

_____

I feel low self-esteem _____

_____

_____

Self-Evaluation: On a scale from one to ten, how much does low self-esteem negatively affect your life? Number one indicates that it has little negative effect. Number ten indicates that it has great negative effect. Circle where you are today.

| 1 | 2 | 3 | 4 | 5 | 6 | 7 | 8 | 9 | 10 |

OVERDEVELOPED SENSE OF RESPONSIBILITY

As children in a dysfunctional home, we felt responsible for our parents' problems. We tried to be "model children" and arrange things the way we thought others wanted them to be. We believed that we were responsible for the emotions and actions of others—even for the outcome of events. Today we remain supersensitive to the needs of others, and we try to assume responsibility for helping them get their needs met. It is important for us to be perfect. We volunteer to do things so people will appreciate us. Our sense of responsibility causes us to overcommit, and we have a tendency to take on more than we can handle effectively.

When we are too responsible, we may:

Take life too seriously	Over-achieve	Appear rigid
Be perfectionists	Manipulate others	Have false pride

List situations where overdeveloped sense of responsibility is a problem for you.

Example: **I feel overly responsible** when things aren't going well at work **because** I think it's my fault. **This affects** my health. I'm extremely tense and I get headaches. **This activates** my resentment and anger. I hate these people for letting me do all the work. **This makes me feel** guilty.

I feel overly responsible_____

_____

_____

I feel overly responsible_____

_____

_____

I feel overly responsible_____

_____

_____

Self-Evaluation: On a scale from one to ten, how much does overdeveloped sense of responsibility negatively affect your life? Number one indicates that it has little negative effect. Number ten indicates that it has great negative effect. Circle where you are today.

1	2	3	4	5	6	7	8	9	10

In childhood, life was so chaotic we felt that nothing we did mattered. The models we had were untrustworthy and irresponsible, so we didn't know what was normal. The expectations placed on us were beyond our ability to achieve. We couldn't be what everyone wanted us to be, so we quit trying. Rather than compete with successful siblings, we unplugged, we gave up. As adults we are irresponsible. We wait for things to change before we begin to take initiative. We believe life has been so unfair to us that we won't claim responsibility for our present condition. We are overwhelmed by our problems, but don't know how we can make a difference.

When we are irresponsible, we may:

Become detached	Feel like victims	Under-achieve
Appear uncaring	Expect others to take care of us	Have false pride

Consider situations where irresponsibility is a problem for you.

Example: **I behave irresponsibly** when too much is expected of me **because** I know that I can't do what my family wants. **This affects** my self-esteem. I want to isolate and hide. **This activates** my resentment and anger. I hate these people for expecting this of me. **This makes me feel** guilty and afraid.

I behave irresponsibly _____

_____

_____

I behave irresponsibly _____

_____

_____

I behave irresponsibly _____

_____

_____

Self-Evaluation: On a scale from one to ten, how much does irresponsibility negatively affect your life? Number one indicates that it has little negative effect. Number ten indicates that it has great negative effect. Circle where you are today.

1	2	3	4	5	6	7	8	9	10

INAPPROPRIATELY EXPRESSED SEXUALITY

We have learned to think of our sexual feelings as unnatural or abnormal. Because it is awkward to share our feelings with others, we have no opportunity to develop a healthy attitude about our own sexuality. As small children, we may have explored our physical sexuality with peers and then been punished severely. The message was "sex is dirty, is not talked about, and is to be avoided." Some of us saw our parents as very disapproving or even as totally nonsexual beings. We may have been molested by a parent or close relative who was out of control. As a result, we are uncomfortable in our sexual roles. We do not freely discuss sex with our partners for fear of being misunderstood and abandoned. As parents, we may avoid discussing sexuality with our children and deny their need for developing a sexual identity.

Due to inappropriately expressed sexuality we may:

Lose our sense of morality	Be lustful	Seduce others
Be frigid or impotent	Avoid intimacy	Feel guilt and shame

List situations where inappropriately expressed sexuality is a problem for you.

Example: **I inappropriately express my sexuality** when my spouse wants intimacy **because** I feel dirty and unlovable. **This affects** our relationship. **This activates** my resentment and anger toward my spouse for not understanding, consequently I hate myself for being this way. **This makes me feel** lonely.

I inappropriately express my sexuality_____

_____

_____

I inappropriately express my sexuality_____

_____

_____

I inappropriately express my sexuality_____

_____

_____

Self-Evaluation: On a scale from one to ten, how much does inappropriately expressed sexuality negatively affect your life? Number one indicates that it has little negative effect. Number ten indicates that it has great negative effect. Circle where you are today.

1	2	3	4	5	6	7	8	9	10

Consider the positive character strengths you already possess in the following areas:

Emotional: Healthy feelings or affective responses to one's self and others (e.g., I am able to feel and express my love for my spouse and my children)._____

_____

Spiritual: The good ways one relates to God (e.g., I have a strong commitment to Jesus Christ)._____

_____

Relational: Positive and supportive interaction with others (e.g., I have a healthy friendship with Robert). _____

_____

Moral: Proper ethics and behavior in thoughts and actions (e.g., I have a clear conscience concerning my business affairs). _____

_____

Intellectual: Quality attention and energy devoted to mental activities (e.g., I devote time to reading and study). _____

_____

Self-care/nurturing: Healthy concern and care for self (e.g., I take time to go fishing). _____

_____

ADDITIONAL INVENTORY

Use the space below to list the strengths and weaknesses you did not list in your Step Four inventory.

Strengths	*Weaknesses*
_____	_____
_____	_____
_____	_____
_____	_____

GROUP ACTIVITIES

ACTIVITY #1: "This Is My Ear"

Objective: To poke fun at our problems with denial.

❏ Stand in a circle and designate someone as *It*.

❏ *It* then touches his ear; he does not say, "This is my ear." Instead, he may say, "This is my elbow." Then he quickly points to someone.

❏ The person *It* points to must then point to his elbow and say, "This is my ear." He must do this before *It* can count to ten. If he fails to do so, he becomes *It*. If he succeeds, *It* must go to someone else. (NOTE: Other body parts should be used for variety. For example, *It* might point to his eye and say, "This is my knee." The other person must respond by pointing to his knee and saying, "This is my eye.")

❏ After the game has been played the group may choose to discuss the absurd ways we deny the truth about our lives.

ACTIVITY #2: "You Did It!"

Supplies Needed: A small soft object such as a beanbag, small pillow, stuffed toy, or wads of paper.

Objective: To have fun with the idea of blaming.

❏ Designate someone as *It* and have him stand with his back to the group.

❏ Pass the soft object to someone in the group and have her throw the object at the person who is *It*.

❏ After *It* has been hit, he turns around and blames the person he thinks hit him. If he guesses correctly, that person becomes *It*. If not, he continues as *It*.

❏ When the game is over the group may want to discuss how we have been hit by others in life and how we waste time blaming and holding resentments.

ACTIVITY #3: "What Would Nathan Say?"

Objective: To identify with King David's hidden faults and denial.

❏ The participants are to close their eyes and assume a meditative posture. Someone should read aloud 2 Samuel 11:1 through 12:14.

❏ Following the reading, share how you identify with David's hidden faults and denial. Complete the following sentence: "If Nathan the prophet were to come to me, he would confront me about…"

STEP FIVE

*Admitted to God, to ourselves, and to another human being
the exact nature of our wrongs.*

. . .

*Therefore confess your sins to each other and
pray for each other so that you may be healed.*

(JAMES 5:16A)

UNDERSTANDING STEP FIVE

Imagine a house that had been shut up for several years. A blanket of dust covers everything. Signs of decay abound: cobwebs in strings like party decorations. Stuffy and stale odors of mildew and mold. Unrecognizable knickknacks on the dust-covered mantle. Forgotten and faded pictures on stained walls. Eerie feelings that hover like ghosts from years gone by. We can't wait to open all the doors, to pull back all the drapes, to vent the shut-up rooms. We turn on every light and expose each darkened, dusty corner. We watch the light of day sweep out the demons of darkness and shadow.

Our lives are like closed-up houses. All our shameful secrets, embarrassing behaviors, and spoiled hopes lie hidden from view. The air of our lives is stale because we have been afraid to open the doors and windows to anyone else lest we be found out, rejected, or shamed. Step Five is our emergence. When we admit the nature of our wrongs to God, ourselves, and another human being, we are opening the doors and windows of our lives. We are displaying our true selves.

WORKING STEP FIVE

We work Step Five by bringing our Step Four inventory to God in prayerful admission. We work Step Five by being honest with ourselves, by looking ourselves in the eye, and reciting our inventory. We work Step Five by sharing our inventory with someone we can trust, someone who will understand, someone who will encourage and not condemn us. The work of confession is our task here. Not easy work, but absolutely necessary.

PREPARING FOR STEP FIVE

We prepare for Step Five by scheduling an undistracted time with God and with ourselves. We prepare by prayerfully searching for another human being with whom to share. And we prepare by asking God for help in completing this step. Sometimes our tendency is to round off the edges and water down the truth of our inventory. God can give us the courage to be brutally honest about ourselves.

PRAYER FOR STEP FIVE

Higher Power,

My inventory has shown me who I am, yet I ask for your help in admitting my wrongs to another person and to you. Assure me, and be with me in this step, for without this step I cannot progress in my recovery. With your help, I can do this, and I will do it.

(Taken from *Prayers for The Twelve Steps—A Spiritual Journey,* page 16)

Step Four laid the foundation for identifying many of our shadowy deeds and thoughts. It also provided an opportunity for recording our strengths. Completing our Step Four inventory made us aware of many truths about ourselves. This realization may have caused us pain. The natural reaction is to feel sadness or guilt or both. We faced ourselves and our history honestly. We courageously identified some behaviors we want to eliminate.

For those of us who have been honest and thorough, Step Four has provided the foundation upon which we will build our recovery. It identified the unresolved feelings, unhealed memories, and personal defects that produced resentment, depression, and loss of self-worth. God's help and light (John 1:5–9) helped us commit our lives to walking in the light of his truth. The acknowledgment of our wrongs and the mending of our self-worth have begun to lift a great burden from our hearts and minds. Now that we have identified our character traits, it is possible to relieve ourselves of the burden of guilt and shame associated with our wrongdoings.

Step Five requires that we engage in honest confrontations with ourselves and others by admitting our faults to God, to ourselves, and to another person. By doing so, we begin the important phase of setting aside our pride so that we can see ourselves in true perspective.

Admitting the exact nature of our wrongs to God is the first phase of Step Five. Here, we confess to God all that we have worked so hard to conceal. It is no longer necessary to blame God or others for what has happened to us. We begin to accept our history for exactly what it is. This process of acceptance brings us closer to God, and we start to realize that he is always there for us. Our confession helps us receive God's love and accept ourselves unconditionally. We must remember that we are all children of God and will never be rejected.

Admitting our wrongs to ourselves began in Step Four, as we wrote our inventory and had the opportunity to see our behaviors for what they really are. In Step Five, we consciously admit our wrongs. This increases our self-esteem and supports us as we move toward Step Seven, in which we ask God to remove our shortcomings.

Telling our story to another person can be a frightening experience. Many of us have spent a major portion of our lives building defenses to keep others out. Living in isolation has been a way of protecting ourselves from further hurt.

Step Five is our pathway out of isolation and loneliness, a move toward wholeness, happiness, and a sense of peace. It is a humbling experience to be totally honest, but we can no longer pretend. It is time to reveal ourselves completely.

We will unveil parts of our nature that we have concealed from ourselves. We may fear the impact that telling the truth will have on our lives. sharing our story with another person may cause us additional fear of being rejected. However, it is essential that we take this important risk and confess our wrongs. With God's help, we will have the courage to reveal our true nature. The result will be worth all the agony of the unburdening process.

Following are some important guidelines to focus on when completing the fifth step:

- Remember that Step Five asks only that we admit the exact nature of our wrongs. We admit how our behaviors have been hurtful to ourselves and others. It is not necessary to discuss how the wrongs came about or how changes will be made. You are not seeking counsel or advice.

- Remember also to share your strengths. The objective is balance. Thank God for the strengths of character that he has nurtured in your life.

- Begin with prayer, calling upon God to be present as you prepare to go through your fourth step revelations and insights. Ask God's Spirit to guide and support you in what you are about to experience.

- After completing your fifth step, take time for prayer and meditation to reflect on what you have done. Thank God for the tools you have been given to improve your relationship with him. Spend time rereading the first five steps and note anything you have omitted. Acknowledge that you are laying a new foundation for your life. The cornerstone is your relationship with God and your commitment to honesty and humility.

- Congratulate yourself for having the courage to risk self-disclosure, and thank God for the peace of mind you have achieved.

Ask for God's help in choosing the person to whom you will admit your wrongs. Remember that the other person should reflect the image of Christ and be a representative for him. God intended us to speak to others, to share our sorrows and joys as members of his family. Look for qualities you admire in the other person that will inspire your confidence. God's Holy Spirit works spiritually through all of his children. Sharing our personal experiences will help us come to know the depth of God's unconditional love for all his human family.

Choose your Fifth Step listener carefully, one who is familiar with Twelve-Step programs. The individual can be:

- A clergyman ordained by an established religion. Ministers of many faiths often receive such requests.

HELPFUL HINT
. . .
Read Step Five Prayers, pages 16–17, *Prayers for The Twelve Steps—A Spiritual Journey*

THE TWELVE STEPS—A SPIRITUAL JOURNEY

- A trusted friend (preferably of the same sex), a doctor, or psychologist.

- A family member with whom you can openly share. Be careful not to reveal information that might be harmful to your spouse or other family members.

- A member of a Twelve-Step program. If you are working with family groups as described in this book, you may find that significant trust already exists in your group. That trust will deepen by doing your fifth step with a group member. In some cases, the family group as a whole can be the listener.

- Choose a listener who is patient and sympathetic. The listener is God's spokesperson and is communicating God's unconditional acceptance.

- Choose a listener who is accepting and understanding.

PERSONAL REFLECTION

Our growing relationship with God gave us the courage to examine ourselves, accept who we are, and reveal our true selves. Step Five helps us acknowledge and discard our old survival skills and move toward a new and healthier life. Being thorough and honest in completing our inventory places us in a position to move forward. And the forward motion in Step Five takes the form of confessing Step Four inventory. We will share all we have learned about ourselves.

1. Describe some feelings you experienced when making your inventory. _____

_____

_____

HELPFUL HINT

• • •

Read "Prayers of Penitence," Chapter Seven, pages 93–103, *Prayers for The Twelve Steps—A Spiritual Journey*

> *Submit yourselves, then, to God. Resist the devil, and he will flee from you. Come near to God and He will come near to you. Wash your hands, you sinners, and purify your hearts, you double-minded.*
> JAMES 4:7–8

2. How did the process of doing your inventory bring you closer to God? _____

_____

_____

Step Five consists of three distinct parts. We will confess our faults to God, to ourselves, and to another human being. For some of us, it will involve telling our life story for the first time. As we do it, we will cleanse ourselves of the excess baggage we have been carrying. As we open our hearts and reveal ourselves, we will achieve a deeper level of spirituality.

3. What are your hopes and fears surrounding Step Five? _____

_____

_____

> *O Lord, we acknowledge our wickedness and the guilt of our*
> *fathers; we have indeed sinned against you.*
> JER. 14:20

4. Which of your faults is the most difficult to acknowledge to another human being? Why? _____

_____

_____

Admitting our defects to God can be very frightening. We may choose to believe that because God is in charge of the universe, all events are his will. In that way blaming God can be a method for us to deny our part in the problem. It is important to understand that God has given us free will. He wants what is best for us, but he allows us to make choices free of his manipulation. As we admit our wrongs to him, we must hold fast to his unconditional and everlasting love for us. He will strengthen and guide us, as we pursue his desire for us to lead a healthy and peaceful life.

> *So then, each of us will give an account*
> *of himself to God.*
> ROM. 14:12

Step Five is for your own benefit—God already knows you. You are beginning a process of living a life of humility, honesty, and courage. The result is freedom, happiness, and serenity.

The following information is helpful when completing your fifth step with God:

- Imagine God sitting across from you in a chair.

- Start with a prayer such as, "Lord, I understand that you already know me completely. I am now ready to reveal myself to you openly and humbly—my hurtful behaviors, self-centeredness, and negative traits. I am grateful to you for the gifts and abilities that have brought me to this point in my life. Take away my fear of being known and rejected. I place myself and my life in your care and keeping."

- Speak audibly, sincerely, and honestly. Share your understanding of the insights you gained from your fourth step inventory. Be aware that emotions may surface as part of the powerful cleansing experience taking place.

IF YOU HAVE NOT ALREADY DONE IT, STOP NOW AND COMPLETE YOUR FIFTH STEP WITH GOD.

---

5. If you admitted your wrongs to God, you can count on his mercy. Describe your experience or understanding of God's mercy for you now. _____

_____

_____

6. In what ways did you feel God's unconditional love for you? _____

_____

_____

Our admission to ourselves is the least-threatening part of Step Five and it can be done with the least risk. However, it is not the easiest part of Step Five because of denial. We use denial as a coping mechanism—an unconscious tool to protect ourselves from pain. Through denial we are protected from facing the truth about ourselves. Denial is not easily conquered, but if we have done an honest Step Four inventory, the barrier of denial is already weakened.

> *If we claim to be without sin, we deceive ourselves and the truth is not in us. If we confess our sins, he is faithful and just and will forgive us our sins and purify us from all unrighteousness.*
> 1 JOHN 1:8-9

7. What are you using to distract yourself from the pain of being broken (e.g., television, radio, music, activities, work, relationships, substance abuse, religion, etc.)? _____

_____

_____

The following information is helpful when completing your fifth step with yourself:

- Writing your fourth step inventory began the process of developing your self-awareness, the first step toward what will become genuine self-love. Solitary self-appraisal is the beginning of your confession, but it is not enough by itself. It is in Step Five is that you turn that knowledge into improved self-acceptance.

- Sit in a chair with your imaginary double seated across from you in an empty chair. Or sit in front of a mirror that allows you to see yourself as you speak.

- Speak out loud. Allow yourself time to hear what you are saying and to note any deeper understanding that occurs.

- Acknowledge your courage for proceeding to this point. This and every part of this process releases excess emotional baggage that you have carried around because of low self-worth.

IF YOU HAVE NOT ALREADY DONE IT, STOP NOW AND COMPLETE YOUR FIFTH STEP INVENTORY WITH YOURSELF.

Admitting our wrongs to another human being is the most powerful part of Step Five. It is a true exercise in humility and will help us break down our defenses. Being rigorously honest with another human being may frighten us and cause us to procrastinate this portion of Step Five. It is tempting to believe that telling God is all that is necessary because he ultimately forgives all sins. While this is true, confession to another person provides special healing and wholeness and releases the grip of hidden sin. According to Scripture, we have God's promise of healing when we confess our sins, faults, and shortcomings to another person and when that person responds by praying for us. The Apostle James said, *"Therefore confess your sins to each other and pray for each other so that you may be healed."* (James 5:16)

8. Which of your character traits or weaknesses cause you to feel fear or embarrassment when you think of sharing your story with another human being?____

> *"When he came to his senses, he said, 'How many of my father's hired men have food to spare, and here I am starving to death! I will set out and go back to my father and say to him: Father, I have sinned against heaven and against you. I am no longer worthy to be called your son; make me like one of your hired men.' "*
> LUKE 15:17–19

9. When confessing his sins, the prodigal son had to admit the terrible error of his ways. What do you most want to tell someone about the error of your ways?

When choosing a person for Step Five, we will want to select a loving, caring person, one who will be there for us and who will provide unconditional acceptance. The person must be dependable, trustworthy, and not shocked or offended by what we reveal. It is wise to choose someone who is familiar with the program. Sharing will flow easily if there is honesty and opportunities for feedback from the other person. Trusting the person with whom we share our story is vital to the success of Step Five and will provide a safe atmosphere.

10. What qualities do you feel are most important in the person with whom you will share your fifth step? _____

_____

_____

HELPFUL
HINT
• • •
Read Recovery Note
for Psalm 32:5–9,
page 610, *Life
Recovery Bible*

> *When I kept silent, my bones wasted away through my groaning all day long. For day and night your hand was heavy upon me; my strength was sapped as in the heat of summer…Then I acknowledged my sin to you and did not cover up my iniquity. I said, "I will confess my transgressions to the Lord"—and you forgave the guilt of my sin…*
> PS. 32:3–5

11. What ill effects do you experience when you conceal your wrongs? _____

_____

_____

In telling our story to another person, we can expect more than just being heard. We must be ready to listen to the other person's response. The interchange can be helpful and productive if we are willing to listen with an open mind to the other person's viewpoint. This broadens our awareness of ourselves and gives us an opportunity to change and grow. Feedback is vital to us as a means of completing the process of revelation. Questions asked in a caring and understanding manner can reveal new insights and feelings. Sharing our life story in this way can be one of the most important interactions in our lives.

12. What type of feedback do you want from the person helping you complete Step Five (e.g., the other person's experience, that person's identification with your story, verbal expressions of acceptance and comfort, affirmations of God's forgiveness, etc.)? _____

_____

_____

13. What do you hope to gain by listening to the other person's viewpoint? ___

_____

_____

> *Therefore confess your sins to each other and pray for each other so that you may be healed. The prayer of a righteous man is powerful and effective.*
> JAMES 5:16

14. List the items from your inventory for which prayer is important to you. ___

_____

_____

> *He who conceals his sins does not prosper, but whoever confesses and renounces them finds mercy.*
> PROV. 28:13

It takes considerable humility to bare ourselves to another person. We are about to reveal our self-defeating, damaging, and harmful character traits. We also will mention our positive strengths and worthwhile traits. We must do this to remove the masks we present to the world. It is a bold step toward eliminating our need for pretense and hiding. Rigorous honesty should be our goal, not personal image. We all want the respect and admiration of others, but the need to be well-thought-of must not interfere with our need for honesty.

The following information is helpful when completing your fifth step with another person:

- Allow ample time to complete each thought and stay focused on the subject. Refrain from unnecessary explanations.

- Eliminate distractions. Telephone calls, children, visitors, and extraneous noises must not disrupt your sharing.

- When Step Five is completed, both parties can share their feelings about the experience. It is now possible to extend to each other the love God extends to us through Christ.

- It is possible that you will not see your fifth step listener again. That's OK. It is your decision to continue the relationship in whatever direction you choose, from casual friendship to deeper spiritual companionship.

IF YOU HAVE NOT ALREADY DONE IT, STOP NOW AND COMPLETE YOUR FIFTH STEP WITH ANOTHER HUMAN BEING.

15. Describe your experience of admitting your wrongs to another human being.

_____

_____

When Step Five is completed, some expectations may remain unfulfilled. God's timing is not always our timing. God works in each one of us according to our own capacity to respond to him. We are not to submit to our anxiety; instead, we are to trust God. The real test of our Step Five admission is our willingness to trust that God will strengthen and develop our capacity to change our lives.

16. What difficulties did you have while sharing with another human being? Were you able to be thorough? Explain. _____

_____

_____

> _"If you have played the fool and exalted yourself, or if you have planned evil, clap your hand over your mouth!"_
> PROV. 30:32

17. In what way has admitting your wrongs helped you accept your past?_____

_____

_____

Upon completion of Step Five, we will realize that we are not always in control. It is not easy to change our old behavior patterns all at once. Admitting the exact nature of our wrongs is no guarantee we will stop acting in our old ways. We can expect to have moments of weakness. But we can also be strong in knowing that our relationship with God can help us overcome them. If we sincerely want to change our ways, God will give us the strength and courage required.

18. How did Step Five bring you closer to God and others?_____

_____

_____

> **For all have sinned and fall short of the glory of God.**
> ROM. 3:23

HELPFUL
HINT
...
Read Meditation for
Romans 3:23, page
72, _Meditations for The
Twelve Steps—A
Spiritual Journey_

19. What do you plan to do when you act in your old ways? _____

_____

_____

PREPARING FOR COMMUNITY

20. Which three questions from this step would you like to share with others?

_____

_____

21. How do you feel toward your family group? _____

_____

_____

22. What have you been unwilling to ask for from your family group? What are you willing to ask them for now? _____

_____

_____

23. What have you been unwilling to give your family group? What are you willing to give to them now? _____

_____

_____

KEY IDEAS

Shadow: In Step Five we come to grips with our shadow. In Step Four we noted the presence of our shadow, but we really didn't confront how it impacted our life. It's like coming to believe that a mouse is at work in our kitchen during the night. In the mornings, we find droppings and teeth marks, but we don't see the mouse itself. In Step Four we noted the evidence and identified the problems, but in Step Five we catch the mouse. We admit to our wrongs openly.

Confession: In Step Five, confession is the act of admitting our wrongs. To confess is to acknowledge openly what we have discovered about ourselves in our Step Four inventory. In confession we speak the truth about ourselves; we tell our story. We end the silence, the isolation, the hiding.

GROUP ACTIVITIES

ACTIVITY #1: "Sharing Our Stuff"

Supplies Needed: A bunch of scratch paper to make into paperwads

Objective: To enjoy paper-wad basketball while thinking about Step Five's admission to another person.

❑ Divide the group into two teams.

❑ Give each team member five paperwads.

❑ A team member from each team serves as the basketball hoop by placing his arms out in front of himself in the form of a hoop. He should stand an agreed-upon distance away from the shooter. Rotate the hoop person so that all can shoot.

❑ The team that tosses the most paper wads through their teammates' arms wins.

❑ When the game is over, discuss the anxieties some may be having about admitting their wrongs to another person.

ACTIVITY #2: "Pinocchio Does Step Five"

Objective: To have fun and learn while role-playing Pinocchio's Step Five work.

❑ Designate three actors to play Pinocchio, Pinocchio's Fairy Godmother, and Pinocchio's Conscience.

❑ The three role players should practice in advance and decide how Pinocchio might do his Step Five admission to the Fairy Godmother. Pinocchio should still be struggling with some denial and deceit. Pinocchio's Conscience should keep Pinocchio on the straight and narrow by encouraging his truth telling. (NOTE: It would be best to designate the role-players a week in advance so they can practice, re-familiarize themselves with the story, and make up Pinocchio's Step Four inventory.)

ACTIVITY #3: "God, Have Mercy"

Objective: To hear and identify with King David's prayer of confession in Psalm 51.

❑ The participants are to close their eyes and assume a meditative posture. Someone should read aloud Psalm 51. Read the Psalm twice.

❑ Following the reading, share how you identify with David's prayer. Share which particular comment or verse you could use as your own and explain why.

Were entirely ready to have God remove all these defects of character.

. . .

Humble yourselves before the Lord, and he will lift you up.

(JAMES 4:10)

UNDERSTANDING STEP SIX

When a farmer works a field, he begins by preparing the soil. The farmer will plow, disc, harrow, fertilize, harrow again, and finally plant the seeds. For a period of time the farmer is visibly active in his field. But after he plants, he stops for a while to allow the new seeds to grow. There is nothing he can do except wait and hope for the best.

In Step Six, activity ceases for a season. The seeds of change that God planted are allowed time to germinate and grow. Our emotions are allowed time to catch up with our new experiences. We have been plowed and prepared, and now we give God's power the necessary time to create in us an internal change. This internal change is a growing readiness and willingness to have God remove all of our defects of character. We might, on the surface, think that this is an easy thing, but many of these defects are deep character traits on which we have depended for survival. To release them means letting go of more than just a defect; it means letting go of a way of life.

WORKING STEP SIX

We work Step Six by being ready to have God bring change into our lives. Becoming ready may not seem a lot like work, but it is—it's spiritual work. God can't change us unless we are willing for him to do so, and so far we have not asked asked God for change. We have only become aware of our condition and admitted our need. In future steps we will ask God to remove our shortcomings and to help us set things straight. In this step we wait for God to do some internal work, and we must be sensitive to the changes he is making in our hearts.

PREPARING FOR STEP SIX

We prepare for Step Six by quieting our minds and opening our hearts. Steps Four and Five required a lot of hard work and brought up some painful discoveries about ourselves. Now we can best prepare for the next leg of the journey by making quiet time for ourselves. We put down the pencils and put on the walking shoes. Taking time to be alone with ourselves and with God helps us to remove the distractions that sometimes shield us from reality.

PRAYER FOR STEP SIX

Dear God,
I am ready for your help in removing from me the defects of character that I now realize are an obstacle to my recovery. Help me to continue being honest with myself and guide me toward spiritual and mental health.

(Taken from *Prayers for The Twelve Steps—A Spiritual Journey*, page 18)

Having completed Steps One through Five, some of us may believe that we can stop here. The truth is much more work lies ahead. The best results are yet to come. In Steps One and Two, we recognized our powerlessness and came to believe in a power greater than ourselves. In Step Three, we turned our wills and our lives over to God's care. In Steps Four and Five we honestly faced the truth about ourselves and admitted that truth to God, to ourselves, and to another person. We may have an illusion that everything is OK and that the remaining steps are less important. If we believe this, we will surely undermine our progress.

Steps One through Five helped to steer us in the right direction as we built a foundation for ultimate surrender. In Step Six, we confront the need to change our attitudes and behaviors. Here, we prepare to make these changes and totally alter the course of our lives.

The changes that are about to take place in our lives require a cooperative effort. God provides the direction and plants the desire. We contribute the willingness to take the action required. Our job is to respond to God's leadership in our journey. God never forces himself on us. We must invite him into our lives. That is why Step Six is so important. This step provides us with the opportunity to become ready for God's deepest work, which is yet to come.

We are not expected to remove our character defects alone. We are expected only to let go and let God. Step Six is not an action step that we actually take. It is a state of preparation that enables us to become ready to release our faults to God. Our willingness to surrender will increase. This enables us to reach the point (in Step Seven) where we are ready to let God take over and remove our faults as he sees fit. We do this by working the program, one day at a time, regardless of whether or not we see any progress.

We must remind ourselves that the character traits we want to eliminate are often deeply ingrained patterns of behavior, developed through many years of struggling to survive. They will not vanish overnight. We must be patient while God is reshaping us. Through our new willingness to let God be in control, we learn to trust him more completely. This frees us to welcome his timetable for our growth.

Step Six is similar to Step Two. Both steps deal with our willingness to allow God to work through us to change our lives. In Step Two, we seek restoration to sanity by coming to believe in a power greater than ourselves. In Step Six, we seek readiness to let God remove our shortcomings. Both steps acknowledge the existence of problems and require that we seek God's help in being freed from them. The fact that we "came to believe" will strengthen our capacity to be "entirely ready."

PERSONAL REFLECTION

To be successful with Step Six, we must sincerely want to change our disabling behaviors. But even this desire to change will come from God's grace as we wait upon his will for our lives. Our past has been dominated by our self-will, through which we sought to control our environment. We victimized ourselves by our self-will, rarely calling on God for help. Our life's condition shows us that self-will has never been enough to help us. Now, honest determination to eliminate our behavior flaws causes us to seek God's will. Before we can accept God's help, we must relinquish our self-destructive natures.

1. Steps Four and Five undoubtedly caused you to recall the pain you have caused yourself and others. Which painful memories tend to increase your readiness to change? _____

_____

_____

> *Therefore, prepare your minds for action; be self-controlled;*
> *set your hope fully on the grace to be given you when*
> *Jesus Christ is revealed.*
> 1 PET. 1:13–14

HELPFUL HINT
...
Read Meditation for 1 Peter 1:13–14, page 76, *Meditations for The Twelve Steps—A Spiritual Journey*

2. Where is your current level of trust? Are you trusting Christ to remove your defects or are you relying on you own willpower to change? Explain. _____

_____

_____

At this point in our program, we see that change is necessary to live life to the fullest. Recognizing the need for change and being willing to change are two different matters. The space between recognition and willingness to change can be filled with fear. As we move toward willingness, we must let go of our fears and remain secure in the knowledge that with God's guidance, everything will be restored to us. We let go of fear by holding on to God's love. The Bible says that perfect love casts out fear. When we firmly hold on to the fact that God loves us, we will find it easier to change.

> *Delight yourself in the Lord and he will give you the desires*
> *of your heart. Commit your way to the Lord;*
> *trust in him and he will do this.*
>
> PS. 37:4–5

3. In what ways are you committing your recovery to God? _____

_____

_____

> *Not that I have already obtained all this, or have already been*
> *made perfect, but I press on to take hold of that for which Christ*
> *Jesus took hold of me. Brothers, I do not consider myself yet to have*
> *taken hold of it. But one thing I do: Forgetting what is behind and*
> *straining toward what is ahead, I press on toward the goal to win*
> *the prize for which God has called me heavenward in Christ Jesus.*
>
> PHIL. 3:12–14

4. Which defects continue to plague your progress? _____

_____

_____

Our character defects are familiar tools to us. They are what we used as coping mechanisms to deal with our surroundings. The loss of these tools threatens our ability to control ourselves and others. The thought of giving up our character defects may cause anxiety. But we can trust that God won't remove a character trait we need. When we place our trust in God we develop a sense of comfort. Even the smallest beginning is acceptable to God. Scripture tells us that if we have *"faith as small as a mustard seed"* nothing is impossible for us (Matt. 17:20). When we have planted the seed of our willingness, we need to look for and protect the tiny sprouts of positive results. We do not want the weeds of self-will to overrun our new garden. These seedlings of "willingness" respond quickly to our nurturing, but they also quickly wilt with self-will. One sure way to hinder our growth is to think we are able to make the necessary changes ourselves. Healing requires God, not self-will.

5. Which character defects are you not entirely ready to have removed? Explain why you are still attached to them. _____

_____

_____

> *Do not conform any longer to the pattern of this world, but be trans-*
> *formed by the renewing of your mind. Then you will be able to test*
> *and approve what God's will is—his good, pleasing and perfect will.*
> ROM. 12:2

6. We draw near God in order to know his will and please him. Explain how you are drawing near to God (e.g., through devotions, prayer, fellowship, journaling, meditations, etc.). _____

_____

_____

Our ability to talk to God is an important part of Step Six. We need to communicate with him in a way that shows our humility and invites his intervention. When we say, "Dear God, I want to be more patient," we are making a demand and telling God what we want. When we say "Dear God, I am impatient," we present the truth about ourselves. When we pray in this manner, we exhibit humility, relinquish our pride, and ask God to act on our behalf.

7. List examples of your prayers that show you are making demands on God, instead of asking for his will to be done in your life or declaring the truth about yourself. _____

_____

_____

HELPFUL HINT
...
Read "Prayers of Declaration," Chapter Three, pages 55–65, *Prayers for The Twelve Steps—A Spiritual Journey*

> *Humble yourselves before the Lord, and he will lift you up.*
> JAMES 4:10

8. The first place to show your humility before God is in prayer. Write a one-sentence prayer in which you humbly tell God the truth about yourself regarding a particular defect._____

_____

_____

> *If any of you lacks wisdom, he should ask God, who gives generously*
> *to all without finding fault, and it will be given to him. But when*
> *he asks, he must believe and not doubt, because he who doubts is*
> *like a wave of the sea, blown and tossed by the wind.*
> JAMES 1:5–6

9. List any doubts you have that are interfering with your readiness to have God remove your shortcomings. _____

_____

_____

This step requires that we look at the shortcomings we will ask to have removed. We may be unwilling to give up some of them. They may seem useful to us, so we respond, "I cannot give up...yet." We have a potential problem if we say "I will never be any different and will never give up." These attitudes shut our minds to God's redeeming qualities and can add to our own destruction. If we respond this way to any behavior, we need to admit our doubts and struggles to God and seek his help in surrendering to his will.

10. What practical wisdom or helpful techniques have you learned from the program that could help you now (e.g., to work the first three steps, to use the Serenity Prayer, to share your struggles in a meeting, etc.)? _____

_____

_____

_____

"BROKEN DREAMS"

As children bring their broken toys
with tears for us to mend,
I brought my broken dreams to God
because He was my friend.
But then, instead of leaving Him
in peace to work alone,
I hung around and tried to help
with ways that were my own.
At last, I snatched them back and cried,
"How can you be so slow?"
"My child," He said,
"What could I do?
"You never did let go."
Author unknown

11. How do you identify with the "Broken Dreams" poem? _____

_____

_____

12. What do you fear will happen when your defects are removed? _____

_____

_____

> *But the Lord is faithful, and he will strengthen and protect you from the evil one.*
> 2 THESS. 3:3

As we follow the principles of the program in our daily lives, we gradually and unconsciously prepare to have our shortcomings removed. Sometimes, we are even unaware of our readiness to have our defects removed. At first, we realize that we are behaving differently—that we have changed. Sometimes, others note the changes before we become aware of them ourselves. Approval seekers begin to function more independently; control addicts become more easygoing and more relaxed; caretakers become more sensitive to their own needs. People who diligently work the program as an integral part of their lives become calmer, more serene, and genuinely happy.

13. What positive changes have you noticed in your behaviors, thought patterns, or relationships? _____

_____

_____

> *In the same way, count yourselves dead to sin but alive to God in Christ Jesus. Therefore do not let sin reign in your mortal body so that you obey its evil desires.*
> ROM. 6:11-12

HELPFUL HINT
• • •
Read Recovery Note for Romans 6:12–14, page 1236, *Life Recovery Bible*

14. Which character defects have caused you the most pain and need to be removed first? _____

_____

_____

A radiant, confident person lives in each of us, hidden under a cloud of confusion and uncertainty, distracted by ineffective behavior. If someone asked us if we wanted to be freed from our character defects, we could give only one answer—we are entirely ready to have God remove them.

15. What does being "entirely ready" mean to you?_____

_____

_____

> *I seek you with all my heart; do not let me stray from your commands. I have hidden your word in my heart that I might not sin against you. Praise be to you, O Lord; teach me your decrees.*
> PS. 119:10–12

16.   Explain how seeking God's will has helped you become more willing to change. _____

_____

_____

> *This is the assurance we have in approaching God: that is if we ask anything according to his will, he hears us. And if we know that he hears us—whatever we ask—we know that we have what we asked of him.*
> 1 JOHN 5:14–15

17. Describe your confidence in God to help you in removing your defects of character. _____

_____

_____

PREPARING FOR COMMUNITY

18. Which three questions from this step would you like to share with others?

_____

_____

19.   What could someone else do to encourage you in your Step Six work and in your recovery? _____

_____

_____

20. What can you specifically do to be of service and encouragement to others in recovery? _____

_____

_____

21. What current event in your life has helped you reinforce your readiness to have God remove all your defects of character? _____

_____

_____

KEY IDEAS

Readiness: Step Six is a time to overcome fear and gather the readiness we need to proceed with our recovery. We now know the truth about ourselves and what faults must be removed. In Step Six we need readiness and willingness to allow God to change us. This step is like bungee jumping. You may be dressed to jump, and have all the facts about the bungee cord. You may even have complete confidence in the operators, but you won't jump until you're ready. And you won't be ready until you overcome your fear. Your defects are a part of you. They have helped you survive. The thought of losing anything, even your damaging defects, tends to produce fear.

Defects of Character: Our defects of character are called many things in the program. They are called character weaknesses, faults, shortcomings, harmful behaviors, survival skills, negative traits, etc. Whatever the name, the point is the same. These undesirable parts of ourselves must be removed and replaced with godly character. These defects of character began innocently in childhood. They were our means of survival. We learned to manipulate in order to have our needs met, to lie to protect ourselves, and to hide our emotions in defense against overwhelming pain. In short, we learned how to survive. These survival skills were tools of control. They were our ways of managing our environment, minimizing our threats, and taking care of ourselves. Eventually, these coping skills break down. It is then we realize that God is the only one able and wise enough to control our lives.

Willingness: Willingness is a state of mind and emotions that propels us into action. We may have the best intentions, but until we are willing to act, we won't. There are many singles today who want to get married, who intend to get married, and who even know whom to marry, but they won't marry because they are not yet willing. In Step Six all of our good intentions simmer and brew until, with God's help, we are entirely ready and willing to change.

READINESS EXERCISE

The following exercise is intended to help you prepare to let go of the character defects you discovered while working Step Four. When necessary, refer to your fourth step written inventory.

Pride: Conceit; disdainful behavior or treatment of others; arrogance.

In what ways are you willing to let go of your constant need to impress others?

_____

_____

What difficulty do you have in letting go of your preoccupation with self? _____

_____

_____

Greed: Selfishness; hoarding; never having enough of anything.

What do you fear losing by letting go of your intense need for material things?

_____

_____

What will you gain by giving up your selfish tendencies? _____

_____

_____

Lust: Lechery; an intense indulgence in inappropriate sexual activity; above-normal desire.

What inappropriate sexual behavior is God asking you to give up? _____

_____

_____

How will removing your lustful tendencies change your current social behavior? __

_____

_____

Dishonesty: Deceit; disposition to defraud or deceive; justifying behaviors by explaining ourselves dishonestly.

What anxieties do you feel when you realize the need to tell the truth?_____

_____

_____

How will honesty improve the quality of your life?_____

_____

_____

Gluttony: Abnormal and distorted appetites; overwhelming need for possessions; excessive eating or drinking.

When changing your habits of overindulgence, what benefits do you hope to gain?

_____

_____

What are you ready to give up? _____

_____

_____

Envy: Jealousy; painful or resentful longing for an advantage or benefit enjoyed by another, combined with a desire to possess the same perceived benefit.

In what ways are you ready to lessen your desires for status and material wealth?

_____

_____

What do you believe your life will be like when you no longer experience jealousy?

_____

_____

Laziness: Not inclined to activity or exertion; not energetic or vigorous; distinct avoidance of responsibility.

In what ways are you willing to heighten your productivity? _____

_____

_____

What are you willing to do to eliminate your habit of procrastination? _____

_____

_____

GROUP ACTIVITIES

ACTIVITY #1: "Get the 'L' Out!"

Objective: To think about having our "defects of character" removed and have fun by trying to talk after a particular letter of the alphabet (like "L") has been removed.

❑ Choose a letter that you would like to remove from the alphabet for a while like the letter "L."

❑ Begin by asking the first person questions. To make the answer difficult, the questions should require the use of the letter "L" (or whatever letter is chosen) in the response. For example, the leader might ask, "What month follows March?" The answer cannot contain a word with the letter "L"; so she may say, "The month before May."

❑ The contestant may continue to answer questions until she makes a mistake and uses the forbidden letter. The game then moves on to the next person in line. The one who responds to the most questions without using the removed letter wins.

❑ After the game, openly discuss the problems group members foresee in removing character defects they have relied upon in their lives. For example: lying to protect ourselves, isolation to feel safe, blaming to cope with our shortcomings.

ACTIVITY #2: "Holy Moses"

Objective: To identify with Moses' journey toward readiness as he struggled to participate with God's plan of deliverance.

❑ The participants are to close their eyes and assume a meditative posture. Someone should read aloud Exodus 3:7 through 4:20. (In this passage, God tells Moses of his plan to use him to deliver Israel from Egypt, but Moses is not sure if he is ready.)

❑ Following the reading, share how you identify with Moses' reluctance to press ahead toward deliverance.

❑ Discuss the things that helped Moses become ready to follow God's plan.

❑ Share what you need from God to become entirely ready for God's deliverance plan.

ACTIVITY #3: "Spelling Bee"

Objective: To have fun and, at the same time, review a number of recovery related words and their meanings.

❑ Prepare in advance a list of recovery- or step-related words. Use the Key Ideas section for words.

❑ Divide the family group members into two teams and have the teams face each other in two lines of chairs.

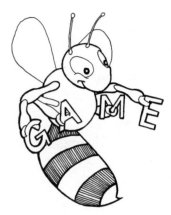

❑ Ask the first team to spell a particular word like "dysfunction." Beginning with the first team member, each team member down the line spells only one letter of the word until the team has correctly spelled the word in order. Each member has only to the count of ten to answer correctly (the leader or facilitator should count or use a stopwatch). After the word has been spelled correctly, the next person in line must define the word.

❑ When a mistake is made or if too much time is taken, the second team tries the same word. Alternate between teams like a real spelling bee.

❑ The team with the most correct spellings wins. A good prize might be to exempt the winners from cleanup. Or the losers might bring the winners a dessert the following week.

Humbly asked Him to remove our shortcomings.
. . .
*If we confess our sins, he is faithful and just and will forgive us our sins
and purify us from all unrighteousness.*
(1 JOHN 1:9)

UNDERSTANDING STEP SEVEN

Anyone who has been seriously ill or injured knows what it's like to need others. It is indeed humbling when we are in that sickbed and unable to move or care for ourselves. Even the simplest of needs must be met by another. By the time we come to Step Seven we realize that we are on a sickbed, and the only one who can meet our needs is God. Every step, up till now, has reinforced the same theme: We are unable, but God is able.

By Step Seven we have abandoned the illusion that we can help ourselves. The pain of our former way of life has caught up to us, and we lie wounded with a self-inflicted injury. We are certainly not interested in self-help now. So as we lie helpless and humbled on the sickbed of our disease, we pray: "Remove my shortcomings."

WORKING STEP SEVEN

Step Seven requires prayer. We work this step on our knees. Our condition, our honesty, and our pain have humbled us so now we must open our mouths and pray. The temptation here is to pray a general prayer. We are tempted to ask God to remove everything as if it were a package deal. But that's not how the program works. If we were thorough, our Step Four inventory listed each character defect separately. Our confession in Step Five was also done item by item, and later our amends will be made individually. So now our Step Seven work is humble prayer for the removal of our shortcomings—one defect at a time.

PREPARING FOR STEP SEVEN

We prepare for Step Seven by holding nothing back from God—no glimmer of hope in our own ability to control. We prepare for Step Seven by making sure that we have resolved the fear of letting go of our defects. We prepare for Step Seven by learning to draw nearer to God, by becoming comfortable in God's presence. We prepare by taking prayer seriously. This is a time to talk to God in a very personal way. We go to him with our Step Four inventory in hand and with a full understanding of our need.

PRAYER FOR STEP SEVEN

My Creator,
I am willing that you should have all of me, good and bad. I pray that you now remove from me every single defect of character that stands in the way of my usefulness to you and my fellows. Grant me strength as I go out from here to do your bidding.

(Taken from *Prayers for The Twelve Steps—A Spiritual Journey,* page 20)

Humility is a recurring theme in the Twelve-Step program and the central idea of Step Seven. By practicing humility we receive the grace necessary to work the program and achieve satisfactory results. We recognize now, more than ever before, that most of our lives have been devoted to fulfilling our self-centered desires. We must set aside these prideful, less-than-nurturing behaviors, come to terms with our inadequacies, and realize that humbly seeking God's will alone will free our spirit. Step Seven requires surrendering our will to God so that we may receive the serenity necessary to achieve the happiness we seek.

We are growing in the wisdom and knowledge of Christ. This growth not only comes because we are seeking it, but also from the insight gained by examining the pain of our past struggles. We gain greater courage by hearing how others cope with their life challenges. As we work through the steps, we recognize the value of acknowledging the truth of our past. Although the pain of this reality may seem unbearable, the insights we achieve are the only means to our release.

Step Six prepared us to let go of our old defective behaviors and freed us to develop the powerful new ones that God intends for us to use. Asking God to remove our faults is a true measure of our willingness to surrender control. For those of us who have spent our lives thinking we were self-sufficient, the surrender of control can be an extremely difficult task—but not impossible. Are we sincerely ready to abandon these deceptions? If so, then we can ask God to help us let go of our past and create new life within us.

Step Seven is a vitally important part of the cleansing process and prepares us for the next stage of our journey. During the first six steps, we became aware of our problems, looked at our lives honestly, revealed previously hidden aspects of ourselves, and became ready to change our attitudes and behaviors. Step Seven presents us with the opportunity to turn to God and ask for removal of those parts of our character that cause us pain.

Before beginning this program, we avoided looking at ourselves honestly and admitting the extent of our disabling behavior. Meditating on the vision of Christ's presence in our lives will focus our attention on living life according to his example and begin to free us from this disabling burden of "self." Our partnership with Christ will increase our concern for the whole human family and put our obsession with "self" into its proper perspective. We will finally recognize the person we have been, understand who we are, and look forward with joy to the person we are becoming.

Preparing to have our shortcomings removed requires willingness to work with God to revise and redirect our attention and activity. Our progress will be halted if we continue our destructive behaviors. We must be ever-vigilant and alert to the possible return of "old behaviors" and work diligently toward eliminating them from our lives. It is wise to be gentle with ourselves and remember that it took us a lifetime to develop these habits. It is not realistic to expect them to disappear overnight.

When looking to God to remove our shortcomings, we do well to remember that God gives grace directly to us through prayer and meditation and also through other people. God often uses outside forces to correct our defects. Ministers, teachers, medical doctors, and therapists can all be instruments of God's grace. Our willingness to seek outside help can be a clear indication of our readiness to change. Compulsive worriers can pray to God to release their worries and, at the same time, seek help from a counselor to relieve their anxiety. Persons who overindulge in food or drugs can seek professional help to gain control over their obsessive habits. We need to pray for God's help in removing our shortcomings, and have the courage to seek appropriate professional help when we know we need it.

PERSONAL REFLECTION

Through working the steps, we are progressing toward a happier and healthier life. We see how the opportunities and blessings that God brings into our lives surpass anything we could ever have created on our own. Having completed the first six steps, we are becoming aware of the multitude of benefits available to us. Through this awareness, we become grateful for God's presence and secure in the knowledge that our lives are improving.

1. What special blessings and benefits, even minor ones, has God sent to you since you began your Twelve-Step program of recovery? _____

_____

_____

> *Good and upright is the Lord; therefore he instructs sinners in his ways. He guides the humble in what is right and teaches them his way. All the ways of the Lord are loving and faithful for those who keep the demands of his covenant. For the sake of your name, O Lord, forgive my iniquity, though it is great.*
> PS. 25:8–11

2. What specific tools has God used to guide you and teach you what is right (e.g., Bible, books, meetings, sponsors, counselors, pastors, etc.)? _____

_____

_____

Step Seven implies that we ask for removal of all our shortcomings. However, the process will be more manageable if we deal with them individually, working on the easiest ones first to build up our confidence and strength. If we are patient, God will see that we achieve our goal at a pace that is comfortable for us. Our willingness to accept God's help builds trust and confidence in ourselves and in God. For now, use your Step Four inventory as your Step Seven guide to prayer. Remember that faith is required when you humbly ask God to remove your shortcomings. Trust that God hears and desires to answer, regardless of your emotions. You may not feel or experience any immediate change after you pray. Be confident, however, that God has heard your request and will work to remove your shortcomings.

> *Do not be anxious about anything, but in everything, by prayer and petition, with thanksgiving, present your requests to God. And the peace of God, which transcends all understanding, will guard your hearts and your minds in Christ Jesus.*
> PHIL. 4:6

3. Does prayer make you feel better? If yes, in what ways do you feel better? If no, what problems do you have with prayer? _____

_____

_____

HELPFUL
HINT
• • •
Read "Prayers of
Complaint," Chapter
Four, pages 67–75,
*Prayers for The Twelve
Steps—A Spiritual
Journey*

We may find that after we ask God to relieve us of a burdensome behavior, it doesn't seem to go away. Becoming angry or discouraged is understandable but self-defeating. It is more productive to reach out and ask for prayer support from a friend in recovery. It helps to express our negative feelings to God in prayer, knowing that he understands. When things do not seem to go according to our timetable, reciting the Serenity Prayer can also work to our advantage. It reminds us that God can give us serenity to accept the things we cannot change.

4. List areas in which you are discouraged about your level of progress in having your defects removed. _____

_____

_____

"PARADOXES OF PRAYER"

I asked God for strength, that I might achieve
I was made weak, that I might learn humbly to obey...
I asked for health, that I might do greater things
I was given infirmity, that I might do better things...
I asked for riches, that I might be happy
I was given poverty, that I might be wise...
I asked for power, that I might have the praise of men
I was given weakness, that I might feel the need of God...
I asked for all things, that I might enjoy life
I was given life, that I might enjoy all things...
I got nothing that I asked for—but everything I had hoped for
Almost despite myself, my unspoken prayers were answered
I am, among all, most richly blessed!
© Universal Press Syndicate

5. How does the "Paradoxes of Prayer" reflect your experiences with prayer?

_____

_____

> *If we confess our sins, he is faithful and just and will forgive us*
> *our sins and purify us from all unrighteousness.*
> 1 JOHN 1:9

6. Although God is faithful to forgive and cleanse us, we still tend to doubt. In which part of your life do you doubt God's ability or willingness to cleanse you?

_____

_____

Letting go of negative behaviors, however destructive they are, may create a sense of loss and require that we allow ourselves time to grieve. Some of our negative character traits are like old friends. They may be inappropriate and even hurtful to us, but we still mourn losing them. It is normal to grieve for the loss of something we no longer have. In our childhood we may have experienced "things" being taken from us abruptly or before we were ready to release them. Now, we may be too sensitive and cling to "things" to avoid the pain of loss. So that we don't avoid or deny the existence of our fear of letting go, we can turn to our Lord for courage and trust the outcome to him. This is an opportunity to rely on our love and trust in God to heal our memories, repair the damage, and restore us to wholeness.

7. What "things" were taken away from you as a child before you were ready to give them up? _____

_____

_____

HELPFUL
HINT
...
Read Meditation for
Matthew 23:12, page
91, *Meditations for The
Twelve Steps—A
Spiritual Journey*

> *For whoever exalts himself will be humbled, and whoever humbles himself will be exalted.*
> MATT. 23:12

8. We show humility first in our relationship with others and then with God. How have you humbled yourself with others? _____

_____

_____

Changing our behavior can be temporarily alarming to our sense of self. Our fear of not knowing what is ahead may cause us to repeat past destructive actions. We may retreat into feeling isolated and lose our sense of belonging. Having faith and trusting in our relationship with God shows our willingness to release the fear of being lost, frightened, or abandoned. God wants to be our new escape, where we run when we experience pain or discomfort. He wants to be our refuge and comfort.

9. What fears surface when you think of trusting God for your future instead of trusting yourself? _____

_____

_____

> *But he gives us more grace. That is why Scripture says: "God opposes the proud but gives grace to the humble." Submit yourselves, then, to God. Resist the devil, and he will flee from you. Come near to God and he will come near to you. Wash your hands, you sinners, and purify your hearts, you double-minded.*
> JAMES 4:6–8

10. Describe your present relationship with God. _____

_____

_____

As we notice our defects being removed and our lives becoming less complicated, we must proceed with caution and guard against the temptation to be prideful. Sudden changes in our behavior can and do happen, but we cannot anticipate them or direct them. God initiates change when we are ready, and we cannot claim that we alone removed our character defects. When we learn to ask humbly for God's help in our lives, change becomes God's responsibility. We cannot accept the credit, but we can give thanks. When good changes begin to happen in our lives, we tend to expect similar changes in others. But our focus needs to remain on ourselves—we still have much to accomplish.

11. Cite examples that show you are focusing more on God and less on yourself.

_____

_____

> *Create in me a pure heart, O God, and renew a steadfast spirit within me. Do not cast me from your presence or take your Holy Spirit from me. Restore to me the joy of your salvation and grant me a willing spirit, to sustain me.*
> PS. 51:10–12

12. How do you feel cast away from God's presence? _____

_____

_____

Destructive behaviors that remain after we complete Step Seven may never be eliminated, but we have an opportunity to transform these aspects of our character into positive traits and learn to use them in a constructive way. Leaders may be left with a quest for power but with no need to misuse it. Lovers will be left with exceptional sensuality but with enough sensitivity to refrain from causing pain to the person they love. Those who are materially wealthy may continue to have plenty, but will set aside their greed and possessiveness. With the help of our Lord, all aspects of our personal lives can be rewarding and fulfilling. By continuing to practice humility and accept the tools God is giving us, we will eventually begin to aspire to a more Christlike life, sharing with others the love we have received.

13. Which of your negative character traits are becoming positive? What changes do you notice? _____

_____

_____

> *Humble yourselves, therefore, under God's mighty hand,*
> *that he may lift you up in due time. Cast all your anxiety on*
> *him because he cares for you.*
> 1 PET. 5:6-7

14. Cite an instance in which you humbled yourself, and God either removed a shortcoming or empowered you to deal with it._____

_____

_____

For the program to be successful, we must practice the steps regularly. When we have moments of inner struggle, we can simply say, "This too will pass"; "I let go and let God"; "I fear no evil"; "I choose to see the good in this experience." These affirmations, as well as affirmations in the Bible, are useful to keep us from reverting to our obsessive/compulsive behaviors. Depression, guilt, and anger can be acknowledged and understood to be temporary reactions.

15. What affirmations do you use as a part of your ongoing commitment to recovery? _____

_____

_____

> *Have mercy on me, O God, according to your unfailing love;*
> *according to your great compassion blot out my transgressions.*
> *Wash away all my iniquity and cleanse me from my sin.*
> PS. 51:1-2

16. What can you do daily to remain humble and aware of your need for God's mercy? _____

_____

_____

We need to stop for a moment and acknowledge ourselves for our commitment to recovery. Note how determination enabled us to break the bonds of our unhealthy habits and behaviors. We can accept the positive, spontaneous thoughts and feelings that occur and see that this acceptance results from our personal relationship with God. We learn that the guidance we receive from our Lord is always available. All we need to do is listen, receive, and act without fear.

17. List examples of your behavior that show you have the courage and commitment to change the things you can. _____

_____

_____

HELPFUL
HINT
· · ·

Read Serenity Prayer
Devotional for Luke
11:37–44, page 1113,
Life Recovery Bible

> **Repent, then, and turn to God, so that your sins may be wiped out,
> that times of refreshing may come from the Lord.**
> ACTS 3:19

PREPARING FOR COMMUNITY

19. Which three questions from this step would you like to share with others?

_____

_____

20. Describe how you personally worked Step Seven. _____

_____

_____

21. What current events in your life helped or hindered your Step Seven work?

_____

_____

KEY IDEAS

Humility: Many of us in recovery misunderstand humility. If we are co-dependent, we might mistakenly think that humility is doing for others and placing ourselves second. If we tend toward manipulation, we might mistakenly think that our "poor me" performances are humility, or simply saying "sorry" is a demonstration of humility. The truth is we don't know what healthy humility is.

True biblical humility implies that we see ourselves as God sees us. It is putting ourself in proper perspective in light of God's plan. Appropriate humility is seen in Christ, who emptied himself to obey God's will, to serve others, and to fulfill God's plan for his life. Christ had every right to approach this world with superiority, but instead, he came as a lowly servant doing God's will. So can we be Christ-like in our humility as we place ourselves under God's control and submit to his will and plan for our lives.

TRAIT REMOVAL EXERCISE

The following exercise is to help you review your success in letting go of your character defects.

Humility: Being aware of one's shortcomings; not proud; not aggressive; modest.

List ways in which you are practicing humility. _____

_____

_____

What new behaviors show your more humble attitude toward God?_____

_____

_____

Generosity: Willingness to give or share; being unselfish.

Cite examples of your willingness to share with others. _____

_____

_____

How does your new behavior help you to care about the happiness and welfare of others? _____

_____

_____

Acceptance Of Sexual Self: Feeling comfortable with your sexual nature, without needing to have it lead to sexual intercourse. Clearly expressing preferences for sexual activity with partner.

How has your sexual behavior improved because of letting go of your inappropriate sexual relating? _____

_____

_____

In what way has your self-esteem been enhanced because of your improved sexuality? _____

_____

_____

Honesty: Telling the truth; being trustworthy. Honestly presenting yourself without creating false illusions for impressions sake. Being truthful about your real feelings.

What feelings surface when you risk being honest in your communication with other people? _____

_____

_____

How has being trustworthy improved your relationship with others?_____

_____

_____

Temperance: Moderation in eating and drinking; control of self-indulgence in all things.

Cite examples that show moderation in your use of food and drink. _____

_____

_____

How do you control self-indulgence in other areas? _____

_____

_____

Amicable: Friendly; harmonious; enthusiastic and helpful toward others.

Explain how being friendly helps you to feel more comfortable with yourself and others? _____

_____

_____

List ways in which your enthusiasm toward others is improving your self-confidence. _____

_____

_____

Energetic: Active interest in ideas and activities; attention to needs at work and play.

In what areas of your life is increased energy noticeable?_____

_____

_____

Cite examples of work habits that show you are being more productive._____

_____

_____

SERENITY PRAYER EXERCISE

The following examples are intended to help you in using the Serenity Prayer as part of your ongoing recovery process. The Serenity Prayer is a tool that can be used daily when seeking God's help. This exercise gives you an opportunity to take a number of situations through the Serenity Prayer.

. . .

God, grant me the serenity to accept the things I cannot change...
...like the way _____ ignores me, especially when I want praise.

The courage to change the things I can...
...like the way I manipulate others to get approval, especially from people I admire.

And the wisdom to know the difference...
...between the lasting satisfaction of reparenting myself with approval and the temporary satisfaction of depending on others for it.

. . .

God, grant me the serenity to accept the things I cannot change...
...like the way my childhood was.

The courage to change the things I can...
...especially the way I distract myself or act out when I have victimized feelings about my childhood.

And the wisdom to know the difference...
...between staying in a victim role and continually turning those years over to God.

. . .

God, grant me the serenity to accept the things I cannot change...
...like my parents' incompatibility with each other.

The courage to change the things I can...
...especially my reaction to feelings of abandonment, anger, isolation.

And the wisdom to know the difference...
...between my parents' love being unavailable to me and God's love, which is always with me.

Select a situation in your life that is currently a source of resentment, fear, or anger. It may involve relationships, work, health, or self-esteem.

God, grant me the serenity to accept the things I cannot change…

State the condition or experience you are aware of that you cannot change._____

_____

_____

The courage to change the things I can…

Indicate the specific condition or situation that you believe can be changed. ___

_____

_____

And the wisdom to know the difference…

Identify your understanding of the difference between what you can and cannot change.

_____

_____

List any insights gained from this exercise. _____

_____

_____

"SERENITY PRAYER"

God, grant me the serenity
to accept the things I cannot change,
the courage to change the things I can,
and the wisdom to know the difference.
Living one day at a time,
enjoying one moment at a time;
accepting hardship as a pathway to peace;
taking, as Jesus did,
this sinful world as it is,
not as I would have it;
trusting that You will make all things right
if I surrender to your will;
so that I may be reasonably happy in this life
and supremely happy with you forever in the next.
Amen
Reinhold Niebuhr

GROUP ACTIVITIES

ACTIVITY #1: "Humility Contest"

Supplies Needed: Six ribbons for each family group member. The ribbons may be cloth, multicolored, award-type ribbons that are pinned on, or they may be paper ribbons that are taped on.

Objective: To have fun testing our humility.

❑ Give every family group member six ribbons.

❑ Have each person spend three minutes sharing a personal story (set the time according to group size). During the story, the word "I" must not be used.

❑ Whoever catches the person using the word "I" takes one of his ribbons.

❑ During the game, no one should be caught using the word "I." Even if it is not a person's turn to tell a story, he may lose a ribbon for saying "I."

❑ The one with the most ribbons at the end is deemed "most humble."

❑ After the game ends, discuss everyone's concept of humility. Ask questions like: What is humility? What is conceit? How do you tell a humble person apart from a conceited person?

ACTIVITY #2: "Become Little Children"

Objective: To consider the childlike humility that Christ says is a requirement for entrance into his kingdom.

❑ The participants should close their eyes and assume a meditative posture. Someone should read Matthew 18:1–4 and Mark 9:33-37 aloud.

❑ Following the reading, discuss the following questions:

– How are we like the disciples in the story?

– Why would Jesus use a child as an example of humility?

– In what ways are children humble?

– In what ways can we become childlike?

ACTIVITY #3: "Buzz"

Objective: To remind ourselves about Step Seven by playing a game that removes the number seven and its multiples.

❑ Divide the family group members into two teams and sequentially count around the circle from 1 to 100. However, the teams are to remove the number

7, any number with a 7, or multiples of 7 from the count. In the place of 7 they are to say "buzz." For example the count up to 21 would go as follows: 1, 2, 3, 4, 5, 6, buzz, 8, 9, 10, 11, 12, 13, buzz, 15, 16, buzz, 18, 19, 20, buzz.

❏ Whenever a mistake is made, the team must start counting again at 1. The first team to successfully count to 100 wins.

❏ When the game is over, discuss your biggest shortcoming.

> *Made a list of all persons we had harmed, and became willing to make amends to them all.*
>
> • • •
>
> *Do to others as you would have them do to you.*
> (LUKE 6:31)

UNDERSTANDING STEP EIGHT

"Mom! Sarah hit me!" R. J. screamed like a siren.

"But he kicked me first," Sarah answered in defense.

"Yeah, but she took my game."

"He shouldn't be so touchy."

And so it goes. Does this sound familiar? Kids love to blame others for their troubles, and they hate to accept any responsibility. We adults might occasionally compel them to accept responsibility and coerce them into a forced apology. But they would never freely choose to say, "I'm sorry. My behavior was out of line."

In Step Eight we begin to grow up. We take responsibility for our actions without consideration for the wrongs done to us by others. In the first seven steps we have dealt with our own stuff. Step Four was *our* moral inventory—nobody else's. Our Step Five admissions were for *our* wrongs. The shortcomings belong to us. In Step Eight, we continue to look at ourselves. But this time, we are considering those people who were harmed by our character defects.

WORKING STEP EIGHT

We work Step Eight with thoughtful reflection. With God's help, we recall the names and faces of people we have harmed. Our job is to write their names down and consider each person carefully. We need to examine our relationship with these people and consider how we have harmed them. We will help ourselves by being as thorough as possible in our considerations and notes.

PREPARING FOR STEP EIGHT

We prepare for Step Eight through practicing humility. The willingness to be humble puts our lives in proper perspective and places us in agreement with God's plan and will for our lives. Step Eight requires that we recognize our part in the harm that has been done to others.

On a practical note, we prepare for Step Eight by making room in our lives for reflection. This may mean attending a retreat or setting aside some time to be quiet and thoughtful.

PRAYER FOR STEP EIGHT

Higher Power,

I ask your help in making a list all those I have harmed. I will take responsibility for my mistakes, and be forgiving to others as you are forgiving to me. Grant me the willingness to begin my restitution. This I pray.

(Taken from *Prayers for The Twelve Steps—A Spiritual Journey,* page 22)

Before entering the Twelve-Step program, many of us blamed our parents, relatives, and friends for the turmoil in our lives. We even held God responsible. In Step Eight, we begin the process of releasing the need to blame others for our misfortune and accepting full responsibility for our own lives. Our fourth step inventory revealed that our inappropriate behavior caused injury not only to us but also to the significant others in our lives. Now we must prepare to accept full responsibility and make amends.

Steps One through Seven helped us to center ourselves in the healing power of Jesus Christ. His Holy Spirit started the process of getting our lives in order. We were given the tools to examine our personal experiences and to see the importance of letting go of the past. We were freed to continue our personal growth by facing our history and putting it behind us. Like barnacles on a ship's hull, our past wrongdoings can prevent us from sailing smoothly to a life filled with peace.

Working Steps Eight and Nine will improve our relationships, both with ourselves and others. These steps also invite us to leave behind our isolation and loneliness. The key factor here is our willingness to make amends to those we have harmed. As we continue to welcome Christ's presence into our hearts, we will develop a new openness with others. This openness will prepare us for the face-to-face amends to follow. In Step Eight, we examine each past misdeed and identify the persons involved. Our intention is to make amends and heal our past so that God can transform the present.

Reviewing our fourth step inventory will help us determine who belongs on our list. Making amends is a difficult task—one that we will execute with increasing skill, yet never really finish. Again, uncomfortable feelings may surface as we come to grips with our past behaviors. As we recognize the damage caused by our actions, we will realize what great relief awaits us when we no longer cause injury to ourselves and others.

For many of us, admitting our misdeeds and making the necessary amends will be difficult. The pattern of our lives has been to blame others and to seek retribution for the wrongs done to us. When we look at ourselves, we see that the retribution we vainly sought only created more havoc. By insisting on our own measure of justice, we lost the ability to set and achieve positive goals. Cycles of hatred and hard feelings were created, and we kept our attention focused away from our own wrongs.

Forgiving ourselves and others helps us overcome our resentments. God has already forgiven us for the harmful actions that separated us from him. Developing the ability to forgive ourselves is an important element in our ongoing recovery. The ability to forgive others is essential. Amends without forgiveness lead to dishonesty and further complicate our lives.

To repair our past wrongdoings, we must be willing to face those wrongs by recording the harm we think we have caused. When preparing the list of people we have harmed, it is best to keep our thoughts directed toward making things right. Although our intentions may be rebuffed, our desire is to obey God and find healing. People on our list may feel bitter toward us and resist our attempts at restitution. They may hold deep grudges and be unwilling to reconcile with us. No matter how we are received, we must be willing to proceed with our amends. The amends we make are principally for our own benefit, not the benefit of those we have harmed.

The following are three main categories in which we may have caused harm and for which we must be willing to make amends.

Material Wrongs: Actions that affected an individual in a tangible way, including: borrowing or spending extravagance; stinginess; spending in an attempt to buy friendship or love; withholding money in order to gratify yourself. Entering agreements that are legally enforceable, then refusing to abide by the terms or simply cheating. Injuring or damaging persons or property because of our actions.

Moral Wrongs: Inappropriate behavior in moral or ethical actions and conduct, including questions of rightness, fairness, or equity. The principal issue is involving others in our wrongdoing: setting a bad example for children, friends, or anyone who looks to us for guidance. Being preoccupied with selfish pursuits and totally unaware of the needs of others. Forgetting birthdays, holidays, and other special occasions. Inflicting moral harm (e.g., sexual infidelity, broken promises, verbal abuse, lack of trust, lying).

Spiritual Wrongs: "Acts of omission" by neglecting our obligations to God, to ourselves, to family, and to community. Making no effort to fulfill our obligations and showing no gratitude toward others who have helped us. Avoiding self-development (e.g., health, education, recreation, creativity). Being inattentive to others in our lives by showing a lack of encouragement to them.

PERSONAL REFLECTION

Step Eight begins the process of healing damaged relationships through our willingness to make amends for past misdeeds. We can let go of our resentments and start to overcome the guilt, shame, and low self-esteem we have found through our harmful actions. We can leave behind the gray, angry world of loneliness and move toward a bright future by exercising our new willingness to make things right. Through the gifts of God's work and the Twelve Steps, we have the necessary tools to overcome past wreckage and mend our broken relationships.

1. List the relationships most severely damaged by your past misdeeds. _____

_____

_____

2. In which relationships do you feel the greatest resentment, guilt, or shame?

_____

_____

> *But Zacchaeus stood up and said to the Lord, "Look, Lord! Here and now I give half of my possessions to the poor, and if I have cheated anybody out of anything, I will pay back four times the amount."*
>
> LUKE 19:8

HELPFUL
HINT
· · ·
Read Meditation for
Luke 19:8, page 100,
*Meditations for The
Twelve Steps—A
Spiritual Journey*

As Christians, we are taught the importance of having and maintaining deep, loving relationships. Through Christ's example, we see how he devoted his ministry to loving people and encouraging them to love one another. Christ taught that being reconciled to God requires reconciliation with other human beings.

3. Progress and growth in God's kingdom requires reconciliation with others. Why do you suppose that is true in your case? _____

_____

_____

> *Dear friends, since God so loved us, we also ought to love one another. No one has ever seen God; but if we love one another, God lives in us and his love is made complete in us.*
>
> 1 JOHN 4:11–12

In Step Eight, we prepare ourselves to continue work on God's master plan for our lives by becoming willing to make amends. Once we have prepared our list of those whom we have harmed, we then begin to ask God for the willingness, love, and courage needed to make the amends. With God's help we will be able to extend love and acceptance not only to the injured persons, but also to others who have been affected by our behavior.

4. We can only love others to the degree we know God's love for us. In what ways have you experienced God's love for you? _____

_____

_____

> *For if you forgive men when they sin against you, your heavenly Father will also forgive you. But if you do not forgive men their sins, your Father will not forgive your sins.*
> MATT. 6:14–15

5. Who are you emotionally unwilling to forgive? How does this interfere with your relationship with God? _____

_____

_____

> *You, therefore, have no excuse, you who pass judgment on someone else, for at whatever point you judge the other, you are condemning yourself, because you who pass judgment do the same things.*
> ROM. 2:1

5. Cite an example of your passing judgment on others and thus harming them and yourself. _____

_____

_____

Forgiveness is a two-way street. As Christ declared in the Lord's Prayer: *Forgive us our trespasses, as we forgive those who trespass against us....* We need to ask forgiveness of those we have harmed. And we need to forgive those who have harmed us. As we reflect on our Lord, we see how he encourages us to turn the other cheek, to love our enemies, and to pray for our persecutors. Only in this manner can we break the cycle of hatred and violence. None of this is possible if we rely on our own strength. God knows how we struggle with these things, and he awaits our honest cry for help.

7.   Which relationships cause you the most pain in terms of unforgiveness and bitterness? Tell God through a written prayer. "God help me forgive...and..."

_____

_____

> *"But I tell you who hear me: Love your enemies, do good to those who hate you, bless those who curse you, pray for those who mistreat you. If someone strikes you on one cheek, turn to him the other also. If someone takes your cloak, do not stop him from taking your tunic. Give to everyone who asks you, and if anyone takes what belongs to you, do not demand it back. Do to others as you would have them do to you."*
> LUKE 6:27–31

8. Name one person with whom you relate frequently, who falls in the category of enemy. What can you do to "do good" and "bless" that person?_____

_____

_____

When making our list, we need to examine our relationships with people at home, in our community, and in the world at large. If we ask God to help us, our task will be much easier. We can ask him for guidance in selecting the names of the persons with whom we need to communicate. If we set aside our pride, we will see that the thoughts and feelings of others have worth and value. We do not have to agree with everyone, nor must they agree with us. But we can stop disliking people for what they think and do. We can stop resenting them because their views are different from ours.

9. Describe a relationship where your pride caused harm to the other person.

_____

_____

HELPFUL
HINT
• • •
Read "Prayers of
Intercession,"
Chapter Nine, pages
115–125, *Prayers for
The Twelve Steps—A
Spiritual Journey*

> *"Do not judge, and you will not be judged. Do not condemn, and you will not be condemned. Forgive, and you will be forgiven. Give, and it will be given to you. A good measure, pressed down, shaken together and running over, will be poured into your lap. For with the measure you use, it will be measured to you."*
> LUKE 6:37–38

10. In what ways do you need to be more tolerant of others? _____

_____

_____

Occasionally we will be prevented from facing the people on our list directly. They may be deceased, separated from us, or unwilling to meet with us. Whatever the situation, we still need to put them on our list. When we make the amends in Step Nine, we will see why amends are necessary, even if they cannot be made face-to-face. Being willing to make the amends will release us from hard feelings and enable us to experience serenity and peace of mind.

11. Name one person with whom you need to make amends but is unavailable to meet face-to-face. What is the amend about? _____

_____

_____

> **Be kind and compassionate to one another, forgiving each other, just as in Christ God forgave you.**
> EPH. 4:32

12. What concerns do you have about how you will be treated when making amends? Who causes you the most concern? _____

_____

_____

When looking at those persons we have harmed, we see how our character defects have played a major part in sabotaging our lives and our relationships. For example:

- When we became angry, we often harmed ourselves more than others. This may have resulted in feelings of depression or self-pity.

- Persistent financial problems resulting from our irresponsible actions caused difficulty with our family and creditors.

- When confronted with an issue about which we felt guilty, we lashed out at others instead of looking honestly at ourselves.

- Frustrated by our lack of control, we behaved aggressively and intimidated those around us.

- Because of our indiscriminate sexual behavior, true intimacy was impossible to achieve or maintain.

• Our fear of abandonment sometimes destroyed our relationships, because we did not allow others to be themselves. We created dependency and attempted to control their behavior by trying to maintain the relationship we wanted.

13. What major character defects caused injury to yourself or others? _____

_____

_____

14. What consequences do you fear in making your amends? _____

_____

_____

HELPFUL
HINT
. . .
Read Recovery Note
for Romans 15:1–6,
page 1250, *Life
Recovery Bible*

> *We who are strong ought to bear with the failings of the weak and not to please ourselves. Each of us should please his neighbor for his good, to build him up. For even Christ did not please himself, but, as it is written: "The insults of those who insult you have fallen on me."*
> ROM. 15:1–3

15. The God-given desire to "build up" another is an indication that we are willing to make restitution. What can you do to build someone else up? _____

_____

_____

When making a list of people for our amends, we need to remember to focus on ourselves. Many of us were victims of self-inflicted pain because we did not have the skills to take care of ourselves appropriately. We spent time and energy trying to be available for everybody and sacrificed ourselves in the process. We may have been our own worst enemy and experienced excessive self-blame, guilt, and shame. Taking time to look at the harm we have inflicted upon ourselves and being willing to forgive ourselves is essential to our continued growth.

16. Why is forgiving yourself an important factor in making amends? _____

_____

_____

17. List the major ways in which you have harmed yourself. _____

_____

_____

> *"Why do you look at the speck of sawdust in your brother's eye and pay no attention to the plank in your own eye? How can you say to your brother, 'Let me take the speck out of your eye,' when all the time there is a plank in your own eye?"*
> MATT. 7:3–4

18. List those situations in which you worried about others, when it would have been healthier to focus on what was happening to you. _____

_____

_____

In Step Nine, we seek out the people we have harmed and make amends wherever necessary. For now, all we need to do is list them and describe the harmful behavior. The consequences of our actions may have produced emotional, financial, or physical pain for others. We need to take as much time as necessary to reflect on our list and be as thorough as possible. Being totally honest with ourselves is a major factor in our ability to make restitution for our past destructive actions.

19. Examine your list and identify behaviors that produced emotional, financial, or physical pain. _____

_____

_____

> *"And when you stand praying, if you hold anything against anyone, forgive him, so that your Father in heaven may forgive you your sins."*
> MARK 11:25

20. Take some time to prayerfully forgive anyone who may have harmed you. Write "I forgive…" If you find this difficult, explain below why you still struggle with forgiveness toward this person or persons. _____

_____

_____

PREPARING FOR COMMUNITY

21. Which three questions from this step would you like to share with others?

_____

_____

22. What contact did you make with your Step Study family during your Step Eight writing work? _____

_____

_____

23. Share what you feel is the degree of openness of communication within your family group. _____

_____

_____

KEY IDEAS

Amends: Within the context of the Twelve-Step program, the idea of amends is broadly defined as "repairing the damage of the past." Amends can be as simple as an apology or as complex as restitution for physical or financial liability.

Forgiveness: Forgiveness is a key part of Step Eight. When we work this step and begin to make a list of the persons we have harmed, we immediately think about how others have harmed us. Perhaps this reaction is a defense mechanism—a way to avoid admitting guilt. It doesn't matter why we feel this way; what matters is that we deal with it. We need to forgive those who have hurt us—our forgiveness, according to Scripture, depends on it.

Forgiveness is not an emotion. It is a decision. Forgiveness can only be real with God's help. God alone can give us the grace, desire, and ability to release those who have hurt us. Left to ourselves, we allow unforgiveness, bitterness, and resentment to fester.

NOTES

_____

_____

_____

_____

Person	Relationship	My wrongdoing	Effects on others	Effects on me
Joan	wife	angry insults	fear, anger	guilt, shame
John	coworker	sexual advances at party	distrust, shame	loss of self-respect

AMENDS LIST EXERCISE

Select the person to whom you have caused the most harm and answer the following questions.

Name: _____

Harm: _____

_____

_____

What is the reason for making the amend? _____

_____

_____

What is your resistance to making the amend? _____

_____

_____

How do you feel about making the amend? _____

_____

_____

What character defects were active in your relationship with this person?_____

_____

_____

When and how do you plan to make the amend?_____

_____

_____

ACTIVITY #1: "Bible Man or Woman?"

Objective: To recall the names of men and women from the Bible as a fun way to remind ourselves that Step Eight is about recalling names from our lives.

❑ Form a circle.

❑ Designate someone as *It.*

❑ Have *It* point to someone in the circle and say either "man" or "woman." The one pointed to must say the name of either a man or woman from the Bible before *It* can count to ten. For example, if *It* points to someone and says, "woman," the one pointed to might say "Eve." (NOTE: Rather than counting you may use a stopwatch.)

❑ If the one pointed to cannot say a name before *It* counts to ten, he becomes the new *It.*

❑ After the game, discuss difficulties you're having in recalling names for your Step Eight list.

ACTIVITY #2: "My Mask"

Supplies Needed: Large brown-paper sacks, marker pens or crayons, and scissors.

Objective: To demonstrate and discuss ways in which we hide who we really are. "Many of us use disguises to hide our pain. Some of us try not to be attractive so no one will notice us like our abuser did. Some of us hide behind humor and happiness or act 'cool,' thinking no one will love us if they see our deeply wounded self. Some of us squelch our wit, intelligence, or energy, hoping we'll feel safer if we're invisible."[1]

❑ Make a mask using a large paper bag. Draw a face on the front of the mask and cut holes for eyes and mouth. Make a mask that represents the way you hide from others.

❑ After the mask is done, put it on and role-play the behavior or character the mask represents. Tell a little bit about the character or role you play when your mask is on.

❑ Next, take off the mask and share about your real self and why you need to hide sometimes.

---

[1] Reinicke, Melinda, *Parables for Personal Growth* (San Diego, CA: RPI Publishing Inc., 1993) p. 115.

ACTIVITY #3: "Who's Missing?"

Supplies Needed: At least twenty small pieces of paper equal in size, a list of common names, and a table.

Objective: To have fun with a list of names, test our memory skills, and remind ourselves about our Step Eight work.

❑ Put one name on each of the twenty pieces of paper. Be sure to use male and female names.

❑ Randomly place ten of the names face up on the table top.

❑ Have one person at a time look at the list and try to remember all the names. After the person has examined the list, have her turn away while one name is taken away. Shuffle the names around so that positions change. And have the person look back and guess which name was removed while the others slowly count to ten (e.g., "one Mississippi, two Mississippi, three Mississippi...").

❑ If the person correctly guesses the missing name, add another name so that there are eleven names. Repeat the process described above. Continue to add names if the person is correct. When the person misses, it becomes someone else's turn. Give everyone a chance. The one who can correctly guess the missing name with the highest number of names on the table is the winner.

STEP NINE

Made direct amends to such people wherever possible, except when to do so would injure them or others.

• • •

Therefore, if you are offering your gift at the altar and there remember that your brother has something against you, leave your gift there in front of the altar. First go and be reconciled to your brother; then come and offer your gift.

(MATT. 5:23–24)

UNDERSTANDING STEP NINE

Natural disasters are always gripping news. Earthquakes, hurricanes, forest or brush fires, and floods capture our attention. For a brief time, they are a major focus of our energy. But rarely do we have an opportunity to see the hard work of rebuilding that takes place after the disaster has past. Lives, homes, businesses, and whole communities are often repaired and revived, but the actual impact on us is not the same.

Step Nine is similar to the repairs and rebuilding that take place after a disaster. The difference is that we are part of the entire event. Through the process of making amends, we begin to make restitution and mend the damage of our past. In Step Eight we surveyed the damage and made a plan. Now, in Step Nine we go into action.

WORKING STEP NINE

Working Step Nine involves making personal or indirect contact with those we have harmed. We review our Step Eight list person by person. We approach each one we can with gentleness, sensitivity, and understanding. God can help us to know the best way to make contact. Some people will require a face-to-face meeting, while other situations may be handled by changing our behavior. In some cases, making a direct amend will not be possible. Whatever the case, God provides us with the wisdom and direction we need.

PREPARING FOR STEP NINE

We prepare for Step Nine by making our Step Eight list as complete as possible. There is no need to hurry. The important thing is that we become willing to make the amends. As we pray over every name, God will give us special insight and direction. He will also help us overcome the fear and apprehension that arises.

PRAYER FOR STEP NINE

Higher Power,

I pray for the right attitude to make my amends, being ever mindful not to harm others in the process. I ask for your guidance in making indirect amends. Most important, I will continue to make amends by staying abstinent, helping others, and growing in spiritual progress.

(Taken from *Prayers for The Twelve Steps—A Spiritual Journey*, pages 8–9)

Step Nine completes the forgiveness process that began in Step Four and fulfills our requirement to reconcile with others. In this step, we clear our garden of the dead leaves—we rake up and discard the old habits that are troublesome to us. We are ready to face our faults, to admit the degree of our wrongs, and to ask for and extend forgiveness. Accepting responsibility for the harm done can be a humbling experience because it forces us to admit the effect we have had on others.

Since we began our recovery, we have come a long way toward developing a new lifestyle. We have seen how the powerlessness and unmanageability of our lives caused havoc and chaos. Our commitment to face our character flaws in Step Four, to admit them to others in Step Five, and, finally, to ask God for their removal in Step Seven, has been a humbling experience for us. In Steps Eight and Nine, we proceed with the final stage of cooperating with God in rebuilding our character—we make amends.

The qualities we need in order to work Step Nine effectively are available from God. He can give us the judgment and careful sense of timing, courage, and stamina we need to accomplish this task. As we become more courageous, it will be easier and safer to talk honestly about our past behavior and admit to others that we have caused them harm.

Making amends helps release us from many of the resentments of our past. We achieve serenity in our lives by seeking forgiveness from those we have harmed and by making restitution where necessary. Without forgiveness, the resentments will continue to undermine our growth. Making amends releases us from guilt and promotes freedom and health in mind and body.

Some people in our lives feel bitter toward us. Others feel threatened by us and resent our changed behavior. We can pray about these people and ask that Christ's wisdom be made known to us. God gives us the discernment to consider the appropriateness of facing these people directly. If we are to forgive ourselves completely, we must first acknowledge the pain that others have endured because of our actions. We can only pray that God will prepare their hearts to receive our amends.

Some stumbling blocks appear in Step Nine. We may procrastinate by telling ourselves "the time is not yet right." We may delay by finding excuses to avoid facing those we have harmed. We must be honest with ourselves and not procrastinate because of fear. Courage is an important requirement for the successful completion of this step. The very spirit of Step Nine is contained in our decision to make restitution and in our readiness to accept the consequences of our past.

Another delaying tactic is the temptation to let bygones be bygones. We rationalize that our past is behind us, that there is no need to stir up more trouble by bringing up issues from our past. We fantasize that amends for past misdeeds are unnecessary, that all we have to do is change our current behavior. It is true that some of our past behaviors may be laid to rest without direct confrontation. Being supported by others during this leg of our journey enables us to face the people and issues on our amends list. Our improved life filled with peace and serenity is closely connected to our being able to confront the fears and resentments of our past.

PERSONAL REFLECTION

In order to complete Step Nine, we need to review our list from Step Eight and decide on the appropriate method to make each amend. Most situations will require direct contact, although some may be handled by simply changing our behavior. Other amends may need to be done indirectly due to circumstances beyond our control. Whichever alternative we choose, it is important that the process of making amends be done when we are ready, and be as complete as possible.

1. Who on your amends list causes you the most anxiety? What is your concern?

_____

_____

> *We love because he first loved us. If anyone says, "I love God," yet hates his brother, he is a liar. For anyone who does not love his brother, whom he has seen, cannot love God, whom he has not seen.*
> 1 JOHN 4:19–21

2. Is there anyone on your amends list for whom you have felt hatred in the past? What are your feelings today? _____

_____

_____

HELPFUL HINT
...
Read Step Nine Devotional on "Making Peace" from Matthew 5:23-25, page 1011, *Life Recovery Bible*

Step Nine has two distinct parts regarding making amends:

"MADE DIRECT AMENDS TO SUCH PEOPLE WHEREVER POSSIBLE"

We make direct amends to people who are readily accessible and who can be approached when we are ready. These people include family members, creditors, coworkers, and others to whom we owe an amend. They can be friends, enemies, or people with whom we do business.

As part of making the amend, we must try to repair to the best of our ability the damage that has been done. The other person's response may be surprising to us, especially if our amend is accepted. We may wonder why we waited so long to resolve the conflict.

3. What is your reaction to the idea of making amends to your enemies? _____

_____

_____

> *"You have heard that it was said, 'Love your neighbor and hate your enemy.' But I tell you: Love your enemies and pray for those who persecute you."*
> MATT. 5:43–44

4. What is interfering with your willingness to make direct amends? _____

_____

_____

There are situations that prevent us from making direct personal contact. These may involve people who are no longer accessible to us or who are deceased. In these cases, indirect amends can satisfy our need for reconciliation. These amends are accomplished through prayer or by writing a letter, as if we were communicating with the absent person. The important thing is that we make the contact necessary to satisfy our need to make the amend. We also can make amends by performing a kindness for someone else we may not even know, but who is connected in some way to the person we have harmed.

5. How do you suppose prayer or writing help you make amends when direct contact is not possible? _____

_____

_____

> *Above all, love each other deeply, because love covers over a multi-tude of sins. Offer hospitality to one another without grumbling. Each one should use whatever gift he has received to serve others, faithfully administering God's grace in its various forms.*
>
> 1 PET. 4:8–10

6. Do you have an indirect amend to make that could be accomplished by offering hospitality to another? Explain. _____

_____

_____

"EXCEPT WHEN TO DO SO WOULD INJURE THEM OR OTHERS"

Step Nine provides for those people to whom we can make only partial restitution because complete disclosure could cause harm to them or others. These people may include spouses, ex-partners, former business associates, or friends. We must analyze the harm they would suffer if complete disclosure was made. This is especially true in cases of infidelity. In such situations, irreparable damage could occur to all parties if a direct amend were made. Even if the matter must be discussed, we should avoid bringing harm to third parties. Amends for infidelity can be made by concentrating sincere affection and attention on persons to whom we have made loving commitments.

7. Who on your amends list falls into this category? How will complete disclosure cause harm? _____

_____

_____

> *Therefore, if you are offering your gift at the altar and there remember that your brother has something against you, leave your gift there in front of the altar. First go and be reconciled to your brother; then come and offer your gift.*
>
> MATT. 5:23–24

8. Describe any difficulties you are having in making amends to those who continue to hold something against you. _____

_____

_____

There are situations where amends could result in serious consequences. In cases involving potential loss of employment, imprisonment, or alienation from one's family, we need to weigh the consequences carefully. If we delay our amends merely out of fear for ourselves or others, we will ultimately be the ones to suffer. In these situations, we can seek outside guidance from a counselor, minister, or close friend to decide how to proceed. Otherwise, we will delay our growth, and also experience stagnation in our progress toward building a new and healthier life.

9. Describe a situation in which you need counsel before proceeding with direct amends. _____

_____

_____

> *...if he gives back what he took in pledge for a loan, returns what he has stolen, follows the decrees that give life, and does no evil, he will surely live; he will not die. None of the sins he has committed will be remembered against him. He has done what is just and right; he will surely live.*
> EZEK. 33:15–16

10. Which amend requires that you give something back (e.g., money, books, furniture, respect, honor)? _____

_____

_____

There are amends that require deferred action. It is wise to seek counsel in situations where deferred action is required. It is seldom advisable to abruptly approach an individual who still suffers deeply from the injustices we have done. In situations where our own pain is still deeply imbedded, patience might be the wise choice. Timing is important. Our ultimate goals are personal growth and reconciliation. Recklessness and haste might create further injury.

11. Who on your amends list falls into this category? What harm can be caused by making an amend too soon? _____

_____

_____

> *Therefore encourage one another and build each other up, just as in fact you are doing.*
> 1 THESS. 5:11

12. Amends ought to encourage and support you and the other person. Have you ever experienced an amend that wasn't uplifting? Explain. _____

_____

_____

> *Therefore let us stop passing judgment on one another. Instead, make up your mind not to put any stumbling block or obstacle in your brother's way.*
> ROM. 14:13

13. Describe a specific situation in which you passed judgment on another and caused that person harm. _____

_____

_____

As we have learned, certain situations require special consideration and timing. It is better to proceed slowly and be complete with the amend, rather than hurry and cause more damage. Here, God can be a great source of aid and comfort. We need to be constantly aware that his presence is with us now and will continue to be with us on our journey. Others may not understand or support our amends process, but God stands ready to help see us through this process.

> *"But love your enemies, do good to them, and lend to them without expecting to get anything back. Then your reward will be great, and you will be sons of the Most High, because he is kind to the ungrateful and wicked."*
> LUKE 6:35–36

14. What rewards do you expect to receive if you are generous with others? (These can be spiritual, emotional, or material.) _____

_____

_____

To help in making the amend, take time to pray and meditate, then prepare a schedule listing the persons to contact, what you will say, how you will say it, and when you will say it. Writing letters and making phone calls are acceptable ways of making amends if face-to-face contact is not possible. Sometimes, meeting in person may not be the most desirable approach. The important thing is to make the amend before it is too late. Successful amends making will improve our relationship with those we have harmed and promote better relationships with others.

HELPFUL
HINT
...
Read Meditation for
Romans 13:8, page
122, *Meditations for
The Twelve Steps—A
Spiritual Journey*

> *Let no debt remain outstanding, except the continuing debt to love one another, for he who loves his fellowman has fulfilled the law.*
> ROM. 13:8

15. List any outstanding debts you have that need to be repaid. How do you plan to make restitution? _____

_____

_____

When working this step, we need to distinguish between amends and apologies. Apologies are appropriate; however, they are not substitutes for making amends. A person can apologize for being late for work, but until the behavior is corrected, an amend cannot be made. It is important to apologize when necessary, but it is more important to commit to changing the unacceptable behavior.

16. List an example in which you apologized, but did not make an amend. ____

_____

_____

> *Do not repay anyone evil for evil. Be careful to do what is right in the eyes of everybody. If it is possible, as far as it depends on you, live at peace with everyone.*
> ROM. 12:17-18

17. Explain how your desire for revenge has prevented you from making a proper amend? _____

_____

_____

Occasional emotional and spiritual relapses are to be expected and should be dealt with promptly. If not, they will block our ability to make successful amends. When these relapses occur, we must accept them as signals that we are not working the program effectively. Perhaps we have turned away from God by not praying or reading Scripture daily and we need to return to Step Three. We may have eliminated something from our inventory and need to return to Step Four. Or we may be unwilling to relinquish a self-defeating behavior and need to return to Step Six.

18. List examples of recent relapses and how you dealt with them. _____

_____

_____

19. Which character defects caused the relapses? _____

_____

_____

> *Do nothing out of selfish ambition or vain conceit,*
> *but in humility consider others better than yourselves.*
> *Each of you should look not only to your own interests,*
> *but also to the interests of others.*
> PHIL. 2:3–4

20. In which areas of your life are you still being selfish? _____

_____

_____

Steps Eight and Nine help us repair the past. Through these steps, we take responsibility for causing injury to others and make restitution where necessary. We have a chance to redeem ourselves for past misdeeds by making amends, and we can look forward to a healthy and rewarding future life. We are now able to rebuild our self-esteem, achieve peaceful relations with ourselves and others, and live in harmony with our own personal world and with God.

21. As you make amends and repair the damage of the past, your self-esteem is allowed to grow. How do you feel about yourself today? _____

_____

_____

22. What difficulties are you having in making direct amends? _____

_____

_____

HELPFUL
HINT
. . .
Read "Finish the
Business," pages
24–25, *Prayers for The
Twelve Steps—A
Spiritual Journey*

161

PREPARING FOR COMMUNITY

23. Which three questions from this step would you like to share with others?

_____

_____

24. Select some highlights from your amends letter to yourself to share with your family group. _____

_____

_____

25. What can your family group do to help you with your Step Nine work? ____

_____

_____

KEY IDEAS

Direct Amends: Direct amends are amends that we make personally to those we have harmed. We schedule appointments or plan to meet personally with them. If physical distance is a problem, we can call them on the phone or write a letter. The amend includes sharing with them that we are in a program that requires us to make amends. We request permission to make our amends to them; then we share our amend without blaming them or others. (See the Amends to Others Exercise on page 163.)

Indirect Amends: Indirect amends are nonpersonal amends that we make to those we have harmed. These include amends to someone who is deceased, whose location is unknown, or who is inaccessible for another reason. We can make indirect amends to these people through letters that are not mailed, through prayer to God, or by doing a kindness to someone else such as a family member of the person we have harmed.

Amends To Self: The one person we have often harmed the most is ourself. The amends process would not be complete without taking time to set things right with ourselves. The best way to accomplish this is to write a letter of amends to ourselves and then read it while sitting in front of a mirror. (See Amends to Self Exercise on page 164.)

AMENDS TO OTHERS EXERCISE

This is a summary of ideas and procedures that have been useful in preparing for and making the amends in Step Nine. To align yourself with God's will, ask God to give you the correct attitude of heart so that you will be able to do the following.

Attitude

- Love and forgive yourself and the person to whom an amend is to be made.
- Be careful not to blame the person with whom you are communicating.
- Take responsibility for what you are going to say.
- Be willing to accept the consequences.
- Resist the desire for a specific response from the other person.
- Be willing to turn your anxieties over to God.

Preparation

- Devote time to prayer and meditation.
- Del— upset.
- tions aren't necessary.
- he other person's part in the situation.
- n to make the amend.

ord, make me a channel of thy peace — that where there is hatred, I may bring love — that where there is wrong, I may bring the spirit of forgiveness — that where there is discord, I may bring harmony — that where there is error, I may bring truth — that where there is doubt, I may bring faith — that where there is despair, I may bring hope — that where there are shadows, I may bring light — that where there is sadness, I may bring joy. Lord, grant that I may seek rather to comfort than to be comforted — to understand, than to be understood — to love, than to be loved. For it is by self-forgetting that one finds. It is by forgiving that one is forgiven. It is by dying that one awakens to Eternal Life. Amen.

St. Francis of Assisi
Eleventh Step Prayer
Twelve Steps and Twelve Traditions

l, feeling abandoned, etc.) when _____
giveness for _____ (harm done) and for
e past through my thoughts, words, or
rgiveness and assure you of my intention
ou."

t _____. For all those words that were
ness, etc.) and confusion, I ask your
ve and caring toward you."

e an amend.

for the amend? _____

_____

_____

How will you communicate the amend? _____

_____

_____

AMENDS TO SELF EXERCISE

The following are some guidelines to use when making amends to yourself.

Attitude

- Be willing to love and forgive yourself.
- Know what you want to say and take responsibility for your actions.
- Have reasonable expectations of yourself.
- Be willing to turn your anxieties over to God.

Preparation

- Devote time to prayer and meditation.
- Delay the amend if you are angry or upset.
- Keep it simple. Explanations are not necessary.
- Remember the amend is to yourself and does not pertain to others.

Sample Amends

- "I was _____ (scared, overwhelmed, feeling abandoned, etc.) when _____ happened. I forgive myself for the _____ (harm done) and anything else I may have done in the past through my thoughts, words, or actions to cause myself harm."

- "I want to make an amend to myself about _____. I forgive myself for all the words that I said out of _____ (fear, thoughtlessness, etc.) and confusion."

Write an amends letter to yourself.

Dear _____,

_____

_____

_____

_____

_____

_____

_____

_____

How do you feel as a result of writing this letter? _____

_____

GROUP ACTIVITIES

ACTIVITY #1: "The Boy Who Cried 'Wolf' Makes Amends"

Objective: To learn about Step Nine by role-playing the amends process "the boy who cried wolf" might have gone through had he lived and been in the program.

❑ Pick at least four people to play the following parts (NOTE: one person can represent a group): the boy who cried wolf, the boy's parents, the townsmen who came to the rescue, and the sheep (talking sheep, of course). Give the role-players a week to prepare if possible.

❑ Act out the boy's amends toward the above mentioned persons/animals. Be sure that the parents, townsmen, and sheep know that appropriate feedback is expected.

❑ After the role-playing is done, discuss how the boy did. Some may have suggestions or alternatives.

ACTIVITY #2: "Breaking the Chains"

Supplies Needed: Construction paper (cut in strips or provide scissors) and staplers.

Objective: To symbolize the bondage that is broken through working Step Nine. Many find that making amends is the process that breaks past bondage more than any other step.

❑ Make a paper chain with strips of construction paper and a stapler. Make the chain approximately 18 inches in length.

❑ Attach the paper chain to your wrists with larger paper loops. Someone else will have to help you accomplish this.

❑ Once everyone has their paper-chain shackles on, share what major bondage you hope to break as a result of making amends.

❑ Have a group prayer. Ask God for help in breaking the bondages that were mentioned. After prayer, break the paper chains to symbolize the deliverance God is providing.

ACTIVITY #3: "Let Me Explain"

Supplies Needed: Paper and pencils for half of the group.

Objective: To test our communication skills by reproducing a drawing through verbal directions only. Step Nine is all about communication, and it is very important we communicate exactly what we mean.

❑ In advance, draw a simple yet abstract line drawing (e.g. a triangle on top of a circle inside a square with an antenna on top). Make copies for half of the group, but be sure that no one sees the drawing.

❑ Divide by twos and seat the couples back to back. Arrange the chairs in advance so that there is a line of chairs back to back.

❑ Give one side of the group blank paper and pencils. Give the other side the drawing. Be sure that the side with the blank paper does not see the drawing.

❑ The ones with the drawing should explain the sketch so their partners can draw the picture from their instructions. Set a time limit of five minutes.

❑ After the time has expired, show the drawings.

❑ Conclude by discussing the difficulties in communicating details such as we might share in our amends.

STEP TEN

Continued to take personal inventory and, when we were wrong, promptly admitted it.

. . .

So, if you think you are standing firm, be careful that you don't fall.

(1 COR. 10:12)

UNDERSTANDING STEP TEN

Anyone who has planted a garden knows the care required to keep it healthy. We must remove the rocks and weeds, enrich the soil with fertilizer, bank it to hold water, plant the seeds, water, and guard against insects. Constant care is required to keep the garden clear of weeds, which could retake the garden if allowed. The garden once belonged to those weeds, and they always seem to want it back.

Our recovery is similar to a garden. Our lives once belonged to the weeds, our self-defeating behavior, but God has helped us plant a garden in our lives. He has pulled the weeds and caused some wonderful things to grow in their place. God used the Steps as tools and raised us to a place where things are different. We are beginning to see the promise of fruit, the promise of lasting change. In the midst of this new garden, we can also see the return of weeds. They don't die easily. In fact, as long as we live, weeds, our old self-defeating ways, will seek to recapture our lives. For that reason we must be ever vigilant to work Step Ten. We must continue to take personal inventory and protect our garden.

WORKING STEP TEN

Step Ten is really a summary of Steps Four through Nine. We take an inventory of our lives and admit what we find. We become willing to have God change us, and then we humbly ask God to remove the shortcomings. We make note of the amends needed and make those amends. The new element in Step Ten is the periodic inventory. We need to set aside regular times for personal inventory.

PREPARING FOR STEP TEN

We best prepare for Step Ten by scheduling time for our inventory. Setting aside time is important, or we may tend to avoid taking an inventory. We might plan for our inventory by setting aside a portion of our daily devotional or journal time. An option is allowing time during lunch or just before bedtime. A more extensive inventory can be made by spending a weekend at a retreat center each quarter or twice a year. Whatever the interval of time, the key is committing to take a regular inventory.

PRAYER FOR STEP TEN

I pray I may continue:
To grow in understanding and effectiveness;
To take daily spot check inventories of myself;
To correct mistakes when I make them;
To take responsibility for my actions;
To be ever aware of my negative and self-defeating attitudes and behaviors;
To keep my willfulness in check;
To always remember I need your help;
To keep love and tolerance of others as my code; and
To continue in daily prayer how I can best serve you, my Higher Power.

(Taken from *Prayers for The Twelve Steps—A Spiritual Journey,* page 26)

In Step Ten, we begin the maintenance part of the Steps. We will learn how to sustain what we have accomplished, become more confident, and proceed with joy along our spiritual journey. The first nine steps put our house in order and enabled us to change some of our destructive behaviors. This journey requires that we continue to rely on God's Holy Spirit and the inspiration of his word. Our work is beginning to pay off when we increase our capacity to develop new and healthier ways of taking care of ourselves and relating to others.

Some of us may wonder if the peace and serenity we are experiencing in our lives is permanent or just temporary. Working the steps has helped us to see how fragile and vulnerable we are. But with daily practice of the steps and with Christ's loving presence in our lives, we will be able to achieve and maintain our newfound balance. Our relating skills will improve, and we will see how our interactions with others assume a new quality.

At this point, we may be tempted to revert to our old bravado and believe we are healed. We may think we have all the answers and can stop here. We feel comfortable with ourselves and see no need to continue with the program. We allow other activities to interfere and find excuses for skipping meetings and abandoning the program. We must resist this temptation to quit and realize that giving in will deprive us of realizing the goal we set for ourselves. Our successes can be maintained only if we are willing to depend upon God and practice the principles of the steps daily for the rest of our lives.

Step Ten points the way toward continued spiritual growth. In the past, we were constantly burdened by the results of our inattention to what we were doing. We allowed small problems to become large by ignoring them until they multiplied. Through our lack of sensitivity and skills to improve our behavior, we allowed our ineffective behavior to create havoc in our lives. In Step Ten, we consciously examine our daily conduct and confess our wrongs where necessary. We look at ourselves, see our errors, promptly admit them, and seek God's guidance in correcting them.

While we are working so carefully to monitor our actions and reactions, we must not judge ourselves too harshly. If we do, we face the possibility of returning to our negative attitudes. We need to recognize that nurturing ourselves emotionally and spiritually requires daily vigilance, loving understanding, and patience. Life is never stagnant; it is constantly changing, and each change requires adjustment and growth.

A personal inventory is a daily examination of our strengths and weaknesses, motives and behaviors. It is as important as prayer and Bible study in nurturing our ongoing spiritual growth. Taking daily inventory is not a time-consuming task and can usually be accomplished within fifteen minutes. When done with discipline and regularity, this is a small price to pay for continuing the good work we have begun.

It's important to monitor ourselves for signs that we are returning to our old attitudes and patterns of behavior. We may be attempting to manage our lives alone, manipulating others, or slipping into old patterns of resentment, dishonesty, or selfishness. When we see these temptations arising, we must immediately ask God to forgive us, then make amends where needed. Daily practice of Step Ten maintains our honesty and humility and allows us to continue our development.

We become more conscious of our strengths and weaknesses when we examine our behaviors by taking regular inventory. We are less inclined to yield to feelings of anger, loneliness, and self-righteousness when we are emotionally balanced. Our personal inventory helps us discover who we are, what we are, and where we are going. We become more focused and better prepared to live the Christian life we desire.

NOTE: Before proceeding, refer to Step Ten Daily Inventory Log on page 178.

PERSONAL REFLECTION

The Twelve-Step program emphasizes the need for taking a regular personal inventory because many of us haven't developed the basic tools for self-appraisal. In time, we will appreciate the value of personal inventory. Although Step Ten inventories require some time and energy, the results are worth the effort. Three types of inventories are recommended; each serves a different purpose. These are **Spot-Check Inventory**, **Daily Inventory**, and **Long-Term Periodic Inventory**.

1. Have you had past success in the development and practice of good personal habits such as devotions, exercise, reading, etc.? Explain. If not, what stops you?

_____

_____

> *Whoever of you loves life and desires to see many good days, keep your tongue from evil and your lips from speaking lies. Turn from evil and do good; seek peace and pursue it.*
> PS. 34:12–14

HELPFUL HINT

• • •

Read "Prayers of Imprecation," Chapter Eight, pages 105–113, *Prayers for The Twelve Steps—A Spiritual Journey*

2. Which of your self-defeating behaviors reappear most often? _____

_____

_____

Spot-Check Inventory

A spot-check inventory involves stopping several times each day to assess our behavior and attitude. It is a short review of our actions, thoughts, and motives. This review can be useful in calming stormy emotions and it keeps us in touch with our behavior. It is a chance for examining situations, seeing where we are wrong, and taking prompt corrective action. Taking frequent inventories and immediately admitting our wrongs keeps us free from guilt and supports our spiritual growth. It is a good way to keep our lives free from anger, resentment, and unforgiveness.

3. Describe a recent situation in which you were wrong and promptly admitted it.

_____

_____

4. What can you do to remind yourself to take spot-check inventories during the day? _____

_____

_____

> *For by the grace given me I say to every one of you: Do not think of yourself more highly than you ought, but rather think of yourself with sober judgment, in accordance with the measure of faith God has given you.*
> ROM. 12:13

5. What is your current opinion of yourself and your progress in the program?

_____

_____

Daily Inventory

It is important to stop at the end of each day or start at the beginning of the next and review what has happened. We should examine our lives daily to remind ourselves that this program is lived one day at a time. This action, with God's guidance, keeps us focused on the present and prevents us from worrying about the future or living in the past. It is an opportunity to keep in touch with our thoughts, feelings, and actions on a daily basis.

6. How do you suppose a daily inventory improves your ability to get along with others? _____

_____

_____

> *"Settle matters quickly with your adversary who is taking you to court. Do it while you are still with him on the way, or he may hand you over to the judge, and the judge may hand you over to the officer, and you may be thrown into prison. I tell you the truth, you will not get out until you have paid the last penny."*
> MATT. 5:25–26

7. Cite an example in which correcting your wrongs saved you from unnecessary consequences and pain._____

_____

_____

The daily inventory can be viewed as a balance sheet for the day—a summary of the good and the bad. It is an opportunity to reflect on our interactions with other people, things that happened, and a reminder of the difficulties we encountered. In the situations where we did well, we can feel good and acknowledge our progress. In those situations where we tried and failed, we need to acknowledge our attempt because we *did* try. We can then make amends and move forward with peace of mind. As we work the program, we can be assured that our number of successes will continue to increase.

8. Cite a recent situation in which you did not behave appropriately. What did you do when you realized you were in error? _____

_____

_____

> *Therefore each of you must put off falsehood and speak truthfully to his neighbor, for we are all members of one body. "In your anger do not sin": Do not let the sun go down while you are still angry, and do not give the devil a foothold. He who has been stealing must steal no longer, but must work, doing something useful with his own hands, that he may have something to share with those in need.*
>
> EPH. 4:25–28

9. Describe a recent situation in which you did not resolve angry feelings. What effect did it have on you? _____

_____

_____

Future situations may arise that will challenge our integrity and commitment. We need to be as honest and clear about our intentions as possible. Taking a few minutes to review our Step Four inventory can provide helpful insights to our recovery. Things to consider are:

- If we are isolating and feeling withdrawn, we need to reach out and share our difficulties with a friend.

- If we are slipping back, trying to control and manipulate others, we need to recognize this and ask God to correct it.

- If we are comparing ourselves to others and feeling inferior, we need to reach out to supportive friends. We can then honestly examine our feelings to renew our own sense of self-worth.

- If we are becoming obsessive or compulsive and not taking care of ourselves, we need to stop and ask our Higher Power for help. We need to decide what unmet needs we are trying to fulfill and understand how to meet these needs.

- If we are fearing authority figures, we need to find the reason for our fear, acknowledge it, and ask our Higher Power for help.

- If we are depressed, we need to discover the central issue causing us to feel withdrawn or sorry for ourselves.

- If we are repressing our feelings, we need to take the necessary risks and express our feelings assertively.

10. Which ineffective behaviors keep showing up on your daily inventory? Why do you think they recur in your life? _____

_____

_____

> *Anyone who listens to the word but does not do what it says is like a man who looks at his face in a mirror and, after looking at himself, goes away and immediately forgets what he looks like. But the man who looks intently into the perfect law that gives freedom, and continues to do this, not forgetting what he has heard, but doing it—he will be blessed in what he does.*
> JAMES 1:23-25

HELPFUL HINT
...
Read Step Ten Devotional on "Looking in the Mirror" from James 1:21–25, page 1403, *Life Recovery Bible*

11. In which area of your life has this program most helped you honestly face yourself in the mirror as suggested in James 1:21–25? _____

_____

_____

Long-Term Periodic Inventory

A long-term periodic inventory can be accomplished by being alone or going away for a time. These are special days that can be set aside for reflection on our lives. We might attend a retreat or simply find a place of solitude. This is an important time that provides an opportunity for us to renew our intention to live healthier and more fulfilling lives.

12. How much time do you spend alone reflecting on your life? In what ways does being alone help you? _____

_____

_____

> *Therefore, if anyone is in Christ, he is a new creation; the old has gone, the new has come!*
> 2 COR. 5:17

13. In what ways do you experience personal fellowship with Christ? If not, what blocks you?_____

_____

_____

This inventory can be done once or twice a year and will give us a chance to reflect on our progress from a clearer perspective. We will have an opportunity to see the remarkable changes we have made and to renew our hope and courage. We must be careful not to inflate our ego and must remind ourselves that our progress is a product of God's help and careful spiritual growth. Long-term inventories help us recognize problem areas in our lives. These inventories enable us to get a larger perspective of our behavior and allow us the chance to make significant changes. During these special inventories, we will discover new defects as well as new strengths.

14. What new defects have you discovered that didn't appear in your Step Four work? _____

_____

_____

15. In what ways is your "new self" different from your "old self?"_____

_____

_____

> *You were taught, with regard to your former way of life,*
> *to put off your old self, which is being corrupted by its*
> *deceitful desires; to be made new in the attitude of your*
> *minds; and to put on the new self, created to be like*
> *God in true righteousness and holiness.*
> EPH. 4:22–24

If we sincerely want to change our lifestyle, we take personal inventory regularly and continue to interact with others in recovery. This reminds us that we are not unique—that everyone gets upset occasionally and no one is always "right." Through this awareness, we develop the ability to be forgiving and understanding and to love others for who they are and where they are. By being kind, courteous, and fair, we will often receive the same in return and can expect to achieve harmony in many of our relationships.

16. What new strengths have emerged because of your recent experiences?____

_____

_____

As we progress in our recovery, we see how pointless it is to become angry or to allow others to inflict emotional pain on us. Taking periodic, regular inventory and promptly admitting our wrongs keeps us from harboring resentments and allows us to maintain our dignity and respect for ourselves and others.

17. How do you deal with anger and resentment today?_____

_____

_____

> *A patient man has great understanding, but a quick-tempered man displays folly. A heart at peace gives life to the body, but envy rots the bones.*
> PROV. 14:29–30

18. List examples where you have been understanding of others. Describe the feelings that resulted from maintaining your composure. _____

_____

_____

The conscientious practice of Step Ten has many benefits; most importantly, it strengthens and protects our recovery. Step Ten keeps us from returning to old patterns or behaviors such as:

- Medicating any discomfort through alcohol or drugs

- Distracting ourselves through compulsive behaviors such as eating or shopping

- Hiding from life through isolation

- Denying our needs through control and manipulation of others

- Escaping reality through fantasies

- Soothing our low self-esteem through people pleasing

19. In which areas are you slipping back into old behaviors?_____

_____

_____

> *So, if you think you are standing firm, be careful that you don't fall.*
> 1 COR. 10:12

HELPFUL
HINT
• • •
Read Meditation for 1 Corinthians 10:12, page 136, *Meditations for The Twelve Steps—A Spiritual Journey*

Working the steps is a way for us to develop a daily discipline that deepens our love for God and enables us to be genuinely sorry for our wrongs. It helps us in continually striving for improvement in our relationships with God and others. Learning to face our faults daily and correct them promptly provides God with the opportunity to mold our character and lifestyle. Delay in admitting our wrongs shows a resistance to working Step Ten. This is harmful and will only make matters worse.

The ongoing practice of Step Ten has many rewards, such as:

- Our relationship problems diminish. Taking inventory and admitting our wrongs promptly dissolves many misunderstandings without further incident.

- We learn to express ourselves and not fear being "found out." We see that, by being honest, we do not need to hide behind a false front.

- We no longer have to pretend we are flawless and can be candid about admitting our wrongs.

- Through admitting our own wrongs, others may become aware of their own behavior difficulties. We develop a better understanding of others and can express ourselves honestly.

20. What success are you having in taking daily inventory, seeing your faults, and then promptly admitting them?_____

_____

_____

> *Be very careful, then, how you live—not as unwise but as wise, making the most of every opportunity, because the days are evil.*
> EPH. 5:15–16

21. Describe the changes you have made in your lifestyle. _____

_____

_____

PREPARING FOR COMMUNITY

22. Which three questions from this step would you like to share with others?

_____

_____

23. Review your actions of last week as recorded on your Daily Inventory Log. In what area did you behave well? In what area did you act poorly?_____

_____

_____

24. Share a situation from this last week in which you experienced God's help in overcoming temptation. _____

_____

_____

Personal Inventory: The Step Ten personal inventory is much like the moral inventory in Step Four. The difference is the ongoing and frequent nature of the Step Ten inventory. The idea of "personal" is a reminder to us that the inventory process is about us, not others.

Spot-Check Inventory: The spot-check inventory is the most frequent self-check. Through this inventory we monitor our actions throughout the day. We might designate objects or times in our day as reminders. For example, a red dot on our desk calendar might serve as a reminder to take a spot-check inventory. Or a prayer taped to our refrigerator might help us remember.

Daily Inventory: Quality time every day needs to be set aside for our daily inventory. This can be a few minutes before bed or early in the morning when our minds are clear. It is best to use a journal or inventory log for this daily inventory. This will serve as a reminder that progress is being made—one day at a time.

Long-Term Periodic Inventory: The long-term periodic inventory is done after a longer period of time. We may take this inventory every quarter, twice a year, or annually—the specific interval is not important. The idea is to occasionally get away and take a thorough inventory that reflects upon longer periods of time. In this way we are able to view patterns and seasons in our lives. If possible, it is helpful to find some form of retreat or solitude for this inventory.

_____

_____

_____

_____

_____

_____

_____

STEP TEN DAILY INVENTORY LOG

This inventory log can be most effectively used by selecting three character weaknesses and three character strengths that you want to focus on during the week. Making copies of this page will enable you to focus on the other behaviors at another time. As you work with the behaviors you have selected, the following ratings will enable you to record your level of functioning when dealing with yourself and others.

Using the following ratings, record your level of functioning each day: 0 = Poor; 1 = Fair; 2 = Average; 3 = Good; 4 = Excellent

CHARACTERISTIC (Weakness)	MON	TUE	WED	THUR	FRI	SAT	SUN
Abandonment							
Anger/Resentment							
Approval seeking							
Caretaking							
Control							
Depression/Self-pity							
Dishonesty							
Frozen feelings							
Isolation							
Low Self-Esteem							
Over Responsibility							
Procrastination							
Worry (past or future)							

CHARACTERISTIC (Strength)	MON	TUE	WED	THUR	FRI	SAT	SUN
Forgiveness							
Generosity							
Honesty							
Humility							
Patience							
Risk-taking							
Self-nurturing							
Tolerance							
Trust							

What were your experiences in completing this exercise? _____

_____

How did it help you be more aware of your behavior? _____

_____

IMPORTANT GUIDELINES
IN EVALUATING PERSONAL GROWTH

The material offered in this guide is intended to help you evaluate your personal growth. The material includes feelings and behaviors from the Step Four inventory exercise. They are presented again to provide you with the opportunity to evaluate your progress in these important areas.

When doing this inventory, choose the traits, feelings, or behaviors that specifically apply to you. Don't tackle them all at once. Use recent events and record words and actions as accurately as possible. Take your time. This process enables you to evaluate your growth. You are the primary beneficiary of your honesty and thoroughness in this inventory.

At the end of each character trait, feeling, or behavior is a self-evaluation exercise. This same exercise was used in Step Four. It is provided again as another opportunity to measure your growth.

RECOVERY FROM RESENTMENT

We experience a release from resentment when we begin to understand that those who mistreated us were also spiritually sick. We extend to them the tolerance and forgiveness that God gives us. When we concentrate on our own inventories in Step Four and Ten, we put the wrongs of others out of our mind, and we focus on our faults, not the faults of others.

As we recover from resentment, we begin to:

Feel tolerance for others   Forgive those who hurt us
Focus on our inventory   Accept some blame
Release the need to retaliate   Feel compassion for others

List specific examples that show you are overcoming resentment. _____

_____

_____

_____

_____

_____

_____

_____

What do you hope to achieve by releasing your resentments? _____

_____

_____

_____

_____

_____

_____

_____

Self-evaluation: On a scale from one to ten, how much does resentment negatively affect your life? Number one indicates that it has little negative effect. Number ten indicates that it has great negative effect. Circle where you are today.

| 1 | 2 | 3 | 4 | 5 | 6 | 7 | 8 | 9 | 10 |

Fear becomes less of a problem for us as our faith in God grows. We list our fears one by one and consider why they have power over us. We especially note the fears that grow out of our failed self-reliance. God is able to manage where we could not. Our faith empowers us to release our need for self-reliance and the fear that goes with it.

As we recover from fear, we begin to:

Feel less threatened   Embrace change
Rely on God   Face our fear honestly
Feel more joy   Pray more

List specific examples that show you are less fearful. _____

_____

_____

_____

_____

_____

_____

_____

What do you hope to achieve as you identify and release your fear?_____

_____

_____

_____

_____

_____

_____

_____

Self-evaluation: On a scale from one to ten, how much does fear negatively affect your life? Number one indicates that it has little negative effect. Number ten indicates that it has great negative effect. Circle where you are today.

| 1 | 2 | 3 | 4 | 5 | 6 | 7 | 8 | 9 | 10 |

RECOVERY FROM REPRESSED OR INAPPROPRIATE ANGER

Learning to express anger appropriately is a major step in our recovery. It releases many hidden emotions and allows healing to take place. Expressing anger lets others know our limits and helps us to be honest with ourselves. As we learn to express anger more appropriately, we are better able to cope with our own hostility and also the anger of others. Our relationships improve as we begin to feel comfortable expressing ourselves. Stress-related problems diminish, and we even feel better physically.

As we recover from repressed or inappropriate anger, we begin to:

Express anger appropriately   Set limits for ourselves
Identify hurt feelings   Enjoy inner peace
Make reasonable requests   Reduce stress and anxiety

List specific examples that indicate you are expressing anger in a healthy way.

_____

_____

_____

_____

_____

_____

What do you hope to achieve when you can release anger appropriately? _____

_____

_____

_____

_____

_____

_____

Self-evaluation: On a scale from one to ten, how much does repressed or inappropriate anger negatively affect your life? Number one indicates that it has little negative effect. Number ten indicates that it has great negative effect. Circle where you are today.

| 1 | 2 | 3 | 4 | 5 | 6 | 7 | 8 | 9 | 10 |

RECOVERY FROM APPROVAL SEEKING

As we begin to rely on our own approval and that of our Higher Power, we understand that wanting approval is OK, and we learn to ask for it and not manipulate others to get it. We accept compliments from others and learn to simply say "thank you," believing that the compliment is sincere. We say "yes" when it is a comfortable answer. We are willing to say "no" when "no" is appropriate.

As we recover from inappropriate approval seeking, we begin to:

Recognize our own needs   Be loyal to ourselves
Tell the truth about how we feel   Build our confidence

List specific examples that show you are recovering from inappropriate approval seeking. _____

_____

_____

_____

_____

_____

_____

_____

What do you hope to achieve as your need for outside approval lessens? _____

_____

_____

_____

_____

_____

_____

_____

Self-evaluation: On a scale from one to ten, how much does approval seeking negatively affect your life? Number one indicates that it has little negative effect. Number ten indicates that it has great negative effect. Circle where you are today.

| 1 | 2 | 3 | 4 | 5 | 6 | 7 | 8 | 9 | 10 |

RECOVERY FROM CARETAKING

As we put aside the role of caretaker, we assume less responsibility for everyone and everything and we allow individuals to find their own way. We give them over to the care of their Higher Power, which is the best source for their guidance, love, and support. By dropping the burden of meeting everyone's needs, we find time to develop our own personalities. Our obsession with caring for others is replaced by an acceptance of the fact that ultimately we have no power over the lives of others. We realize that our main responsibility in life is for our own welfare and happiness. We turn other people over to God's care.

When we stop being caretakers, we begin to:

Stop rescuing others   Develop our own identity
Take care of ourselves   Recognize dependent relationships

List specific examples that show you are lessening your role as caretaker. _____

_____

_____

_____

_____

_____

_____

_____

What do you hope to achieve when you are more aware of your own needs and stop being a caretaker? _____

_____

_____

_____

_____

_____

Self-evaluation: On a scale from one to ten, how much does caretaking negatively affect your life? Number one indicates that it has little negative effect. Number ten indicates that it has great negative effect. Circle where you are today.

| 1 | 2 | 3 | 4 | 5 | 6 | 7 | 8 | 9 | 10 |

As we become more aware of the ways we have attempted to control people and things, we begin to realize that our efforts have been useless. We did not control anything or anyone except ourselves. We discover more effective ways to get our needs met when we start accepting God as the source of our security. As we begin to surrender our wills and our lives to his care, we will experience less stress and anxiety. We become more able to participate in activities without being primarily concerned with the outcome. Saying the Serenity Prayer is helpful whenever we begin to recognize the reappearance of our need for control.

As we learn to give up control, we begin to:

Accept change	Reduce our stress levels
Trust in ourselves	Find ways to have fun
Empower others	Accept others as they are

List specific examples that show you have less of a need to be in control. _____

_____

_____

_____

_____

_____

_____

What do you hope to achieve when you are less controlling? _____

_____

_____

_____

_____

_____

_____

Self-evaluation: On a scale from one to ten, how much does controlling negatively affect your life? Number one indicates that it has little negative effect. Number ten indicates that it has great negative effect. Circle where you are today.

| 1 | 2 | 3 | 4 | 5 | 6 | 7 | 8 | 9 | 10 |

RECOVERY FROM FEAR OF ABANDONMENT

As we learn to rely more upon the ever-present love of God, our confidence in life and the future increases. Our fear of abandonment diminishes and is replaced by the feeling that we are worthy people in our own right. We seek out healthy relationships with people who love and take care of themselves. We feel more secure in revealing our feelings. We transfer our old dependence on others to trust in God. We learn to understand and accept a nurturing and loving fellowship within our community. Our self-confidence grows as we begin to realize that with God in our lives, we will never again be totally alone.

As fear of abandonment diminishes, we begin to:

Be honest about our feelings   Consider our own needs in a relationship
Feel comfortable being alone   Reduce our caretaking traits

List specific examples that show your fear of abandonment is decreasing. _____

_____

_____

_____

_____

_____

_____

What do you hope to achieve as your fear of abandonment lessens? _____

_____

_____

_____

_____

_____

_____

Self-evaluation: On a scale from one to ten, how much does fear of abandonment negatively affect your life? Number one indicates that it has little negative effect. Number ten indicates that it has great negative effect. Circle where you are today.

| 1 | 2 | 3 | 4 | 5 | 6 | 7 | 8 | 9 | 10 |

RECOVERY FROM FEAR OF AUTHORITY FIGURES

As we begin to feel comfortable with people in roles of authority, we learn to put our focus on ourselves and discover that we have nothing to fear. We recognize others to be like us, with their own fears, defenses, and insecurities. Others' behavior no longer dictates how we feel about ourselves. We start acting and not reacting when responding to others. We recognize that our ultimate authority figure is God and that he is always with us.

As we become comfortable with authority figures, we begin to:

Act with increased self-esteem   Accept constructive criticism
Stand up for ourselves   Interact easily with people in authority

List specific examples that show you are gaining confidence around people in authority. _____

_____

_____

_____

_____

_____

_____

What do you hope to achieve when you are more confident and secure around people in authority?_____

_____

_____

_____

_____

_____

_____

Self-evaluation: On a scale from one to ten, how much does fear of authority figures negatively affect your life? Number one indicates that it has little negative effect. Number ten indicates that it has great negative effect. Circle where you are today.

| 1 | 2 | 3 | 4 | 5 | 6 | 7 | 8 | 9 | 10 |

RECOVERY FROM FROZEN FEELINGS

As we get in touch with our feelings and learn to express them, strange things begin to happen. Our stress levels decrease as we become able to express ourselves honestly, and we begin to see ourselves as worthy. We learn that expression of true feelings is the healthy way to communicate, and we find that more of our own needs are being met. All we have to do is ask. As we begin to release our feelings, we experience some levels of pain. But, as our courage increases, the pain goes away, and we develop a sense of peace and serenity. The more willing we are to take risks in releasing our emotions, the more effective our recovery will be.

As we experience and express our feelings, we begin to:

Feel free to cry   Experience our true self
Feel healthier   Express our needs to others

List specific examples that show you are more aware of your feelings and are able to express them more easily. _____

_____

_____

_____

_____

_____

What do you hope to achieve as you become more capable of expressing your feelings? _____

_____

_____

_____

_____

_____

Self-evaluation: On a scale from one to ten, how much do frozen feelings negatively affect your life? Number one indicates that they have little negative effect. Number ten indicates that they have great negative effect. Circle where you are today.

| 1 | 2 | 3 | 4 | 5 | 6 | 7 | 8 | 9 | 10 |

As we begin to feel better about ourselves, we become more willing to take risks and expose ourselves to new surroundings. We seek friends and relationships that are nurturing, safe, and supportive. We learn to participate and to have fun in group activities. It becomes easier to express our feelings as we develop a stronger sense of self-esteem. We recognize that people will accept us for who we really are. Our self-acceptance allows us to experience the precious gift of living more comfortably and serenely.

As we isolate less often, we begin to:

Accept ourselves   Cultivate supportive relationships
Freely express our emotions   Actively participate with others

List specific examples that show you isolate less frequently._____

_____

_____

_____

_____

_____

_____

What do you hope to achieve when you are more confident about situations from which you would usually isolate yourself?_____

_____

_____

_____

_____

_____

_____

Self-evaluation: On a scale from one to ten, how much does isolation negatively affect your life? Number one indicates that it has little negative effect. Number ten indicates that it has great negative effect. Circle where you are today.

| 1 | 2 | 3 | 4 | 5 | 6 | 7 | 8 | 9 | 10 |

RECOVERY FROM LOW SELF-ESTEEM

As we work with our Higher Power to build confidence in ourselves and our abilities, our self-esteem increases. We are able to interact with others and accept ourselves as we really are. We see our strengths as well as our limitations. We learn to accept ourselves at face value. We become more willing to take risks, and we realize we can achieve many things that we had never dreamed possible. Sharing feelings with others becomes more comfortable. We feel safer as we come to know others and allow them to know us. Relationships become healthier because we are able to trust and validate ourselves. We no longer need to look to others for validation.

As our self-esteem increases, we begin to:

Be more confident   Love ourselves
Act more assertively   Openly express feelings
Easily interact with others   Take risks

List specific examples that show your self-esteem is improving. _____

_____

_____

_____

_____

_____

_____

What do you hope to achieve as you feel better about yourself? _____

_____

_____

_____

_____

_____

_____

Self-evaluation: On a scale from one to ten, how much does low self-esteem negatively affect your life? Number one indicates that it has little negative effect. Number ten indicates that it has great negative effect. Circle where you are today.

| 1 | 2 | 3 | 4 | 5 | 6 | 7 | 8 | 9 | 10 |

RECOVERY FROM OVERDEVELOPED
SENSE OF RESPONSIBILITY

Accepting the fact that we are not responsible for the actions and feelings of others forces us to focus on ourselves. We understand that we can't force others to change and that people are responsible for themselves. As we assume responsibility for our own actions, we become aware that we must rely on God for guidance and take care of our own needs. Then we will find time and energy to support and nurture ourselves.

As we stop being too responsible, we begin to:

Take care of ourselves   Accept our limitations
Enjoy leisure time   Delegate responsibility

List specific examples that show you are feeling less responsible for others.____

_____

_____

_____

_____

_____

_____

What do you hope to achieve by allowing others to take responsibility for themselves and begin taking care of yourself? _____

_____

_____

_____

_____

_____

_____

Self-evaluation: On a scale from one to ten, how much does overdeveloped sense of responsibility negatively affect your life? Number one indicates that it has little negative effect. Number ten indicates that it has great negative effect. Circle where you are today.

| 1 | 2 | 3 | 4 | 5 | 6 | 7 | 8 | 9 | 10 |

RECOVERY FROM IRRESPONSIBILITY

As we understand that God will help us achieve realistic goals, we begin to work in partnership with God for our future. We place less value on the expectations others have of us and more value on our own desires to achieve goals in life. We understand that we are competing only with ourselves, and God will enable us to do what is needed to win at life. God brings order to our lives as we give him control, and he makes it possible for us to contribute in meaningful ways.

As we recover from irresponsibility, we begin to:

Keep commitments   Accept responsibilities
Set goals for ourselves   Feel better about ourselves

List specific examples that show you are less irresponsible. _____

_____

_____

_____

_____

_____

_____

_____

What do you hope to achieve by being more responsible? _____

_____

_____

_____

_____

_____

_____

_____

_____

Self-evaluation: On a scale from one to ten, how much does irresponsibility negatively affect your life? Number one indicates that it has little negative effect. Number ten indicates that it has great negative effect. Circle where you are today.

| 1 | 2 | 3 | 4 | 5 | 6 | 7 | 8 | 9 | 10 |

RECOVERY FROM INAPPROPRIATELY
EXPRESSED SEXUALITY

As we rely upon the constant love of our Lord, our self-worth increases, and we see ourselves as worthy in his eyes and in the eyes of others. As we increase our self-love and our ability to take care of ourselves, we seek to be with other healthy people who love and take care of themselves. We fear commitment less and are better prepared to enter a healthy relationship—emotionally, intellectually, and sexually. We feel more secure in sharing our feelings, strengths, and weaknesses. Our self-confidence grows and allows us to be vulnerable. We give up the need for perfection in ourselves and others and, in so doing, open ourselves to growth and change. We are honest about our own sexuality with our children. We accept their need for information and also their need for a healthy sexual identity.

When we accept our sexuality, we begin to:

Discuss sex openly   Consider our own sexual needs
Accept our sexual self   Share intimate feelings

List specific examples that show you are becoming more comfortable with your sexuality. _____

_____

_____

_____

_____

_____

What do you hope to achieve as you feel more confident with your sexuality? __

_____

_____

_____

_____

Self-evaluation: On a scale from one to ten, how much does inappropriately expressed sexuality negatively affect your life? Number one indicates that it has little negative effect. Number ten indicates that it has great negative effect. Circle where you are today.

| 1 | 2 | 3 | 4 | 5 | 6 | 7 | 8 | 9 | 10 |

GROUP ACTIVITIES

ACTIVITY #1: "Sour Puss"

Supplies Needed: Stopwatch.

Objective: To try to elicit a smile from family group members. This activity is intended for fun; however, it is also a playful reminder that in Step Ten we continue to inventory such things as frozen emotions.

- ❏ Designate someone as *It*.

- ❏ Form a line and have *It* face each person, one at a time, for 15 seconds. During those 15 seconds *It* must try to make that particular family group member smile, and the group member must try not to smile.

- ❏ If *It* is successful in making someone smile within 15 seconds, the one who smiled becomes *It*.

- ❏ After the game, discuss your emotional health. For example, are you finding it easier to smile and enjoy life?

ACTIVITY #2: "Paper Planes"

Supplies Needed: Plain white paper.

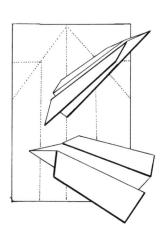

Objective: To fold, fly, and fix paper planes with a goal to fly the farthest by making improvements and corrections to airplane design and construction. This activity is a metaphor for our Step Ten work as we improve life through continuous inventory and improvement.

- ❏ Fold a paper airplane and mark it. The goal will be to fly your plane the farthest.

- ❏ Throw your plane in a distance test. Note whose plane went the farthest.

- ❏ Retrieve your airplane and make modifications to increase its distance. It's OK to start over with a new piece of paper. It's also OK to borrow good ideas from someone whose design worked well. Repeat the test.

- ❏ After about four or five test flights, hold the final contest. Reward the winner.

- ❏ Discuss what sort of mid-course corrections and changes you have made in your life. Discuss how you learn about and borrow good ideas from others.

ACTIVITY #3: "Association Recreation"

Supplies Needed: Paper and pencils for everyone.

Objective: To do word association for fun and think about why we choose certain words.

❑ In advance prepare a list of words (ten to twenty) to be read as word-association cues. Do not show the words in advance.

❑ Once everyone is ready with paper and pencil, read the list one word at a time. Pause at lease five seconds between words.

❑ Particpants should write down whatever word pops into their mind after the reading of each cue word. For example, if the word "moonlight" is read, they might think "bay" or "sunlight." Whatever they think first is what they write down.

❑ After the list is read and the participants have written their responses, go over the list again and have the participants share what they wrote for each word. Have them guess why they might have chosen certain words in response.

❑ Finally, discuss some of the lingering character defects that pop up in the form of conditioned responses (e.g., angry comebacks, sarcasm, cutting humor, etc.).

Sought through prayer and meditation to improve our conscious contact with God as we understood Him, praying only for knowledge of His will for us and the power to carry that out.

. . .

Let the word of Christ dwell in you richly.
(COL. 3:16A)

UNDERSTANDING STEP ELEVEN

Vital to a healthy relationship is honest communication and a willingness to be ourselves. If partners choose not to talk honestly with each other, their relationship will suffer in every area and may eventually fail. On the other hand, when communication and honesty exist, relationships are strengthened, and broken relationships can be healed.

Our relationship with God is our most important asset. And having a relationship with God is impossible without communication. As we draw nearer to God in prayer and meditation, we draw closer to our source of power, serenity, guidance, and healing. To ignore the need to communicate with God is to unplug our power source.

WORKING STEP ELEVEN

We work Step Eleven through the routine practice of prayer and meditation. Through prayer we talk to God and petition to him. Through meditation we listen to God and hope to hear the message he has for us. Many of us, however, struggle with the idea of prayer and meditation as a way to maintain contact with God. We know prayers, but we don't know how to pray. Many of us may be unfamiliar with meditation and resistant to trying it. Step Eleven is communicating with God. It is the work of learning the intimacy and power of prayer and meditation. It is the act of drawing near God, and seeking his will for us.

PREPARING FOR STEP ELEVEN

We prepare for Step Eleven by taking prayer and meditation seriously. Many of us have a tendency to put prayer and meditation on the second shelf, to treat both as nonimportant or unnecessary. We need to prepare for this step by developing an understanding appreciation for prayer and meditation. If we struggle in this area, we might counsel with a minister, talk with an experienced program member, or otherwise seek help and insight from a close friend.

PRAYER FOR STEP ELEVEN

Higher Power, as I understand you,

I pray to keep my connection with you open and clear from the confusion of daily life. Through my prayers and meditations, I ask especially for freedom from self-will, rationalization, and wishful thinking. I pray for the guidance of correct thought and positive action. Your will, Higher Power, not mine, be done.

(Taken from *Prayers for The Twelve Steps—A Spiritual Journey,* page 28)

Steps Ten and Eleven are the tools that help us trust God more fully and sustain the progress we have made in Steps One through Nine. In the first three steps, we recognized the seriousness of our condition and established the foundation for dealing with our problems. In Steps Four through Nine, we experienced a process similar to that of taking our car to the garage for a long-overdue, major overhaul. We devoted the time and energy required to make the necessary repairs and restore our "engine" to its proper running condition. In Steps Ten and Eleven, we have the opportunity to keep ourselves in tune by devoting time to regular service and maintenance. As we continue in this direction, we learn to recognize problems, to correct them promptly, and to continually seek God's guidance. This enhances our ability to improve our new skills for living life to the fullest. If we provide the required maintenance, we will find that our lives will run smoothly.

Prior to Step Eleven, we made contact with God in Steps Three, Five, and Seven. In Step Three, we made a decision to turn our wills and our lives over to his care. In Step Five, we admitted our wrongs to him. In Step Seven, we humbly asked him to remove our shortcomings. And now in Step Eleven, we use prayer and meditation to improve our conscious contact with God and to become more sensitive and responsive to his guidance.

Through the progress we have made in working the steps, we are learning more about what we want to achieve in the program. To protect what we have learned, we must continually seek to know God's will for us. A daily regimen of prayer and meditation makes it clear that relief from pain of the past is just a day-to-day reprieve. We must relentlessly seek to know God's will for us and how we are to live our lives.

Those of us who have experienced the hell and chaos caused by our willful acts realize that we worshiped false gods such as drugs, sex, money, or addictive relationships. Surrendering to the Twelve-Step process was not the step that led us to heaven, but was, in fact, the step that led us out of the hell that our lives had become.

Spiritual growth and development occur slowly and only through discipline and reliance upon God. The best example of the discipline of prayer is that of Jesus as he prayed frequently to know his Father's will. In the Lord's Prayer, the singularly most important petition is "Thy will be done, on earth as it is in heaven." This might be interpreted as "May your will be realized throughout all of space, time, and creation. God, if it is to be done, it is for you to bring it about." As our self-esteem increases and our Higher Power becomes a trusted friend, we grow more confident in the fact that he is ever present with us especially when we pray. And we grow more confident that his will is what we want for our lives.

Meditation is an important way of seeking God's will for us, of setting aside our own intentions, and of receiving God's guidance. Meditation on Scripture is our best way to know God's will. Other forms of meditating can quiet our minds and remove the barriers of our conscious thoughts. When properly done, this process will calm us emotionally and relax us physically. We will release the energy we expend keeping our emotions in high gear and our bodies tense with anxiety.

Our approach to Step Eleven will vary in intent and intensity—it shows our commitment to a prayerful life. If we are communicating with God, his joy will infuse our fellowship and friendship with others. We will reap rich benefits. Ideally, we should practice this step throughout the day. The Apostle Paul encouraged believers to "pray without ceasing." But until we reach that goal, we should practice Step Eleven upon awakening and retiring. This discipline at the beginning and end of each day reminds us that we sincerely and humbly want God's will for our lives.

Note: Before proceeding, refer to Guidelines for Prayer and Meditation on page 208.

PERSONAL REFLECTION

Praying only for knowledge of God's will for us and the power to carry it out helps us set aside our self-serving motives and interact well with others. We receive the reassurance of God's presence and the knowledge that his will is for us to be restored to health. Scripture gives examples of how we might behave when we allow God's will to work through us. In Luke 6:35–38, we are told: *"Love your enemies, do good to them, and lend to them…be merciful…do not judge…do not condemn…forgive…give…"* When we follow Christ's teachings and observe God's will for our lives, we experience peace and serenity.

1. What are you hoping to gain from Step Eleven? _____

_____

_____

2. What is your prior experience of learning God's will for your life?_____

_____

_____

> *"The good man brings good things out of the good stored up in his heart. For out of the outflow of his heart his mouth speaks."*
> LUKE 6:45

3. If the mouth speaks from the overflow of the heart, what does your mouth (communication) say about your heart? _____

_____

_____

> *"Therefore I tell you, whatever you ask for in prayer, believe that you have received it, and it will be yours. And when you stand praying, if you hold anything against anyone, forgive him, so that your Father in heaven may forgive you your sins."*
> MARK 11:24

Spending time in meditation enables us to become better acquainted with God in the same way that we become acquainted with someone we would really like to know. Meditation can be difficult at first. We are accustomed to being active and may feel uncomfortable with sitting still and calming our busy thoughts. We may feel we are wasting time, instead of doing something productive. Actually, nothing could be more productive.

4. What has been your experience of meditation? _____

_____

_____

HELPFUL
HINT
. . .
Read Meditation for
Hosea 6:3, page 144,
*Meditations for The
Twelve Steps—A
Spiritual Journey*

> *"Let us acknowledge the Lord; let us press on to acknowledge him. As surely as the sun rises, he will appear; he will come to us like the winter rains, like the spring rains that water the earth."*
> HOS. 6:3

5. What difficulties do you have in opening your heart to God? What do you believe is causing this? _____

_____

_____

In the act of meditating, we ponder and apply our knowledge of God's ways. It is contemplation done in the presence of and with the help of God. It is two-way communion with him. Meditation's purpose is to clear our mental and spiritual vision and to let God's truth make its full and proper impact on our minds and hearts. Meditation humbles us as we contemplate God's greatness and glory and allow his Spirit to encourage, reassure, and comfort us.

> *"But when you pray, go into your room, close the door and pray to your Father, who is unseen. Then your Father, who sees what is done in secret, will reward you."*
> MATT. 6:6

6. What do you experience while privately praying to God? Describe any feelings of discomfort you have in doing this. _____

_____

_____

> *"Show me your ways, O Lord, teach me your paths; guide me in your truth and teach me, for you are God my Savior, and my hope is in you all day long."*
> PS. 25:4–5

7. Cite a situation in which God showed you the correct path to follow. How did God reveal his will? _____

_____

_____

In developing a routine for prayer and meditation, we seek times and places to invite God's presence. Our desire is to be available for him. Some simple guidelines for learning to pray and meditate are:

- Pray, meditate, and study Scripture in solitude. Be alone and undisturbed, so you can be totally free from distractions.

- Pray and meditate in silence, or talk quietly to God without interruptions. Outside influences disrupt your concentration and inhibit your ability to tell God your thoughts and feelings.

- Set aside quality time. Do not wait until you are tired or your ability to clear your mind is hindered.

- Listen carefully. God has messages for you, just as you have messages for him.

- Review your daily inventory with God. Admit your wrongs, ask for forgiveness, and make amends to him as needed.

- End your session by asking for knowledge of God's will for you and the power to carry it out.

8. What is your current routine of prayer and meditation? How can you improve it? _____

_____

_____

> *"Ask and it will be given to you; seek and you will find; knock and the door will be opened to you."*
> MATT. 7:7

9. Write down a current request you have made of God. How does this request show that you are seeking God's will rather than your own? _____

_____

_____

If we are progressing satisfactorily with Step Eleven by praying and meditating daily, we will see signs along the way. We will feel more at peace in our daily affairs. We will experience deep gratitude for our ongoing healing. We will feel as though we have finally achieved a rightful place in the world. Feelings of self-worth will replace feelings of shame. These signs tell us that God is guiding and sustaining our recovery.

10. What events in your life suggest that you are having some success in practicing Step Eleven? _____

_____

_____

> *"Blessed is the man who does not walk in the counsel of the wicked or stand in the way of sinners or sit in the seat of mockers. But his delight is in the law of the Lord, and on his law he meditates day and night. He is like a tree planted by streams of water, which yields its fruit in season and whose leaf does not wither.*
> *Whatever it does prospers."*
> PS. 1:1–3

11. What events indicate that you are yielding to God's will, and not your own idea of what is right? _____

_____

_____

When we combine prayer and meditation with self-examination, we discover the secret to successfully working the steps. We also discover an effective means for maintaining a rewarding spiritual life. No matter how dedicated we are to recovery, we all have moments of doubt about the direction of our lives. We may even question the need to continue working the steps. Sometimes, we are tempted to regress to our old compulsive behavior. We tend to be especially vulnerable when we feel pressured for accomplishment or when we expect events to follow our own time schedule. In our frustration, we seize control from God's hands and attempt to hasten the process through our own willfulness. When we do this, we are not following God's guidance and must renew the commitment we made in Step Three.

12. Describe a recent, stressful situation in which you took control away from God because of your doubts. _____

_____

_____

> *"Your word is a lamp to my feet and a light for my path. I have taken an oath and confirmed it, that I will follow your righteous laws."*
> PS. 119:105–106

HELPFUL
HINT
...
Read "Peace in God's
Will," page 39, *Prayers
for The Twelve
Steps—A Spiritual
Journey*

Our power to carry out God's will can be challenged in those moments when our lives seem to be crumbling. Again, the best example of faithfulness is found in Christ. He persevered during the challenges of his ministry, passion, and crucifixion. The strength of his faith can be summarized by the prayer he prayed in Gethsemane. He was overwhelmed by what lay before him: "...*My Father, if it is possible, may this cup be taken from me. Yet not as I will, but as you will.*" (Matt. 26:39) During stressful moments, reflecting on Steps Three and Eleven can help us maintain our peace and serenity.

13. Do you believe that God's will is best for you? Describe your feeling. _____

_____

_____

> *"Do not be anxious about anything, but in everything, by prayer and petition, with thanksgiving, present your requests to God."*
> PHIL. 4:6

14. List an area of your life where anxiety is a problem. Tell God about it in simple prayer. (Write the prayer in the space below.) _____

_____

_____

Routine practice of prayer and meditation give us an opportunity to ask God for knowledge of his plan for us, and the power to carry it out. He gave us intellect and free will, through which we have the ability to think and act. As part of practicing Step Eleven, we must not create excuses to delay our actions or rationalize that we are "waiting" for God's will. Part of doing God's will is taking action and trusting that God's Holy Spirit is working through us.

15. Describe a recent situation in which you delayed taking action because you were "waiting" for God's will. What were the consequences? _____

_____

_____

HELPFUL
HINT
• • •
Read Recovery Note
for Matthew
21:18–22, page 1035,
Life Recovery Bible

> *"If you believe, you will receive whatever you ask for in prayer."*
> MATT. 21:22

In unclear situations, it is sometimes wise to seek outside counsel. As God continues to reach out to us in different ways, revelations may come to us through other people or new experiences. After careful review of the situation, our guidance may be obvious and compelling or still unclear. If unclear, we must be patient and wait for more direction to be revealed to us. If we cannot wait, we should select the best course of action and trust that God is with us, guiding us as we go. Our faith in his guidance will allow us to receive what needs to be revealed to us. The way we feel and function clearly shows if God's will is being done, or if we are trying to control the outcome.

16. Cite an example in which God answered your prayers through another individual or a new experience._____

_____

_____

> *"But the one who hears my words and does not put them into practice is like a man who built a house on the ground without a foundation. The moment the torrent struck that house, it collapsed and its destruction was complete."*
> LUKE 6:49

17. List an example of your doubting God. What were the consequences of your doubt?_____

_____

_____

Our earthly walk with God, as exemplified by Jesus Christ, is designed to bring us a life that is fulfilling. This is God's will for us as described in the teachings of Jesus. We can practice Jesus' teaching by praying the prayer he taught, "...your kingdom come, your will be done..." If we will begin our day with that attitude of prayer, our daily lives will exemplify what Step Eleven means.

18. What is your opinion of your life today? How has the quality of your life improved because of working the steps?_____

_____

_____

> *Whether you turn to the right or to the left, your ears will hear a voice behind you, saying, "This is the way; walk in it."*
> ISA. 30:21

19. Describe how you are learning to hear God's voice. How is he speaking to you?_____

_____

_____

PREPARING FOR COMMUNITY

20. Which three questions from this step would you like to share with others?

_____

_____

_____

"PRAYER OF SAINT FRANCIS OF ASSISI"

Lord, make me an instrument of your peace!
Where there is hatred—let me sow love
Where there is injury—pardon
Where there is doubt—faith
Where there is despair—hope
Where there is darkness—light
Where there is sadness—joy
O Divine Master, grant that I may not so much seek
To be consoled—as to console
To be loved—as to love
for
It is in giving—that we receive
It is in pardoning—that we are pardoned
It is in dying—that
we are born to eternal life.
Amen

21. Discuss any insights about prayer for God's will that you get as you reflect on the Prayer of Saint Francis of Assisi. _____

_____

_____

22. Are you involved in a situation where there is hatred? How can you sow love?

_____

_____

23. Are you aware of a situation where there is injury? How can you bring peace?

_____

_____

24. Do you know someone presently experiencing despair? How can you share hope? _____

_____

_____

Prayer: Our Higher Power is more than an idea or a force. Our Higher Power is Jesus Christ. Prayer is not merely an exercise in spiritual discipline. Prayer for us is conversation with one who loves us very much. Prayer is the communication we need to maintain a living relationship with our Savior. For help with prayer in its many forms, see *Prayers for The Twelve Steps—A Spiritual Journey.* It was written and compiled by Friends in Recovery to aid you in your spiritual journey.

Meditation: The word "meditation" implies various things to various people. Some seem frightened of meditation while others glorify it. But meditation itself is neither intrinsically good nor bad. It is a tool that is as effective or ineffective as the one using it. If practiced regularly, meditation will improve our relationship with God and increase our insight into Scripture.

Meditation must be approached spiritually. It is not an exercise for our minds, it is a practice for our spirits. Our overworked mental processes have sustained our distraction; our meditative practice will serve our spiritual needs. Meditation has often been called listening prayer because in meditation, we quiet our hearts and minds and open our spirits to God.

Conscious Contact: Communication with God is called many things. In the seventeenth century, a monk named Brother Lawrence coined the phrase "practicing the presence of God." The Apostle Paul referred to this communication as unceasing prayer. Step Eleven calls this prayerful communion "conscious contact with God." Whatever we call it, the idea is fellowship and connection with God. Prayer and meditation draw us into this relationship with God and enable us to understand his ways and his will.

God's Will: Every human being created by God has a will of his or her own. In the beginning that free will was used to rebel against God. The result was sin, disease, pain, death, and trouble of every kind. The only way to reverse the misery, which began in the Garden of Eden and bore fruit in us, is to choose God's will over our own. Step Eleven reminds us that the best prayer we can pray is for knowledge of God's will and the power to carry that out.

NOTES

_____

_____

_____

_____

_____

GUIDELINES FOR PRAYER AND MEDITATION

The wisdom and guidance contained in God's word is available to us any time of the day or night. The principles of the Twelve Steps are woven throughout the Bible. Both God's word and the steps are useful tools for us wherever we are in our spiritual journey. An overview of prayer and meditation for a given day may be outlined as follows:

At the beginning of the day, review your plans and:

- Ask God for direction in your thoughts and actions, to keep you free from self-pity, dishonesty, or self-righteousness.

- Ask God to provide the guidance needed to take care of any problems.

- Pray for freedom from self-will and selfishness.

During the day, in moments of indecision or fear:

- Ask God for inspiration and guidance.

- Reflect on Step Three and turn it over.

- Notice feelings of tension or stress in your body and identify what you can do that is both nurturing and relaxing.

- Pray to God as often as necessary during the day, even if the prayer is as short as "God, please help me, I feel _____ (fear, panic, out of control)."

- Make contact with a support person to identify and share what is happening.

At the end of the day, review the events that happened and:

- Review Step Ten and take a personal inventory.

HELPFUL
HINT
• • •
Read pages 151–155,
*Prayers for The Twelve
Steps—A Spiritual
Journey*

- Ask God for guidance in taking corrective action.

- Pray for knowledge of God's will for you.

- Ask God's forgiveness where needed, and acknowledge that this review is not intended to cause obsessive thinking, worry, remorse, or morbid reflection.

- Give thanks to God for the guidance and blessings that were part of the day.

GROUP ACTIVITIES

ACTIVITY #1: "Roadblocks"

Supplies Needed: Two blindfolds and a stopwatch.

Objective: To verbally direct a blindfolded family group member through a maze of obstacles. This activity illustrates the principle of hearing and following God's will.

❑ Divide the family group members into two teams.

❑ Designate someone as *It* in each group.

❑ Send both *Its* out of the room while the others create a maze of obstacles in the room using chairs, tables, wastepaper baskets, etc.

❑ Have the first team's *It* return blindfolded. He is to be verbally directed through the obstacles in the room by his teammates. However, the opposing team will create a noisy distraction to interfere. Spin *It* around a few times before he starts and keep track of his time from start to finish.

❑ Bring in the second team's *It* and repeat the above process. Which team had the best time?

❑ Do this all again, but this time, don't have the opposing team create a noise distraction. Allow *It* to clearly hear every instruction. Still spin *It* around a few times before she starts and keep track of her time from start to finish.

❑ After the exercise, discuss how difficult hearing God's will can be when life's distractions get in the way. Discuss which distractions create the most trouble. Also discuss how prayer and meditation can reduce distractions.

ACTIVITY #2: "This is how it is, God"

Supplies Needed: Paper, pencils, candles, and matches.

Objective: To write and pray a prayer that describes our present condition to God.

❑ Allow participants ten minutes to write individual prayers that describe the present conditions of their lives. In the prayers, they should tell God how they feel in general, how their relationships with others are, how they feel spiritually, how their recovery is going, where they feel they need help or improvement, etc. Also, have them express their need for God's direction and knowledge of his will in their lives.

❑ Form a circle to read the prayers one by one. If the group desires, the prayers could be read by candlelight to create a special atmosphere.

ACTIVITY #3: "Candle Relay"

Supplies Needed: Two candles and matches.

Objective: To run a relay with lit candles. This activity helps remind us that to maintain our contact with God we need to take it easy.

❏ Divide the family group members into two teams.

❏ Have each team line up and give the first runner in each line a lit candle.

❏ When the relay starts the runners must run to a prescribed point and then return without extinguishing the candle. The runner cannot cup the candle with her other hand to protect it from the wind. If the candle blows out, the runner must return to the starting point, relight the candle, and start over.

❏ The first team to successfully run all its members wins.

❏ Discuss the problems with a hurried lifestyle. Ask why meditation and conscious contact with God cannot be hurried.

STEP TWELVE

---

*Having had a spiritual awakening as the result of these Steps,
we tried to carry this message to others, and to practice
these principles in all our affairs.*
• • •
*Brothers, if someone is caught in a sin, you who are spiritual should restore
him gently. But watch yourself, or you also may be tempted.*
(GAL. 6:1)

UNDERSTANDING STEP TWELVE

In most every house with children there is a certain wall or a doorpost with pencil marks. These pencil marks, which have dates or ages next to them, keep track of growth. Every few months the kids back up against the wall while mom or dad mark their height. Sometimes the growth is barely noticeable and other times the growth is drastic.

Step Twelve is a time for noticing growth. We realize in this step that we have had a spiritual awakening. Through God's grace and our commitment to work the steps, we have had a life-changing spiritual experience. We began this journey as frightened tyrants clinging to control our own little kingdoms. But we end this round of our journey with a new king on the throne: God. We experienced a rebellion that we led against ourselves. With God's help, we removed our own kingdom and established God's. Although we know we have grown through this process, the mark on the wall is a little shorter—it's minus the crown.

WORKING STEP TWELVE

Step Twelve involves taking time to appreciate the spiritual growth in our lives. We work this step by sharing the program with others and continuing to practice the principles of the steps in every area of our lives.

PREPARING FOR STEP TWELVE

We can prepare for Step Twelve by ensuring that God has been a part of every aspect of our program. If we have merely added God as an ingredient to our recovery, we will not notice any spiritual awakening in Step Twelve. If we have maintained control throughout the steps and worked them with rigorous zeal, we will find no spiritual awakening now. However, the spiritual awakening of Step Twelve will be ours if we have done all of the following: relied upon God's presence, worked the steps in partnership with him, and given him control of our will and lives.

PRAYER FOR STEP TWELVE

Dear God,

My spiritual awakening continues to unfold. The help I have received I shall pass on and give to others, both in and out of the fellowship. For this opportunity I am grateful.

I pray most humbly to continue walking day by day on the road of spiritual progress. I pray for the inner strength and wisdom to practice the principles of this way of life in all I do and say. I need you, my friends, and the program every hour of every day. This is a better way to live.

(Taken from *Prayers for The Twelve Steps—A Spiritual Journey,* page 30)

The Twelfth Step completes the climb of this particular mountain. Remembering the milestones during this adventure reminds us of the pain and joy we have experienced while accomplishing our objective. Our experiences have been unique and personal to each of us. We now realize that all the events of our lives have pulled together to show us our connection to God and creation. Our spiritual awakening has changed us, so now we have the capacity to live our lives as an expression of God's will. An example of this type of transformation is beautifully captured in Titus 3:3–7:

> *"At one time we too were foolish, disobedient, deceived and enslaved by all kinds of passions and pleasures. We lived in malice and envy, being hated and hating one another. But when the kindness and love of God our Savior appeared, he saved us, not because of righteous things we had done, but because of his mercy. He saved us through...rebirth and renewal by the Holy Spirit, whom he poured out on us generously through Jesus Christ our Savior, so that, having been justified by his grace, we might become heirs having the hope of eternal life."*

Step Twelve requires that we are instrumental in helping others receive God's message of hope and healing through working the Twelve Steps. Many of us were introduced to this program by someone who was working Step Twelve. Now we have the opportunity to promote our own growth by helping others. We look for ways to share our new confidence because of our commitment to recovery and our growing awareness of God's presence in our lives. This program calls us to live our program daily and testify to the effectiveness of the Twelve-Step principles. The Apostle Peter instructed us in this action by saying: *"But in your hearts set apart Christ as Lord. Always be prepared to give an answer to everyone who asks you to give the reason for the hope that you have. But do this with gentleness and respect..."* (1 Pet. 3:15).

This step reminds us that we have not yet completed our journey to wholeness. To continue our process of growth, we need to be aware that we have just begun to learn the principles that will enhance our walk with the Lord. Each of the Twelve Steps is a vital part of fulfilling God's plan for us. When our daily challenges distract and separate us from God, we can use the steps as tools for coping with our problems and drawing us back to God. Step One reminds us of our powerlessness. Steps Two and Three show us the ongoing need for God's help. Steps Four through Nine guide us through self-examination and making amends. Steps Ten and Eleven help us minimize our slips and keep us in touch with God. We are blessed through our conscientious attention to seeking God's will and to working the steps. Our blessings may include a level of love, acceptance, honesty, and peace of mind that we never experienced before. The hardest part of any journey is the beginning, and this step is our milestone. By reaching Step Twelve, we have shown our commitment to God's will in our recovery.

Our spiritual awakening is a gift that instills in us a new perspective. It is usually accompanied by a significant change in our value system. Our pursuit of worldly goals has been subdued and redirected. We now look for fulfillment from things with real and lasting value. For most of us, the awakening is subtle and best seen in hindsight. It seldom has a distinct beginning and ending. We also realize it took hard work to get us here. As we awaken to the presence of God's love for us, our lives become filled with new purpose and meaning. In Romans 13:11, Paul tells us: *The hour has come for you to wake up from your slumber, because our salvation is nearer now than when we first believed.*

PERSONAL REFLECTION

"Actions speak louder than words" is an accurate description of how we should carry the Twelve-Step message to others. It is more effective to witness a principle being applied than to hear lectures on theory alone. For example, sharing our own experiences of prayer and meditation has more meaning than simply lecturing and explaining why everyone should meditate and pray. Telling our story will help others recognize their need for a relationship with God and encourage the growth of our own humility. Carrying the message gives us an opportunity to describe the ways in which God's Spirit works through the Twelve Steps to transform our lives. Each day our life experiences remind us how we are renewed in our relationship with God, our Higher Power. Through our sharing, we can convey the message of our experience, strength, and hope.

1. Describe a recent situation in which you carried the Twelve-Step message to another person by your actions, example, or story. _____

_____

_____

2. Describe how the Twelve Steps have changed your life and renewed your relationship with God._____

_____

_____

HELPFUL
HINT
• • •
Read "Prayers of
Praise," Chapter
Eleven, pages
137–145, *Prayers for
The Twelve Steps—A
Spiritual Journey*

> *Finally, brothers, whatever is true, whatever is noble, whatever
> is right, whatever is pure, whatever is lovely, whatever is
> admirable—if anything is excellent or praiseworthy—think
> about such things. Whatever you have learned or received
> or heard from me, or seen in me—put it into practice.
> And the God of peace will be with you.*
> PHIL. 4:8–9

3. Describe a praiseworthy thing you have accomplished. Indicate why you believe this can be an example of God working through you, and how it can help others discover the same blessings in their lives. _____

_____

_____

Scripture contains dramatic examples of the results of personal testimony about God's interaction in human affairs. John 4:28 and John 9:17 are accounts of personal experiences with Jesus Christ and their impact on the lives of others. Those who knew the speakers were convinced of the power of Christ's presence by the changes they witnessed. We cannot separate Twelve-Step work from our Christian walk; they are connected by our Lord's guiding hand. The action segment of Step Twelve is perfectly described in Romans 10:10: *"For it is with your heart that you believe and are justified, and it is with your mouth that you confess and are saved."*

4. What connection do you see between the Twelve Steps and your Christian walk? _____

_____

_____

> *Be wise in the way you act toward outsiders; make the most of every
> opportunity. Let your conversation be always full of grace, seasoned
> with salt, so that you may know how to answer everyone.*
> COL. 4:5–6

5. Name one person who would benefit from the Twelve-Step program. How can you best share your experience with that person? _____

_____

_____

> *Jesus did not let him, but said, "Go home to your family and tell them how much the Lord has done for you, and how he has had mercy on you."*
> MARK 5:19

6. How has Christ's example in the gospels helped you spread the message of the Twelve Steps? In what way has God empowered or equipped you to share?

_____

_____

Working with newcomers to the program can be very rewarding. Many of them are troubled, confused, and resentful. They need guidance and help to understand that God will strengthen and change them through their Twelve-Step work. Through their willingness and commitment, they will experience rewards and miracles that far outweigh their present pain. We can encourage newcomers to be gentle with themselves and to work the program one day at a time. This can be a growth experience for us. As we reflect on where we were when first introduced to the program, we see how far we have come. When carrying the message, we can emphasize an important point about our decision to join the program. We made the decision only after we suffered enough, were discouraged, were tired of hurting, and had "hit bottom."

7. Cite a recent situation in which you helped a newcomer. Describe your feelings that resulted from this. _____

_____

_____

> *Preach the word; be prepared in season and out of season; correct, rebuke and encourage—with great patience and careful instruction.*
> 2 TIM. 4:2

HELPFUL
HINT
...
Read Recovery Note
for 2 Timothy 4:1–5,
page 1366, *Life
Recovery Bible*

8. What do you most comfortably tell newcomers that encourages them? _____

_____

_____

> *Be imitators of God, therefore, as dearly loved children and live a
> life of love, just as Christ loved us and gave himself up for us
> as a fragrant offering and sacrifice to God.*
> EPH. 5:1–2

9. What can you do to model Christ's love to others? _____

_____

_____

Our relationship with God is the key to our success in everything, particularly in working the steps and applying the principles in our daily affairs. We cannot allow ourselves to drift into indifference and neglect our commitment to living according to the teachings of Christ. Scripture reminds us of the mandate to live a Christlike life. Scripture also tells us how we will know if we fail: *"No one who lives in him keeps on sinning. No one who continues to sin has either seen him or known him."* (1 John 3:6) Life constantly reminds us that we need to be prepared to face temptations and trials. But, with God's help, we can transform them into occasions for growth and comfort to ourselves and to those around us. We will never achieve peace and serenity independently of God's grace and Holy Spirit.

10. In what ways are you experiencing more peace and serenity? _____

_____

_____

> *If anyone speaks, he should do it as one speaking the very words
> of God. If anyone serves, he should do it with the strength God
> provides, so that in all things God may be praised through Jesus
> Christ. To him be the glory and the power forever and ever. Amen.*
> 1 PET. 4:11

11. In what ways does your relationship with God help you practice the principles of the steps in all your affairs? _____

_____

_____

Sometimes we become discouraged and lose sight of our progress. If this happens, we compare our past to our present and ask ourselves:

- Are we less isolated and no longer afraid of people in authority?

- Have we stopped seeking approval from others and accepted ourselves as we really are?

- Are we more selective of the people with whom we develop relationships, and more able to keep our own identity while in a relationship?

- Have we developed the ability to express our feelings?

- Have we stopped trying to dominate others?

- Are we no longer behaving childishly by turning friends or spouses into protective parents and being too dependent?

- Have we become attentive to the needs of our innerchild?

Affirmative answers show the extent of our progress toward a healthier and better way of living.

12. Which of the above situations is still causing you difficulty? Explain._____

_____

_____

13. With which of the above situations have you been most successful in changing your behavior? Explain. _____

_____

_____

> **Brother, if someone is caught in a sin, you who are spiritual should restore him gently. But watch yourself, or you also may be tempted.**
> GAL. 6:1

HELPFUL
HINT
• • •
Read Meditation for
Galatians 6:1, page
164, *Meditations for
The Twelve Steps—A
Spiritual Journey*

14. Cite an example in which you realized that someone was behaving inappropriately and you were able to help that person take corrective action._____

_____

_____

An important achievement in working the steps occurs when we become accustomed to "living" the steps. We do this by habitually taking a problem or concern through the steps, while acknowledging our need for God's support and guidance. The result is peace and serenity and a new confidence that we can deal directly with the problems. Any action we take is then guided by God's will and our honest appraisal of the consequences. We can act confidently and without fear, affirming *"The Lord is my light and my salvation—whom shall I fear? The Lord is the stronghold of my life—of whom shall I be afraid?"* (Ps. 27:1)

15. List a problem area in your life. Describe how you dealt with this problem before you came into the program. _____

_____

_____

16. Describe how you would face the above problem now by applying the Twelve Steps to it. _____

_____

_____

> *Two are better than one, because they have a good return for their work: If one falls down, his friend can help him up. But pity the man who falls and has no one to help him up! Also, if two lie down together, they will keep warm. But how can one keep warm alone?*
> ECCLES. 4:9–11

17. Describe a situation in which you and another person shared the Twelve-Step message with someone who needed help. How did the results impact you and the other person? _____

_____

_____

At this point, we begin to identify the many areas of our lives that are being affected by working the Twelve Steps. Our success with handling new problems is linked to our willingness to thoughtfully take action, while remembering to let go and turn it over to God. Our faith grows as we learn to relinquish control and allow God to be the director of our lives. The process is gradual, regenerative, and neverending. We slowly become more God-centered as we learn the true meaning of God's love, our surrender, and spiritual serenity. Paul captured the heart of this Twelve-Step process when he said: *"Brothers, I do not consider myself yet to have taken hold of it. But one thing I do: Forgetting what is behind and straining toward what is ahead, I press on toward the goal to win the prize for which God has called me heavenward in Christ Jesus."* (Phil. 3:13–14).

18. Describe a current situation in your life where you felt that God directed the course of activity. _____

_____

_____

> *"No one lights a lamp and hides it in a jar...he puts it on a stand, so...those who come in can see... there is nothing hidden that will not be disclosed...or brought out into the open. Therefore consider carefully how you listen. Whoever has will be given more; whoever does not have, even what he thinks he has will be taken from him."*
> LUKE 8:16-18

19. Explain how you experience God's Holy Spirit guiding your new behavior. In what way is your new behavior positively influencing the lives of others? ____

_____

_____

20. Explain how your new behavior may confuse or frustrate those people who knew you before your spiritual awakening. _____

_____

_____

PREPARING FOR COMMUNITY

21. Which three questions from this step would you like to share with others?

_____

_____

22. Turn to page 222 and complete the Twelve-Step Exercise. In what way did this exercise empower you to handle a life situation more effectively?_____

_____

_____

23. Complete the following statements as you now view your life:
When I was a child, I _____

_____

_____

As I grew into adulthood, I _____
_____
_____

When I became aware of my behavior traits, I _____
_____
_____

Having completed the Step Study, I _____
_____
_____

As we may view our lives now, we are the pens through which the ink of our Higher Power flows to write the story of our lives. Our step work and family group have contributed to our deeper contact with God. Sharing each other's experience, strength, and hope has enabled us to expand our faith in our Higher Power and experience unconditional love.

24. What do you want to say to your family members or the other individuals in the Step Study about:

Your spiritual awakening _____
_____
_____

Your gratitude for their coaching you _____
_____
_____

Your commitment to continue working the steps_____
_____
_____

Spiritual Awakening: The spiritual awakening that Step Twelve speaks of is a gradual change in the control of our lives. This change eventually produces a realization that we sincerely trust God and can depend on him. We also realize that this new trust and dependence brings a peace and serenity that we have never experienced before. We come to Step Twelve with confidence that God can be trusted, miracles do happen, and prayer works.

Carrying the Message: In Step Twelve we are encouraged to carry the message of the Twelve Steps to others. If we have read the *The Big Book of Alcoholics Anonymous,* we realize that early program members always understood that they were carrying a spiritual message. The message we carry is that God can save us from our sin, from our self-defeating behavior, from our despair, from our torment—God can save us from ourselves. We carry a spiritual message that only God is able to control our lives and heal us. We will live more productive and healthy lives if we yield to a power greater than ourselves.

PRAYER FOR STEP TWELVE

Heavenly Father,

I dedicate myself to the love and care of my Higher Power, Jesus Christ. All healing work is carried on with his guidance. I am committed to surrendering all concerns, from the largest to the smallest, to him. I accept that with your help, my self-will no longer needs to control my beliefs, thoughts, or actions. Each day I give thanks for your Holy Spirit, which is healing my life more deeply. I cooperate with this healing by agreeing to face any pain, knowing you are there. I know that my healing testifies to humanity the power of your grace, and is a source of joy and serenity to me. I am ever open for the opportunity to spread the truth and the joy of my recovery, one day at a time.

This is the final Step. It is an opportunity for you to acknowledge yourself for having the courage to stay and work with other committed people who are seeking a healthier way of life.

TWELVE-STEP EXERCISE

Identify a situation or condition in your life that is currently a source of resentment, fear, sadness, or anger. It may involve relationships (family, work, or sexual), work environment, health, or self-esteem. Write a concise statement describing the situation and identify your concern.

Use the following exercise to apply the principles of the Twelve Steps to the above situation or condition.

Step One: Describe the ways in which you are powerless in this situation. How does this situation show you the unmanageability of your life? _____

_____

_____

Step Two: How can your Higher Power restore you to sanity? _____

_____

_____

Step Three: Write an affirmation in which you state your decision to turn this situation over to God (e.g., I am no longer willing to fret over my boss's behavior. I decide now to turn my anxiety, my concerns, and my need for security over to God). _____

_____

_____

Step Four: What character defects have surfaced (e.g., fear of abandonment or authority figures, control, approval seeking, obsessive/compulsive behavior, rescuing, excessive responsibility, unexpressed feelings)? _____

_____

_____

Step Five: Admit your wrongs to God, to yourself, and to another person. _____

_____

_____

Step Six: Reflect upon your willingness to have God remove the character defects that have surfaced. Describe your willingness or reasons for not being willing to have them removed. _____

_____

_____

Step Seven: Write a prayer in which you humbly ask od to remove the specific shortcomings relating to this situation (You can be most humble when you are honest about your shortcomings and your needs). _____

_____

_____

Step Eight: Make a list of the persons you have harmed. _____

_____

_____

Step Nine: Describe how you intend to make the necessary amends. _____

_____

_____

Step Ten: Review the above to be sure that nothing has been overlooked. What new issues have surfaced that require attention? _____

_____

_____

Step Eleven: Take a moment for prayer or meditation, asking God for knowledge of his will for you. What is your understanding of God's will for you in this situation? _____

_____

Step Twelve: In this situation have you come to sense a spiritual awakening? Who is in charge now, you or God? Explain. (Your attitude and emotions are good indicators.)_____

_____

NOTES

_____

_____

_____

_____

_____

_____

_____

GROUP ACTIVITIES

ACTIVITY #1: "Spiritual Graph"

Supplies Needed: Pencils and graph paper (regular paper will do).

Objective: To make a graph of our spiritual lives, noting the high and low points.

❏ Using the graph paper, make a line graph of your spiritual life noting the highs, lows, and flat times. For example, your first spiritual high might be infant baptism or dedication. Other highs might include a conversion experience, confirmation, a relationship with a spiritual mentor, a meaningful camp or spiritual retreat experience, etc. Spiritual lows might include periods of loss, disillusionment, doubt, backsliding, rebelliousness, or apathy.

❏ Label each of your highs and lows with a note regarding each particular circumstance.

❏ Finally, share your graph with the group explaining the ups and downs.

ACTIVITY #2: "Pass It On"

Objective: To try to keep *It* from knowing who has the electricity. This activity is a fun reminder that Step Twelve is about "passing it on."

❏ Designate someone as *It*.

❏ Everyone except *It* should join hands in a circle. *It* stands in the center of the circle.

❏ *It* closes her eyes while someone is designated as having the electricity.

❏ After *It* has opened her eyes, the person with the electricity must pass the electricity on to the next person by squeezing that person's hand. The trick is not to let *It* see who has the electricity. The electric current moves around the circle continuously from one person to the next with only one person at a time having the current—the current cannot jump over a person. Someone may hold the current for a moment to prevent *It* from seeing, but he must keep the current going once *It* looks away.

❏ If *It* correctly discovers who has the electric current, *It* returns to the circle and the one caught holding the current becomes *It* and stands in the center.

❏ Discuss how you can practice the Twelve-Step principles in such a way that others do notice.

ACTIVITY #3: "Balloons and Spoons"

Supplies Needed: Balloons and large spoons.

Objective: To do a relay race carrying balloons on spoons and trying not to drop the balloons. This activity can remind us that when we carry the Twelve-Step message to others we need to proceed with sensitivity and focus on our own lives.

❑ Divide the family group members into two teams.

❑ Line up the teams and give the first runner in each line a balloon and a large spoon. The balloon must be balanced or held in the cup of the spoon.

❑ When the relay starts, the runners must run to a prescribed point and then return without losing the balloon. The runner cannot hold the balloon on the spoon with his other hand. If the balloon falls off, the runner must return to the starting point, reposition the balloon on the spoon, and start over.

❑ The first team to successfully run all its members wins.

❑ After the relay, discuss why you must be careful or sensitive when carrying the Twelve-Step message to others. The best way to carry the message is to tell our own story. Discuss some possible situations that would be appropriate for sharing our story with others.

The revised edition of *The Twelve Steps—A Spiritual Journey* contains a number of new features. These features are listed below with suggestions on how they might be best used within the family groups:

Step Overview

At the beginning of each step there is an overview that provides insights into understanding, working, and preparing for the step work. These sections can be read prior to group discussion as a way to encourage discussion and to remind the participants of the step's major themes.

Step Prayer

Immediately following the overview, there is a prayerwhich can also be used as a closing prayer or prior to the sharing time.

Helpful Hints

Helpful Hints are included in each step to provide program and Scripture-oriented resources for prayer, meditation, and Bible study. Reference is made to *The Life Recovery Bible* by Tyndale House Publishers, Inc. and *Prayers for The Twelve Steps—A Spiritual Journey* and *Meditations for The Twelve Steps—A Spiritual Journey* by RPI Publishing, Inc. The last two books were written specifically as companion books to *The Twelve Steps—A Spiritual Journey*.

Preparing for Community

The section entitled Preparing for Community is provided to support family group discussion. The first question asks the participant to list three questions he or she would like to discuss. The remaining questions encourage discussion about the application of the steps in daily life.

Key Ideas

The Key Ideas section that follows Preparing for Community highlights major themes that were covered in the step. This section can be used as a tool to review the step or to probe the understanding of the participants.

Suggested Meeting Formats

Meeting formats are offered only as suggestions. Each group has its own uniqueness, and the facilitator should be sensitive to this and follow a meeting format that best serves the needs of the group.

Group Activities

The Group Activities that follow each step offer a change of pace. The activities include a number of lighthearted opportunities for playful group interactions, involving everything from art to role playing and games.

FACILITATOR ROLE

Significant value can be gained if a recovering person who is familiar with this material acts as a group facilitator and has at least one co-facilitator. The facilitator's role is to provide support, direction, and encouragement to the participants. It is important to realize that this is not group therapy where professional advice is given; it is an arena where individuals can share their own experience, strength, and hope.

Even though you start the workshop and may function as facilitator or co-facilitator, be sure to have a different leader each week. It is recommended that leadership rotate by "family group" rather than by individuals. This gives each family group an opportunity to provide leadership. The recommended meeting formats are in Appendix One beginning on page 235. They are intended as suggestions only.

Previous workshops have revealed that trust develops most quickly in small family groups with a maximum of seven individuals. For example, if twenty-four people participate, divide into four family groups with six members each. The family groups will congregate to discuss the writing exercise and to share within their group for a specified period of time. The final portion of the meeting is devoted to sharing in one large group. It is best to keep the family groups small.

The facilitator serves as a resource in answering questions relative to working the material. This individual offers an element of security wherein group members have someone to turn to when problems arise. The facilitator is not assigned to a specific family group, but rotates each week and participates with the group leading the meeting. This gives the facilitator the opportunity to relate with all members and be attentive to everyone's needs.

A facilitator should be sensitive to those who experience stress or discomfort as a result of group participation. When people touch upon painful issues, especially for the first time, they may become emotional and begin to cry. The facilitator and other group members should be patient, accepting the sadness as a natural and appropriate part of the healing process. It is important to offer them support (e.g., being held, provided tissue for tears, being allowed to leave the room with a safe companion). Rather than interrupt the session, the facilitator should ensure that sharing continues. If the situation appears serious, the facilitator should urge the individual to seek professional help.

The Twelve-Step process is rooted in the belief that God is guiding the entire process and is the ultimate authority inherent and present in the group. Your role of facilitator enhances one's own recovery and serves as a model to the group to "carry the message to others."

Listen to What is Said

Spoken messages contain three essential parts: words, tone of voice, and non-verbal cues or body language. Consider what the person is saying with words and with non-verbal cues.

Establish Group Guidelines

Group guidelines create safety and encourage deeper sharing, and will vary according to the group needs. Establish mutually agreed upon guidelines in advance, so that participants know what to expect. Some basic fundamentals are:

- No probing or judging
- No cross-talk, fixing or advice-giving
- No judging
- No interrupting

Model Spiritual Character

Group members will feel safe when the facilitator models spiritual virtues such as patience, kindness, and love. Showing concern and sensitivity for others helps members grow in empathy for one another.

Reward Honesty and Openness with Affirmations

Affirm group members with praise, encouragement, appreciation, and acknowledgement. Guard against mixed messages, such as, "Jim, you add so much to this group by your presence, you just need to be here more often." A brief affirmation such as, "I'm glad you're here, Jim" or "Thanks for sharing" or "Good insight" is effective and supportive.

Use Personal Experiences as Teaching Tools

Encourage group members to value and learn from the experience, strength, and hope shared by others in the group. Life's most important lessons are best shared as stories.

Encourage Appropriate Trust and Loyalty

Group loyalty and trust is a result of members feeling safe with one another. When the members feel safe, they become more open and honest. As the facilitator, describe your personal understanding of confidentiality within the group, explain the damage that gossip causes, and emphasize the benefits of maintaining privacy.

Focus on Harmony as a Group Priority

Without harmony, group members will not feel comfortable expressing their feelings. Encourage harmony by helping the members focus on their attitudes and conduct. Remind the group to treat others with dignity and respect, to promote acceptance and tolerance, and to seek unity even in conflict.

Relate to the Here and Now

Sharing one's current story and experience promotes growth. War stories from the past and hopes for the future can either retard growth or encourage denial. But "telling it like it is" today encourages honesty.

Promote Sharing on a Feeling Level

To share feelings is to communicate on a deeper level. Most people are comfortable repeating clichés, reporting facts, and sharing judgments. They are unwilling to include feelings as a part of their story, for fear of becoming vulnerable. Help participants feel safe to share feelings by modeling this type of sharing and acknowledging those who do the same.

Confront in a Loving Way

Without confrontation, injuries, offenses, and differences can fester into destructive and divisive forces. It is important to confront potential problems promptly. If someone is giving advice during the meeting, give a gentle reminder that this is inappropriate. If the problem persists, talk to the person privately. Confrontation is appropriate when someone:

- gives unsolicited advice or gossips about others
- dominates others and doesn't listen when others share
- doesn't observe group's guidelines

Have a Plan for Conflict

Conflicts are a natural part of the small group process. The facilitator's role is to help the group resolve the conflict among themselves. The following are guidelines for the group to follow in addressing conflict among the members:

Check Your Attitude: When a problem arises, have the group members ask themselves, "What is my attitude toward this person and this situation?"

Define the Problem: The problem that first arises is rarely the real issue. People are affected by past feelings, hidden agendas, and many other situations. Group members should state the problem using the word "I."

Report Your Feelings: The best way to get to the heart of any issue is to express feelings. Participants can more easily focus on feelings by using statements, such as, "I feel...when this happens..." rather than "You make me feel...."

State Your Request: Requests should focus on a change in behavior and not on another person's character. Requests should be as simple as possible, such as, "I would feel better if you came to the meeting on time," rather than "I wish you weren't so tardy."

Negotiate and Affirm: Conflicts should be resolved in ways that benefit both parties and affirm everyone who makes an attempt at change. Requests should be made in such a way that there is always room for compromise.

Adapted from *The Pocket Facilitator: Training Tools for Building Teams and Leading Small Groups* by David M. Gutknecht, M.S., © 1992.

The Thirty-Week Meeting Schedule on page 233 shows a series of introductory meetings followed by a study of the Common Characteristics and then a two-week study of each step for a total of thirty weeks. This format either can be shortened or lengthened depending upon the intended use of the material and commitment of the participants.

The optional ways to use this workbook are as follows:

Sixteen-week format:

- One meeting for the introductory material.
- One week for the Common Behavior Characteristics.
- One week for each step.
- One week for a break or special event after Step Five.
- One meeting for closing.

Thirty-week format:
- Three meetings for the introductory material.
- One week for the Common Behavior Characteristics.
- Two weeks for each step.
- One meeting for a break after Step Five.
- One week for closing.

One year format:
- Four meetings for the introductory material.
- Two weeks for the Common Behavior Characteristics.
- Three weeks for each step.
- Breaks and special events planned after Steps Three, Five, and Nine.
- Two weeks for closing.
- Holidays (allow for approximately 5 weeks).

MEETING ANNOUNCEMENT

THE TWELVE STEPS
A SPIRITUAL JOURNEY
STEP STUDY WRITING WORKSHOP

_____

(Church or Organization)

is sponsoring a Step Study Writing Workshop for individuals who grew up in less-than-nurturing or chaotic homes. This workshop uses the Twelve Steps in a Christian context.

Beginning Date: _____

Day: _____ Time: _____

Location of Meeting: _____

Contact Person: _____ Phone: _____

The Twelve Steps—A Spiritual Journey is a working guide based on Bible truths, and emphasizes self-understanding and the unchanging love of God for all humanity.

This workshop

- offers tools to restore the fruits of the Spirit.

- provides a workable formula for confronting the past.

- is a model for surrendering one's life to God.

- reaffirms God's right and power to rule over all of life.

- emphasizes the relationship between the Twelve Steps and the practice of Christian living.

WORKSHOP OVERVIEW

- During the first three weeks, the meeting remains open for people interested in experiencing the meeting format.

- After the third week, small family groups are formed. These groups encourage the development of trusting, supportive relationships during the weeks that follow.

- On the fourth week, the meeting is closed to newcomers.

- Two weeks are devoted to each steps.

- Workbook material is completed during the week between meetings.

- The weekly meetings focus on the questions completed during the week.

THE TWELVE STEPS—A SPIRITUAL JOURNEY
STEP STUDY WRITING WORKSHOP
THIRTY-WEEK MEETING SCHEDULE

WEEK	DATE	IN-CLASS EXERCISES	AT-HOME WORK
1	_____	Overview and Intro	Starting the Journey
2	_____	Starting the Journey	Support & Community
3	_____	Support & Community	Common Characteristics
		(Meeting is now closed to newcomers)	
4	_____	Common Characteristics	Step One
5	_____	Step 1 Week 1	Step One
6	_____	Step 1 Week 2	Step Two
7	_____	Step 2 Week 1	Step Two
8	_____	Step 2 Week 2	Step Three
9	_____	Step 3 Week 1	Step Three
10	_____	Step 3 Week 2	Step Four
11	_____	Step 4 Week 1	Step Four
12	_____	Step 4 Week 2	Step Five
13	_____	Step 5 Week 1	Step Five
14	_____	Step 5 Week 2	Get Current
15	_____	Special Program	Step Six
16	_____	Step 6 Week 1	Step Six
17	_____	Step 6 Week 2	Step Seven
18	_____	Step 7 Week 1	Step Seven
19	_____	Step 7 Week 2	Step Eight
20	_____	Step 8 Week 1	Step Eight
21	_____	Step 8 Week 2	Step Nine
22	_____	Step 9 Week 1	Step Nine
23	_____	Step 9 Week 2	Step Ten
24	_____	Step 10 Week 1	Step Ten
25	_____	Step 10 Week 2	Step Eleven
26	_____	Step 11 Week 1	Step Eleven
27	_____	Step 11 Week 2	Step Twelve
28	_____	Step 12 Week 1	Step Twelve
29	_____	Step 12 Week 2	Prepare for completion
30	_____	Closing Meeting	

WEEK ONE
OVERVIEW AND INTRODUCTION

Have the following materials available for purchase:

The Twelve Steps—A Spiritual Journey
Prayers for The Twelve Steps—A Spiritual Journey
Meditations for The Twelve Steps—A Spiritual Journey
The Life Recovery Bible

[Meeting length is 2 hours. Reward promptness by starting on time.]

[Allow 20 minutes for welcome, prayer, and readings]

Welcome: "Good evening! Welcome to the Step Study Writing Workshop. My name is_____. During my childhood, I was influenced by a less than nurturing family environment in which the compulsive or obsessive behavior of an adult seriously wounded me. As a result, my self-esteem was negatively affected. I recognize that dysfunctional behavior is generational, and it is my intention to stop it in my lifetime."

"It is possible to identify with the 'Common Behavior Characteristics' without having biological parents who are, themselves, chemically dependent, outwardly abusive, or violent. The characteristics could have been passed down by grandparents or significant others in our lives."

Prayer: "Please join me for a moment of silence, after which we will recite the Serenity Prayer."

Readings: "I have asked _____ to read Common Behavior Characteristics."
"I have asked _____ to read The Twelve Steps."
"I have asked _____ to read Related Scriptures for The Twelve Steps
"I have asked _____ to read Milestones in Recovery."

[Allow 35 minutes for introducing the program]

Introducing the Program: "I welcome each of you. A Step Study Writing Workshop is not easy. You will find that the writing we do on each of the Twelve Steps is a powerful healing tool. Working the steps can be extremely difficult in the beginning stages of recovery. We suggest you seek other outside support, attend open Step Study meetings, and read additional materials. This will broaden your understanding and enhance your ability to participate in the Twelve-Step process. One of the first lessons in recovery is to know your own limitations and participate only in those activities that support your recovery."

"During the first three weeks, you will have an opportunity to experience the process used in this workshop. You will be asked to make a decision about your personal commitment by the third meeting. The full program requires thirty weeks of work, study, reflection, and growth."

"As the facilitator of the meeting, my purpose is to be your trusted servant. I will work the steps with you. Understand that I am here, as I believe you are, to share my experience, strength, and hope. I will lead only the first three meetings. By the fourth meeting, family groups will have been formed, and each group will be responsible for leading the meeting on a rotating basis."

"This is an introductory meeting intended to provide an overview of the Step Study Writing Workshop using *The Twelve Steps—A Spiritual Journey.*"

"The principal commitment required to successfully complete this work is a willingness to engage in the process one day at a time, one meeting at a time. It is also vital to trust that God will take care of the outcome."

"10 minutes is allocated to review the questions and responses in each Step, followed by 35 minutes of family group sharing about the questions and responses."

"Following the family group sharing, the meeting is open for 30 minutes of larger group sharing or for a group activity."

"The meeting lasts two hours, from 7:00 to 9:00."

"You will find new relationships opening up to you as you spend time with the group and share your experience, strength, and hope. The quality of these relationships may be unlike any other you have experienced."

"The principal purpose of this workshop is to facilitate healing and recovery. You will be asked to do some unfamiliar things, such as trusting others, practicing healthy dependence and interdependence, listening carefully, and sharing your feelings. You will have the opportunity to experience what life within a healthy family can be like."

(Refer to the Overview and Introduction to the Journey in the beginning of the book for further introductory material. These two sections are intended to give an overview of the recovery process. The questions in these two sections introduce the participant to the value of written responses to questions.)

[10-Minute Break]

[Allow 40 minutes for introductions and discussion]

(If the group is not too large [less than 10] introductions can be done in one group. Otherwise divide into smaller groups after the facilitator and co-facilitator introductions.)

Introductions: "Let's take time to go around the room and introduce ourselves by first name only. This respects the anonymity of those who are present. Tell a little about your background, what has brought you here, and what you hope to achieve. I'll start."

Discussion: "At this time the meeting is open for discussion on questions relative to the Step Study."

[Allow 15 minutes for contributions and closing]

Contributions: "Our tradition is to be self-supporting through our own monetary contributions. We ask for your contribution at this time."

Closing: "Prior to next week's meeting, please read the material in Weeks One and Two on pages 1–14 and respond to the questions. Pay particular attention to the 'Participation Agreement' on pages 11-14. The next meeting will focus on this material."

"Are there any announcements?"

"Reminder! What you hear at this meeting is confidential; leave it at this meeting! It is not for public disclosure or gossip. Please respect the privacy of those who shared with us tonight."

"Will everyone please clean up after themselves and help rearrange the room?"

"Please join me in the closing prayer."

[Adjourn]

[Allow 15 minutes for welcome, prayer, and readings]

Welcome: "Welcome to the _____ Step Study Writing Workshop. My name is _____, and I am your trusted servant for tonight."

Prayer: "Please join me for a moment of silence, after which we will recite the Serenity Prayer."

Readings: "I have asked _____ to read Common Behavior Characteristics."
"I have asked _____ to read The Twelve Steps."
"I have asked _____ to read Related Scriptures for The Twelve Steps
"I have asked _____ to read Milestones in Recovery."

[Allow 15 minutes for contributions and introductions]

Contributions: "Our tradition is to be self-supporting through our own contributions. We ask for your contribution at this time."

Introductions: "Please introduce yourself by giving your first name only. This respects the anonymity of those who are present."

"I welcome each of you. A Step Study Workshop is not easy. You will find that the writing we do on each of the Twelve Steps is a powerful healing tool. Working the steps can be extremely difficult in the beginning stages of your recovery. We suggest you seek other outside support, attend open Step Study meetings, and read additional materials. This will broaden your understanding and enhance your ability to participate in the Twelve-Step process. One of the first lessons in recovery is to know your own limitations and participate only in those activities that support your recovery."

"During this meeting and the one next week, you will have an opportunity to experience the process used in this workshop. You will be asked to make a decision about your personal commitment by the third meeting. The full program requires thirty weeks of work, study, reflection, and growth."

[Allow 10 minutes for reflection and preparation]

Please break into small groups of four to six. Before starting the writing exercise, I will read aloud the 'Participation Agreement' on pages 11–13. The agreement will be signed during Week Four.

Reflection and Preparation: Tonight we will be sharing on the materials in Weeks One and Two on pages 1–14. Please use the next few minutes to review the questions and your responses. Make note of the ones you would like to share.

[Allow 35 minutes for small group sharing]

Small Group Sharing: "Sharing your responses to the questions will last 35 minutes. Focus on your written responses, one at a time, and allow everyone to share. Please do not cross talk. Cross talk is when two people enter into a dialogue that excludes other group members. Limit your comments or observations to your own personal experience, and try not to intellectualize when sharing. To the best of your ability, share the feelings you experienced while writing (e.g., joy, sadness, anger, love, guilt, hurt, loneliness). I'll give a three-minute warning to allow you to complete the sharing."

[Allow 35 minutes for large group sharing]

Large Group Sharing: "Please rearrange your chairs into one large circle. The meeting is now open for sharing tonight's experiences."

[Allow 10 minutes for closing]

Closing: "The material used each week will guide you through the writing processes dealing with each step. It is not intended to provide all the possible information on each step or Bible citation."

"Prior to next week's meeting, please read the materials in Week Three on pages 15–22 and respond to the questions."

"Are there any announcements?"

"Newcomers are invited to remain after the meeting to discuss any questions they may have about the Step Study."

"Reminder! What you hear at this meeting is confidential; please leave it at this meeting! It is not for public disclosure or gossip. Please respect the privacy of the persons who have shared here tonight."

"Will everyone please clean up after themselves and help rearrange the room?"

"Please join me in the closing prayer."

[Adjourn]

[Have 3x5 cards available for Step Study enrollment]

[Allow 15 minutes for welcome, prayer, and readings]

Welcome: "Welcome to the _____ Step Study Writing Workshop. My name is _____, and I am your trusted servant for tonight."

Prayer: "Please join me for a moment of silence, after which we will recite the Serenity Prayer."

Readings: "I have asked _____ to read Common Behavior Characteristics."
"I have asked _____ to read The Twelve Steps."
"I have asked _____ to read Related Scriptures for The Twelve Steps"
"I have asked _____ to read Milestones in Recovery."

[Allow 10 minutes for contributions and introductions]

Contributions: "Our tradition is to be self-supporting through our own contributions. We ask for your contribution at this time."

Introductions: "Please introduce yourself by giving your first name only. This respects the anonymity of those who are present."

[Allow 20 minutes for enrollment]

"I will now pass out 3x5 note cards for each individual to complete. Please list your first name, last initial, and telephone number. These cards will be used to form family groups and create a group roster prior to the next meeting. Make note of friends or relatives who are participating so they can be assigned to different groups. Also, please indicate if you prefer to be in an all male or all female group."

"Families are selected at random by dividing the name cards equally into groups. This procedure may sound controlling, but it has been proven to be a safe and 'nonjudgmental' approach to 'family group' selection. It is a big step toward 'letting go.' "

[Allow 10 minutes for reflection and preparation]

Reflection and Preparation: "Tonight we will be sharing on the materials in Week Three on pages 15–22. Please use the next few minutes to review the questions and your responses. Make note of the ones you would like to share. "

[Allow 35 minutes for small group sharing]

Small Group Sharing: "Sharing your responses to the questions will last 35 minutes. Focus on your written responses, one at a time, and allow everyone to share. Please do not cross talk. Cross talk is when two people enter into a dialogue that excludes other group members. Limit your comments or observations to your own personal experience, and try not to intellectualize when sharing. To the best of your ability, share the feelings you experienced while writing (e.g., joy, sadness, anger, love, guilt, hurt, loneliness). I'll give a three-minute warning to allow you to complete the sharing."

[Allow 30 minutes for large group sharing]

Large Group Sharing: "Please rearrange your chairs into one large circle. The meeting is now open for sharing tonight's experiences."

[Allow 10 minutes for closing]

Closing: "The material used each week will guide you through the writing processes dealing with each step. It is not intended to provide all the possible information on each step or Bible citation."

"Prior to next weeks meeting, please read the material in Week Four on pages 23-29 and respond to the questions."

"Are there any announcements?"

"Reminder! What you hear at this meeting is confidential; please leave it at this meeting! It is not for public disclosure or gossip. Please respect the privacy of those who shared here tonight."

"Will everyone please clean up after themselves and help rearrange the room?"

"Please join me in the closing prayer."

[Adjourn]

MEETING PREPARATION FOR WEEK 4

Assign family groups by sorting the 3 x 5 cards randomly into family groups. Prepare a group roster of all participants, divided into family groups. The list is to include first name, last initial, and telephone number. Have copies of the group roster available to distribute. If possible, participants who have indicated a desire to be in an exclusively female or male group should be in one group. It is recommended that relatives or close friends are in separate groups.

Arrange chairs for small family group seating before the meeting begins. For this meeting, assign numbers to each group for easy identification. After the groups have been seated, allow them the option to choose a name for their group (i.e. Kings, Steppers, God's Instruments, etc.).

[Have the family group roster available for distribution.]

[Allow 15 minutes for welcome, prayer, readings and contributions]

Welcome: "Welcome to the _____ Step Study Writing Workshop. My name is _____, and I am your trusted servant for tonight."

Prayer: "Please join me for a moment of silence, after which we will recite the Serenity Prayer."

Readings: "I have asked _____ to read Common Behavior Characteristics."
"I have asked _____ to read The Twelve Steps."
"I have asked _____ to read Related Scriptures for The Twelve Steps."
"I have asked _____ to read Group Participant Guidelines."

Contributions: "Our tradition is to be self-supporting through our own contributions. We ask for your contribution at this time."

[Allow 10 minutes for reflection and preparation]

"I will now distribute the family group roster. Please join with your assigned family group."

Reflection and Preparation: "Tonight we will be sharing on the Common Behavior Characteristics on pages 23–29. Please use the next few minutes to review the questions and your responses. Make note of the characteristics about which you would like to share."

[Allow 35 minutes for small group sharing]

"Prior to sharing, please take a few minutes and sign the Participation Agreement with your family group."

Small Group Sharing: "Focus on your written responses when sharing. Respond to one question at a time and allow time for everyone to share. Please do not cross talk. Cross talk is when two people enter into a dialogue that excludes other group members. Sharing is most valuable when you limit your comments or observations to your own personal experience, using the word "I." I'll give a three-minute warning to complete the sharing. Please introduce yourself before you speak."

[Allow 15 minutes for group prayer]

Group Prayer: "Allow time to offer prayers for yourself and one another. Note especially issues raised during the sharing time."

[Allow 35 minutes for large group sharing]

Large Group Sharing: "Please rearrange your chairs into one large circle. The meeting is now open for sharing tonights experiences."

[Allow 10 minutes for closing]

Closing: "Next week we begin our work on the Twelve Steps. You are encouraged to attend other Twelve-Step meetings and read materials that will broaden your understanding of the steps and related Scriptures."

"Are there any announcements?"

"The family group leading next week is number_____. Please phone those who are absent tonight and encourage their attendance. Try to meet during the week to process writing and to deepen family group bonding and trust. An alternative is telephone contact."

"Reminder! What you hear at this meeting is confidential. Leave it at this meeting! It is not for public disclosure or gossip. Please respect the privacy of those who shared with us tonight."

"Please join me in the closing prayer."

WEEKS FIVE THROUGH TWENTY-NINE
STEPS ONE THROUGH TWELVE

[Allow 15 minutes for welcome, prayer, readings, and contributions]

Welcome: "Welcome to the _____ Step Study Writing Workshop. My name is _____, and I am your trusted servant for tonight."

Prayer: "Please join me for a moment of silence, after which we will recite the Serenity Prayer."

Readings: "I have asked _____ to read (Common Behavior Characteristics, Milestones in Recovery, or Group Participant Guidelines)."
"I have asked _____ to read The Twelve Steps."
"I have asked _____ to read Related Scriptures for The Twelve Steps."

Contributions: "Our tradition is to be self-supporting through our own contributions. We ask for your contribution at this time."

[Allow 10 minutes for reflection and preparation]

Reflection and Preparation: "Tonight we will be sharing on step _____ on pages _____ through _____. Please use the next few minutes to review the questions and your responses. Make note of the questions and responses you would like to share."

[Allow 35 minutes for small group sharing]

Small Group Sharing: "Focus on your written responses when sharing. Respond to one question at a time and allow time for everyone to share. Please do not cross talk. Cross talk is when two people enter into a dialogue that excludes other group members. Sharing is most valuable when you limit your comments or observations to your own personal experience, using the word "I." I'll give a three-minute warning to complete the sharing."

[Allow 15 minutes for group prayer]

Group Prayer: "Allow time to offer prayers for yourself and one another. Note especially issues raised during the sharing time."

[Allow 35 minutes for large group sharing or group activities (ask for group conscience or alternate weekly)]

[Allow 10 minutes for closing]

Closing: "All of you are encouraged to make telephone contact or meet at other times during the week to discuss your writing, deepen family group relationships, and encourage one another. You are also encouraged to attend other Twelve-Step meetings and read materials that will broaden your understanding of the steps and related Scriptures."
"Are there any announcements?"

"The family group leading next week is _____. Please phone those who are absent tonight and encourage their attendance."

"Reminder! What you hear at this meeting is confidential. Leave it at this meeting! It is not for public disclosure or gossip. Please respect the privacy of those who shared with us tonight."

"Please join me in the closing prayer."

NOTE: For your convenience, a copy of this meeting schedule is located on the inside back cover.

[Allow 15 minutes for welcome, prayer, readings, and contributions]

Welcome: "Welcome to the _____ Twelve-Step Writing Workshop. My name is _____, and I am your trusted servant for tonight. This meeting will complete the work you have done with your family group and the Twelve Steps."

Prayer: "Please join me for a moment of silence, after which we will recite the Serenity Prayer."

Readings: "I have asked _____ to read Milestones in Recovery."
"I have asked _____ to read The Twelve Steps."
"I have asked _____ to read Related Scriptures for The Twelve Steps."

Contributions: "Our tradition is to be self-supporting through our own contributions. We ask for your contribution at this time."

[Allow 10 minutes for reflection and preparation]

Reflection and Preparation: "Tonight each person has the opportunity to gently say good-bye with joy, acknowledgement, and love. Spend the next ten minutes reflecting on and responding to the statements below. Saying 'thank you' individually and specifically is not necessary. Your feelings of gratitude can be communicated within the written responses."

I want to complete this experience by acknowledging that it has had the following meaning for me: _____

_____

_____

_____

_____

As part of saying goodbye, I want to acknowledge my feelings. Feel free to express your present emotional state, as it is a healthy part of accepting closure (e.g., loss, sadness, fear, joy, anticipation, gratefulness). _____

_____

_____

_____

_____

[Allow 35 minutes for small group sharing]

Small Group Sharing: "Focus on your written responses when sharing. Respond to one question at a time and allow time for everyone to share. Please do not cross talk. Cross talk is when two people enter into a dialogue that excludes other group members. Sharing is most valuable when you limit your comments or observations to your own personal experience, using the word "I." I'll give a three-minute warning to complete the sharing. Please introduce yourself before you speak."

[Allow 15 minutes for group prayer]

Group Prayer: "Allow time to offer prayers for yourself and one another. Especially note issues raised during the sharing time."

[Allow 35 minutes for large group sharing]

Large Group Sharing: "Please rearrange your chairs into one large circle. The meeting is now open for sharing your closing thoughts. You are to be congratulated for the hard work and committment in completing this Step Study. Take time to recognize and congratulate one another. Fill out the Certificate of Recognition on page 247 as acknowledgment of your accomplishment."

[Allow 10 minutes for closing]

Closing: "You are encouraged to attend other Twelve-Step meetings and continue to read other materials that will broaden your understanding of the steps and related Scripture."

"Are there any announcements?"

"If the group wants further informal contact, this meeting is an opportunity to schedule a reunion date."

"Reminder! What you hear at this meeting is confidential. Leave it at this meeting! It is not for public disclosure or gossip. Please respect the privacy of those who shared with us tonight."

"Please join me in the Prayer for Step Twelve on page 221."

Certificate

of

Recognition

Name

is recognized for commitment, courage,
and completion of work in
The Twelve Steps—A Spiritual Journey

Great Job

Facilitator and Family Group Members

Certificate

of

Recognition

Name

is recognized for commitment, courage,
and completion of work in
The Twelve Steps—A Spiritual Journey

Facilitator and Family Group Members

Great Job

APPENDIX TWO

Books designed for support groups
> InterVarsity Press
>> *Life Recovery Guides,* Dale and Juanita Ryan
>
> RPI Publishing, Inc.
>> *The Twelve Steps for Christians,* Friends in Recovery
>> *When I Grow Up…I Want To Be An Adult,* Ron Ross
>> *Parables for Personal Growth,* Melinda Reinecke
>> *Meditations for The Twelve Steps—A Spiritual Journey,* Friends in Recovery with Jerry S.
>> *Prayers for The Twelve Steps—A Spiritual Journey,* Friends in Recovery with Jerry S.
>> *From Victim to Victor,* Yvonne Martinez

Reference books
> RPI Publishing, Inc.
>> *Divine or Distorted?,* Jerry Seiden
>> *The Gospel and the Twelve Steps,* Martin M. Davis
>> *Jesus and Addiction,* Don Williams

Spanish Language resources
> InterVarsity Press
>> *Guias De Recuperacion Vivencial,* Dale and Juanita Ryan
>
> RPI Publishing, Inc.
>> *Los Doce Pasos Para Los Cristianos,* Friends in Recovery

Videos with Workbooks
> Beloved Ministry
>> *The Truth Will Set You Free,* Fr. Jack McGinnis and Barbara Shlemon
>
> HarperCollins
>> *Hunger for Healing,* J. Keith Miller

Videos
> InterVarsity Press
>> *Ripped Down the Middle*
>> *Picking Up the Pieces*

Instructional Books to Start Self-Help Support Groups
> RPI Publishing, Inc.
>> *Living Free: A Guide to Forming and a Recovery Ministry,* Ron Halvorson and Valerie Deilgat
>
> Thomas Nelson
>> *The Complete Workbook for Recovery Ministry in the Church,* Bill Morris

SUPPORT GROUPS

Christian Groups

Alcoholics Victorious
National Headquarters
9370 S.W. Greenburg Rd., Suite 411
Tigard, Oregon 97323
(503) 245-9629

Confident Kids
720 W. Whittier Blvd. #H
La Habra, CA 90631
(310) 690-9701

Liontamers
2801 North Brea Blvd.
Fullerton, California 92635-2799
(714) 529-5544

Living Free
P.O. Box 1026
Julian, CA 92036
(619) 765-2703

National Association for
Christian Recovery
721 W. Whittier Blvd. #H
La Habra, California 90631
(310) 697-6201

Overcomers, Inc.
4235 Mt. Sterling Avenue
Titusville, Florida 32780
(407) 264-0757

Overcomers Outreach, Inc.
2290 West Whittier Blvd.
La Habra, California 90631
(310) 697-3994

Recovery Works
c/o Church of the Good Shepherd
805 South East Ellsworth Ave.
Vancouver, WA 98664
(206) 893-7770

Homosexuals Anonymous
H.A.F.S.
P.O. Box 7881
Reading, PA 19603
(610) 376-1146

Secular Groups

Adult Children of Alcoholics
Central Service Board
P.O. Box 3216
Torrance, California 90505
(310) 534-1815

Al-Anon/Alateen
Family Group Headquarters, Inc.
862 Midtown Station
NY, NY 10018
(212) 302-7240

Alcoholics Anonymous
World Services, Inc.
468 Park Avenue South
New York, New York 10016
(212) 686-1100

Co-Dependents Anonymous
P.O. Box 33577
Phoenix, Arizona 85067-3577
(602) 277-7991

Debtors Anonymous
P.O. Box 20322
New York, New York 10025-9992
(212) 642-8220

Emotions Anonymous International
P.O. Box 4245
St. Paul, Minnesota 55104
(612) 647-9712

Gamblers Anonymous National
P.O. Box 17173
Los Angeles, California 90017
(213) 386-8789

Narcotics Anonymous
P.O. Box 9999
Van Nuys, California 91406
(818) 780-3951

National Association for
Children of Alcoholics
11426 Rockville Pike, Suite 100
Rockville, MD 20852
(301) 468-0985

Overeaters Anonymous
World Service Office
2190 190th Street
Torrance, California 90504
(310) 618-8835

Sexaholics Anonymous
P.O. Box 300
Simi Valley, California 93062
(805) 581-3343

SERENITY PRAYER

God, grant me the serenity

to accept the things I cannot change,

the courage to change the things I can,

and the wisdom to know the difference.

Living one day at a time,

enjoying one moment at a time;

accepting hardship as a pathway to peace;

taking, as Jesus did,

this sinful world as it is,

not as I would have it;

trusting that You will make all things right

if I surrender to your will;

so that I may be reasonably happy in this life

and supremely happy with you forever in the next.

Amen

Reinhold Niebuhr

"PRAYER OF SAINT FRANCIS OF ASSISI"

Lord, make me an instrument of your peace!

Where there is hatred—let me sow love

Where there is injury—pardon

Where there is doubt—faith

Where there is despair—hope

Where there is darkness—light

Where there is sadness—joy

O Divine Master, grant that I may not so much seek

To be consoled—as to console

To be loved—as to love

for

It is in giving—that we receive

It is in pardoning—that we are pardoned

It is in dying—that

we are born to eternal life.

Amen

GROUP PARTICIPANT GUIDELINES

❑ *Recognize that the Holy Spirit is in charge.*
- Gratefully acknowledge the Holy Spirit's presence and pray for his guidance and direction.

❑ *Make a point of ministering love in an appropriate manner.*
- Respect the needs of others by asking permission to express concern with a hug or a touch. Many are uncomfortable with physical contact.

❑ *Focus individual sharing on the step being worked.*
- Focus sharing on individual experience, strength, and hope in working the steps being discussed.
- Allow equal time for everyone in the group to share.

❑ *Limit talking and allow others to share.*
- Keep your comments brief, take turns talking, and don't interrupt others.
- Respect each person's right to self-expression without comment.

❑ *Encourage comfort and support by sharing from one's own experience.*
- Do not attempt to advise or rescue them.
- Accept what others say without comment, realizing it is true for them.
- Assume responsibility only for your own feelings, thoughts, and actions.

❑ *Refrain from "cross talk."*
- Cross talk occurs when two or more people engage in dialogue that excludes others. It may also involve advice giving.

❑ *Maintain confidentiality.*
- Keep whatever is shared within the group to ensure an atmosphere of safety and openness.

❑ *Avoid gossip.*
- Share your own needs and refrain from talking about a person who is absent.

❑ *Refrain from criticizing or defending others.*
- Lovingly hold others accountable for their behavior only if they ask you to do so. Otherwise, recognize that we are all accountable to Christ, and it is not our place to defend or criticize others.

❑ *Come to each meeting prepared and with a prayerful attitude.*
- Before each meeting, read designated materials and complete any written exercises.
- Pray for guidance and a willingness to share openly and honestly when you communicate with at least one other group participant.

MILESTONES IN RECOVERY

❏ We feel comfortable with people, including authority figures.

❏ We have a strong identity and generally approve of ourselves.

❏ We accept and use personal criticism in a positive way.

❏ As we face our own life situation, we find we are attracted by strengths and understand the weaknesses in our relationships with other people.

❏ We are recovering through loving and focusing on ourselves; we accept responsibility for our own thoughts and actions.

❏ We feel comfortable standing up for ourselves when it is appropriate.

❏ We are enjoying peace and serenity, trusting that God is guiding our recovery.

❏ We love people who love and take care of themselves.

❏ We are free to feel and express our feelings even when they cause us pain.

❏ We have a healthy sense of self-esteem.

❏ We are developing new skills that allow us to initiate and complete ideas and projects.

❏ We take prudent action by considering alternative behaviors and possible counsequences.

❏ We rely more and more on Christ as our Higher Power.

THE TWELVE STEPS
AND RELATED SCRIPTURE

Step One

We admitted we were powerless over the effects of our separation from God—that our lives had become unmanageable.

> *I know nothing good lives in me, that is, in my sinful nature. For I have the desire to do what is good, but I cannot carry it out.* (Rom. 7:18)

Step Two

Came to believe that a Power greater than ourselves could restore us to sanity.

> *For it is God who works in you to will and to act according to his good purpose.* (Phil. 2:13)

Step Three

Made a decision to turn our will and our lives over to the care of God *as we understood Him.*

> *Therefore, I urge you, brothers, in view of God's mercy, to offer your bodies as living sacrifices, holy and pleasing to God—which is your spiritual worship.* (Rom. 12:1)

Step Four

Made a searching and fearless moral inventory of ourselves.

> *Let us examine our ways and test them, and let us return to the Lord.* (Lam. 3:40)

Step Five

Admitted to God, to ourselves, and to another human being the exact nature of our wrongs.

> *Therefore confess your sins to each other and pray for each other so that you may be healed.* (James 5:16a)

Step Six

Were entirely ready to have God remove all these defects of character.

> *Humble yourselves before the Lord, and he will lift you up.* (James 4:10)

Step Seven

Humbly asked Him to remove our shortcomings.

> *If we confess our sins, he is faithful and just and will forgive us our sins and purify us from all unrighteousness.* (1 John 1:9)

Step Eight

Made a list of all persons we had harmed, and became willing to make amends to them all.

> *Do to others as you would have them to do you.* (Luke 6:31)

Step Nine

Made direct amends to such people wherever possible, except when to do so would injure them or others.

> *Therefore, if you are offering your gift at the altar and there remember that your brother has something against you, leave your gift there in front of the altar. First go and be reconciled to your brother; then come and offer your gift.* (Matt. 5:23–24)

Step Ten

Continued to take personal inventory and, when we were wrong, promptly admitted it.

> *So, if you think you are standing firm, be careful that you don't fall.* (1 Cor. 10:12)

Step Eleven

Sought through prayer and meditation to improve our conscious contact with God *as we understood Him,* praying only for knowledge of His will for us and the power to carry that out.

> *Let the word of Christ dwell in you richly.* (Col. 3:16a)

Step Twelve

Having had a spiritual awakening as the result of these steps, we tried to carry this message to others, and to practice these principles in all our affairs.

> *Brothers, if someone is caught in a sin, you who are spiritual should restore him gently. But watch yourself, or you also may be tempted.* (Gal. 6:1)

COMMON BEHAVIOR CHARACTERISTICS

❑ We have feelings of low self-esteem that cause us to judge ourselves and others without mercy. We cover up or compensate by trying to be perfect, take responsibility for others, attempt to control the outcome of unpredictable events, get angry when things don't go our way, or gossip instead of confronting an issue.

❑ We tend to isolate ourselves and to feel uneasy around other people, especially authority figures.

❑ We are approval seekers and will do anything to make people like us. We are extremely loyal even in the face of evidence that suggests loyalty is undeserved.

❑ We are intimidated by angry people and personal criticism. This causes us to feel anxious and overly sensitive.

❑ We habitually choose to have relationships with emotionally unavailable people with addictive personalities. We are usually less attracted to healthy, caring people.

❑ We live life as victims and are attracted to other victims in our love and friendship relationships. We confuse love with pity and tend to "love" people we can pity and rescue.

❑ We are either overly responsible or very irresponsible. We try to solve others' problems or expect others to be responsible for us. This enables us to avoid looking closely at our own behavior.

❑ We feel guilty when we stand up for ourselves or act assertively. We give in to others instead of taking care of ourselves.

❑ We deny, minimize, or repress our feelings from our traumatic childhoods. We have difficulty expressing our feelings and are unaware of the impact this has on our lives.

❑ We are dependent personalities who are terrified of rejection or abandonment. We tend to stay in jobs or relationships that are harmful to us. Our fears can either stop us from ending hurtful relationships or prevent us from entering healthy, rewarding ones.

❑ Denial, isolation, control, and misplaced guilt are symptoms of family dysfunction. Because of these behaviors, we feel hopeless and helpless.

❑ We have difficulty with intimate relationships. We feel insecure and lack trust in others. We don't have clearly defined boundaries and become enmeshed with our partner's needs and emotions.

❑ We have difficulty following projects through from beginning to end.

❑ We have a strong need to be in control. We overreact to change over which we have no control.

❑ We tend to be impulsive. We take action before considering alternative behaviors or possible consequences.